The End of Illusions

The End of Illusions

Politics, Economy, and Culture in Late Modernity

Andreas Reckwitz

Translated by Valentine A. Pakis

polity

Originally published in German as *Das Ende der Illusionen – Politik, Ökonomie und Kultur in der Spätmoderne* © Suhrkamp Verlag Berlin 2019. All rights by and controlled through Suhrkamp Verlag Berlin.

The translation of this work was supported by a grant from the Goethe-Institut.

Figure 2.1 'Hausmodell' from Ralf Dahrendorf: Gesellschaft und Demokratie in Deutschland © 1965 Piper Verlag GmbH, München

Figure 3.3 from Maarten Goos and Alan Manning, "Lousy and Lovely Jobs: The Rising Polarization of Work in Britain," *The Review of Economics and Statistics*, 89:1 (February, 2007), pp. 118–33. © 2007 by the President and Fellows of Harvard College and the Massachusetts Institute of Technology.

Polity Press
65 Bridge Street
Cambridge CB2 1UR, UK

Polity Press
101 Station Landing
Suite 300
Medford, MA 02155, USA

ISBN-13: 978-1-5095-4569-8
ISBN-13: 978-1-5095-4570-4 (paperback)

A catalogue record for this book is available from the British Library.

Library of Congress Cataloging-in-Publication Data
Names: Reckwitz, Andreas, author.
Title: The end of illusions : politics, economy, and culture in late
    modernity / Andreas Reckwitz ; translated by Valentine A. Pakis.
Other titles: Ende der Illusionen. English
Description: Cambridge, UK ; Medford, MA : Polity Press, [2021] | Includes
    bibliographical references and index. | Summary: "A leading social
    thinker examines the key structural features of our disillusioned age"--
    Provided by publisher.
Identifiers: LCCN 2021000323 (print) | LCCN 2021000324 (ebook) | ISBN
    9781509545698 (hardback) | ISBN 9781509545704 (paperback) | ISBN
    9781509545711 (epub) | ISBN 9781509548057 (pdf)
Subjects: LCSH: Social history--21st century. | Social conflict. | Social
    change. | Populism. | Capitalism--Social aspects. | Culture. |
    Civilization, Modern--21st century.
Classification: LCC HN18.3 .R43413 2021 (print) | LCC HN18.3 (ebook) |
    DDC 306--dc23
LC record available at https://lccn.loc.gov/2021000323
LC ebook record available at https://lccn.loc.gov/2021000324

Typeset in 10.5 on 11.5 pt Times New Roman MT
by Fakenham Prepress Solutions, Fakenham, Norfolk NR21 8NL
Printed and bound in the UK by CPI Group (UK) Ltd, Croydon

For further information on Polity, visit our website: politybooks.com

Contents

Figures and Tables

Tables

Introduction: The Disillusioned Present

It's a strange thing. Some events that are retrospectively considered epoch-changing are perceived as merely marginal when they occur, whereas, in the case of others, one can remember precisely – even years later – the moment when "it happened," and also one's own feelings of bafflement, helplessness, fear, or incredulous joy in response to something seemingly impossible taking place.

Just as I still have vivid memories of "my" November 9, 1989 (the day the Berlin Wall came down) and "my" September 11, 2001 (the day of the terrorist attacks on the World Trade Center), the morning of November 9, 2016 is still present in my mind. Like many other people around the world, I felt a growing sense of unease during the months leading up to the American presidential election, which featured the surprising nomination of Donald Trump as the candidate for the Republican Party and his ugly, brutal campaign against Hillary Clinton, the candidate for the Democrats. On that morning, I checked the news on my tablet and was forced to accept that something had happened which, until the very last moment, I had been loath to admit as a real possibility: the populist candidate, who had made the headlines mostly because of his misogynistic and xenophobic demagoguery and his deep distrust of international cooperation and democratic institutions, and who seemed utterly unpredictable, had just been elected as the 45th President of the United States, thereby becoming the commander-in-chief of the leading Western nation.[1] My reaction on that morning, and even weeks later, was one of horror. I had the feeling that things could fall apart, without knowing where this might lead: How was this possible, and how would things now proceed? It felt like a historical rupture.

Trump's election, however, was not the only political earthquake that we have experienced in recent years. Elsewhere, too, elections and referenda have shaken up seemingly stable political orders. In June of 2016, a majority of British citizens voted for their country's exit from the European Union. In the French presidential election of 2017, none of the candidates from established parties made it to the second round of voting, but the right-wing populist Marine Le Pen did. She then lost to Emmanuel Macron, the founder of the new liberal party En Marche!, who then in 2018 and 2019 had to confront large-scale protests by the *gilets jaunes*. In Italy, a (right-wing) populist government came to power in 2018, and in Hungary and Poland, two former model democracies in post-communist Europe, democratic institutions are now under attack. The European Union, which had been regarded by many as the inevitable outcome of political development on a continent that had learned from its past wars, as well as the traditional left–right schema for the landscape of the political parties have suddenly proved to be fragile. And we have experienced further uncertainties: in 2007, a system that many economists had extolled as a reliable money-making machine was brought to the brink of collapse by the global financial crisis. Terrorist attacks, such as the attack in Paris in 2015 (by the "Islamic State") and the attack in Christchurch, New Zealand, in 2018 have demonstrated the fragile nature of everyday life in Western societies. There is a widespread feeling that, clearly, the danger is closing in.

Why do these events make people feel so unsettled? The answer may be painful. We no longer perceive these events as individual incidents that would allow us swiftly to return to our daily routines. Rather, a clear pattern has emerged: the hopeful expectations about the development of society, which many people in Western countries had harbored since the end of the Cold War in 1989/90, have been fundamentally disappointed, or at least relativized. Today, these expectations have been revealed to be illusions, and the result of this is disillusionment. This is true not only in Germany but, rather, in all Western societies, and in many respects it is even the case for global society. After 1990, the general tendency in the media, in politics, in business, and even in large swaths of intellectual debate was to weave a grand narrative of progress: of economic, political, social, cultural, and technological advancement. Borrowing from Hegel and Alexandre Kojève, the American political scientist Francis Fukuyama encapsulated this narrative with his concept of the "end of history." It seemed as though we had come to the home stretch of world history and had achieved a condition in which the institutional orders of politics and economics had taken on a form that no longer needed to be changed – or even one that was impossible to change.[2] From today's perspective, this narrative seems rather naïve.

The essentially liberal narrative of progress over the last 30 years is supported by an abundance of empirical evidence, and this should not be forgotten. Regarding political progress, one can point to the pro-democracy movements in Eastern Europe, Latin America, and Africa, which led to the replacement of authoritarian regimes by largely liberal-democratic systems. In addition, global cooperation between nations also intensified, and the European Union is just one example of this. There is plenty of evidence, too, of economic progress. Globalization and the integration of large parts of the global South into the world market have accelerated industrialization, especially in emerging countries such as China and India, and this has led to a significant reduction of poverty and to the rise of a strong middle class. In North America and Europe, a post-industrial knowledge economy has been established, and the latter has profited considerably from the digital revolution.

The process of digitalization – the defining technological development of the last two decades – at first seemed to fit seamlessly into this narrative of progress. A network of individuals and organizations, the internet as an experimental space for new identities and cooperation, and finally a borderless form of communication that vitalizes democracy – such were the expectations of tech euphoria. Lastly, the narrative of progress also has a socio-political component. Consider the great gains that have been made in liberalization and emancipation over the last few decades: a shift toward gender equality, toward the equal rights of sexual minorities (gay men, lesbian women, and the transgender community, for instance), and toward a transformation of the Western way of life, which has become more hedonistic and cosmopolitan in the best sense and thus left behind so much of the rigidity of postwar society. In particular, the new and young middle class moves around in the globalized world like a fish in water. A sense that the world is fundamentally *open* has been spreading over the past few decades, and by now this seems like a firmly established attitude toward life.

Of course, these developments *have happened*, and they are significant. The liberal narrative of progress is not false. It does not, however, tell the whole truth. Whoever believes that the idea of progress can ever correspond perfectly to social reality is prey to an illusion. Moreover, it is also an illusion that processes, once set in motion, will somehow naturally be perpetuated. The financial crisis, Brexit, terrorist attacks, Trump's election, and other events of the recent past illustrate that social reality is more contradictory and fragile than the narrative of progress would have us believe. Furthermore, it should be assumed that these events are ultimately expressions of or reactions to contradictions, conflicts, and moments of crisis that have long been developing on the structural level of late-modern society.

Progress, Dystopia, Nostalgia

The fact that, until recently, the liberal narrative of progress was able to seem so ubiquitous is not especially unusual if we broaden our perspective and consider the cultural history of modernity as a whole. Over the course of industrialization, democratization, urbanization, marketization, emancipation, and the rise of science, modern society has been developing slowly but steadily since the eighteenth century (and at first in Western nations), and it has always been inextricably linked to a vision of making progress: to the "project of modernity." As Reinhart Koselleck observed, the rise of the semantics of progress coincided with the reality of (political, economic, and technological) revolutions at the end of the eighteenth century; the semantics of progress accompanied these revolutions and, in part, actively impelled them.[3] In a sense, modernity converted the religious belief in the assurance of salvation into a firm belief in progress.

Of course, throughout the history of modernity in the nineteenth and twentieth centuries, there were often heated debates over what, exactly, this realized or desired progress ought to be about: technology, freedom, equality, welfare and comfort, self-determination, or emancipation? In addition, there have always been alternating phases of progressive optimism and cultural-critical self-doubt. In nineteenth-century Europe, the Napoleonic Wars were followed by a long phase of bourgeois self-confidence and the unwavering hope for civilizational progress (accompanied, not coincidentally, by imperialism and colonialism). At the beginning of the twentieth century, the baton of progressive optimism was passed on to burgeoning socialist movements. The First World War was then followed by a phase of gnawing intellectual uncertainty and widespread skepticism, which gave rise, among certain thinkers, to an outright catastrophic outlook concerning the downfall of European modernity. In this regard, it is enough to read Oswald Spengler's *The Decline of the West* or José Ortega y Gasset's *The Revolt of the Masses.*[4] After the civilizational upheaval of fascism, the Holocaust, and the Second World War, liberal progressive optimism resurfaced astonishingly quickly in Western Europe and North America. What followed was the *trente glorieuses* (as Jean Fourastié called these three decades), which were characterized by the rise of affluent societies in the West and by visions of creating a perfect form of industrial-technical modernity. In the 1970s, these societies were confronted with economic and ecological debates over the "limits to growth" and with the discomforting social critique in the wake of 1968. Then the communist system collapsed, the final and most radical thrust toward globalization commenced, and the digital revolution began, thus initiating a renewed phase of the liberal narrative of progress in an era of presumably unlimited opportunity. Today, this narrative is stridently being called into question.

It is instructive to keep in mind these previous upsurges of the social discourse of progress. A historical perspective relativizes many things – both the blind faith that people sometimes have in the conflict-free progress of human development, and the defeatist and catastrophic attitude that inevitably follows. Our current situation, at any rate, is characterized by the genre of *dystopia*.[5] For many people, the sense of disappointment over the failure of the liberal ideal of progress is so great that now, driven by strong emotions such as rage or despair, they tend to fall into the opposite extreme. If public discourse were a psychiatric patient, we would have to say that it displays symptoms of manic depression: boundless euphoria is immediately followed by feelings of profound hopelessness (which, in many people, seem to be accompanied by a quiet sense of pleasure about the impending disaster).

The current dystopias point in different directions. Enormously present in the media – particularly in the digital world, but also in the popular book market – are the diagnoses of downfall from members of the New Right. They have ultimately revived the cyclical philosophy of history found in Spengler's *The Decline of the West*. In contrast, one hears entirely different opinions from left-wing critics who, in the wake of the financial crisis, have been gathering evidence for the imminent implosion of capitalism – a collapse that many of these authors themselves, owing to the lack of a socialist alternative, can only imagine as a hopeless ongoing crisis. On top of this, the public discourse about digitalization has meanwhile almost fully transformed from one of tech euphoria into a sweeping critique of technology. The latter discourse now prefers to associate the digital revolution with the all-encompassing control of users by business-related or government data collectors, with filter bubbles and caustic communication, and finally with automation and the threat of mass unemployment.

In light of these catastrophic scenarios, today's public and political discourse often grasps at the straws of *nostalgia*. In particular, the period of industrial modernity between 1945 and 1975, which just a few years ago seemed like an entirely distant past, has meanwhile been transformed into a projection screen for various sorts of nostalgic longing – nostalgia from the right, from the left, and from the center. Right-wing nostalgia in the United States, France, or Germany glorifies the traditional family values and gender roles that were still dominant in those years, as well as the era's conservative morality and supposed cultural homogeneity. Left-wing nostalgia looks back to that period and yearns for its greater social equality, for its strong industrial workforce, and for the welfare state of the old industrial society. Finally, centrist nostalgia looks wistfully back to an era of people's parties, the large middle class, and a presumably more leisurely pace of life. Such trips down memory lane often have less to do with politics than they do with retro aesthetic trends, but they can also serve the ends of various forms of political populism in an effective way.

Disillusionment as an Opportunity

The transformation of public debate from unwavering progressive optimism into dystopia and nostalgia – from one selective view to the next – does not exactly make it easier for us to understand and deal with the structures of contemporary society. However, the end of illusions does not necessarily have to lead to all-encompassing pessimism. The absence of illusions can also be a virtue that enables sober realism and opens up space for analysis. Beyond becoming mired in dystopian and nostalgic moods, it is possible to develop an undogmatic and differentiated perspective that can be critical without drifting into an untenable general account of the present. This is where sociology comes into play, because it can provide just such a sober analysis of the present. Unencumbered by belief in progress, sociology as I understand it does not, in its analysis of social structures and transformational processes, gloss over the contradictions and ambivalences that define late modernity; sociology neither whitewashes over such things in the name of morality, nor dwells on scenarios of social collapse. Rather, a realistic "socio-analysis" shares, in many respects, parallels with psychoanalysis, which Sigmund Freud developed to study individuals and culture. Psychoanalysis similarly makes no promise to resolve contradictions into a reconciled, harmonious existence. Gaining clarity – that is, making analytical progress – rather involves bringing paradoxes and ambivalences to light in order to reflect upon them and to encourage the patient, with the help of this newfound perspective, to take realistic steps toward changing his or her circumstances.

In this sense, the chapters of this book are attempts to examine the contradictory structures of contemporary society in a way that avoids both the overly simplistic narrative of progress and alarmist diagnoses of social decay. Unambiguous assessments and simple solutions are therefore not to be expected. On the contrary, whoever can tolerate ambivalences and deal with them productively is clearly at an advantage in late modernity. In today's climate of debate, however, with its clear distinctions between friend and foe, the elementary psychological ability to tolerate ambiguity is in a sorry state.[6] In my book *The Society of Singularities*, I attempted to develop a systematic theory of late-modern society that takes into account its ambivalences.[7] In the present book, I intend to refine certain aspects of this theory. Here, I will be equally concerned with political, economic, and cultural dimensions. My analysis of contemporary society, moreover, is not restricted to Germany but, rather, pertains to the Western world as a whole, which – despite national differences – is presently undergoing similar transformations and facing similar problems throughout Europe and North America. The transformation of the West, in turn, can only be understood within a global framework.

From Industrial Modernity to the Society of Singularities

The point of departure for my perspective on today's society is that, over the last 30 years, we have been experiencing a profound structural shift, over the course of which classical *industrial modernity* has transformed into a new form of modernity, which I call *late modernity*. Our understanding of the structures of late modernity, however, is still underdeveloped.

Industrial modernity first took shape at the beginning of the twentieth century, and it reached its zenith in the affluent postwar societies of the aforementioned *trente glorieuses*, which extended into the 1970s. This was a form of society based on rationalization, mechanization, and planning. Industrial mass production in large factories was just as characteristic of this society as large-scale housing projects, Keynesian economic planning, the expansion of the welfare state, and the firm belief in technical progress. For individuals, industrial modernity meant existing in an affluent society (in John Kenneth Galbraith's terms) with a relatively egalitarian standard of living. Social control, cultural homogeneity, and cultural conformism were at a high; a clear division of gender roles and discrimination against sexual and ethnic minorities were not the exception but the rule. Following the French historian Pierre Rosanvallon, one could say that this was a "society of equals," with all its bright and dark sides: a society governed by the rules of the general and the collective.[8]

This classical industrial society no longer exists, even though certain thinkers still regard it as a guiding light. Of course, many of its elements persist; there is, after all, some overlap between historical periods. However, it has been supplanted as the dominant form of society by another form that some sociologists have designated postmodern and others have called high-modern, hyper-modern, or the second modernity. I prefer the term "late modernity." This structural shift was already well on its way in the 1970s and 1980s, and its emblematic events include the student revolts of 1968, the oil crisis and the collapse of the Bretton Woods financial system in 1973, and the development of the Apple I (the first affordable personal computer) in 1976. Late modernity has been maturing since the 1990s. It is characterized by, among other things, radical globalization, which has dissolved the formerly clear separation between the "first," "second," and "third" world, and which increasingly blurs the boundaries between the global North and the global

South. In regions of the South, rapid modernization is now taking place, while regions of the North are losing their traditional status.

It remains challenging to formulate a coherent understanding of the structural features of late modernity. The liberal narrative of progress, which I discussed above, might focus here on globalization (understood positively), democratization, the expansion of markets, liberalization, and digital networking. In this way, the structural shift at hand could be understood from one side as a linear development. We have to learn, however, to understand late modernity as a contradictory and conflicted societal formation that is characterized simultaneously by social growth and decline, by cultural valuation and devaluation, and ultimately by processes of polarization. This, in essence, is what makes it explosive. In large part, these asymmetries and structural disparities have been neither planned nor consciously brought about; rather, they are what sociologists refer to as unintended consequences. For this very reason, they are irritating. Unlike industrial modernity's society of equals, late modernity has increasingly been taking on the form of a *society of singularities*.[9] In short, this means: whereas industrial modernity was based, in so many facets of life, on the reproduction of standards, normality, and uniformity – and one could say that "generality" reigned supreme – late-modern society is oriented toward the production of unique and singular entities and experiences and it values qualitative differences, individuality, particularity, and the unusual. If one would prefer to use more familiar terms from sociological and political debates, one could loosely describe late modernity as a society of radicalized individualism. In a sense, it takes this individualism, which has been a part of modernity from the beginning, to an extreme level. To me, however, the traditional concept of "individualism" – as well as that of "individualization" – seems both too broad and too narrow to describe the social and political processes that characterize late modernity.[10]

I therefore prefer the term "singularization." It more accurately denotes the social processes in which particularity and uniqueness, non-exchangeability, incomparability, and superlatives are expected, fabricated, positively evaluated, and experienced.[11] In late modernity, a social logic of singularization has been established on a large scale, whereas during earlier phases of modernity such logic was only able to exist in small segments of society. It has an inevitably paradoxical structure: core areas of society have now developed *general* structures and practices whose interest is systematically oriented toward the *particular*. Thus, singularities neither exist outside of the social world nor are they directed against it – rather, they are at its center. They are not "released into the wild." On the contrary, they are produced by and are part of the everyday praxis of society.

Unlike the processes of individualization, those of singularization are not restricted to human individuals. Of course, late-modern society admires the particularity of individual people – an excellent performance at work, a top athlete, a prominent environmental activist, or an extraordinary blogger, for instance – but it also admires the singularity of things and objects, such as the authenticity and non-exchangeability of sought-after goods and brands, which are now in part esteemed like works of art. These processes also subject spatial entities to singularization – such as cities or landscapes as recognizably "valuable" places – and they do the same to temporal entities, which can interest us as singular events or memorable moments. Finally, late-modern society even singularizes its collectives: from projects and networks to voluntarily chosen "neo-communities" (of a religious or regional sort, for instance), each of which promises to be incomparable. Late modernity's systems of evaluation typically frown upon that which is merely standardized and functional – "average" individuals who are mere role players, things that are industrial goods bought "off the rack," spaces that are "faceless," and temporal routines that are dull and forgettable – and instead direct society's interest toward that which is felt to be singular and is valorized as such. Only the latter is attributed *value* in the true sense.

Broadly speaking, late modernity has thus turned out to be an extremely ambitious form of society in which it is no longer sufficient for anything to be average. Instead, it is expected of individuals, things, events, places, and collectives that they leave the average in the dust. It is only the singularization of the social that promises contentment, prestige, and the power of identification; it alone, from the perspective of late-modern culture, makes people and the world *valuable*. The transformation from the society of equals to the society of singularities has several causes: the most important among them are the structural shift of the economy from industrial to cognitive-cultural capitalism, the technological revolution of digitalization, and finally the socio-cultural process in which a new urban middle class of highly qualified and educated people, who are oriented toward self-development and individual prestige, has advanced to become society's new leading milieu.

The "singularistic" structure of late-modern society, however, necessarily comes with its reverse side: that which is unable or unwilling to be singular (or forbidden from being so). Such entities are disdained; they remain invisible in the background, and they receive only minimal – if any – recognition. Inevitably, there are thus winners and losers; there is appreciation and *devaluation*. This insight is central: the singularization of the social is not a linear process in which everyone and everything receives recognition for his, her, or its uniqueness. Processes of singularization have not caused us to enter a postmodern "realm of freedom" on the heels of industrial modernity's "realm of necessity." Rather, society's valorization of the singular entails the devaluation of that which is standardized and common (and therefore disappears into the background). Under today's conditions, the ubiquitous singularization of the social inexorably and systematically generates structural asymmetries and disparities.

This *dual structure of singularization and polarization* applies to every dimension of the tectonic shift that late modern societies have been experiencing. Some of these dimensions will be discussed in the chapters of this book.

Regarding the *economy*, today's ambitious and globally networked cognitive-cultural capitalism, which is oriented toward developing complex goods – things, services, events, media formats – that are highly innovative, creative, and appealing, has the reverse side that so-called simple services (routine and repetitive jobs held by low-qualified individuals, whose prestige and social security are minimal) have become more widespread. Conversely, cognitive-cultural capitalism is governed by market structures that follow a winner-take-all logic, so that extremely lucrative goods – from high-tech pharmaceuticals and top football players to globally renowned artwork and desirable real estate – lead to an excessive production of wealth.

In the late-modern *educational system*, the rapidly growing number of university graduates and the heated profile competition between schools, between universities, and between graduates for excellence and unique selling points is only one side of things. The reverse side of this is the indirect devaluation of lower or mid-rank educational degrees. Today, what was once a normal level of achievement is regarded as no more than average.

High ambition and devaluation also go hand in hand in the area of *lifestyles*. The lifestyle model of "successful self-actualization," which strives for uniqueness and the accumulation of singularity capital, turns daily life, work, leisure, and family life into an ambitious challenge. The new middle class rises to this challenge. The reverse side of this process is the subtle cultural devaluation or massive social downgrading that the traditional middle class and the precarious class have been experiencing. In addition, however, there is also a great deal of frustration among members of the new middle class who have failed to live up to their own ambitious standards: the singularistic lifestyle is systematically prone to cause disappointment.

The *digital world*, too, is based on a fundamental asymmetry: between those individuals (and also goods, places, institutions) that attract attention and appreciation (occasionally in excess), and those that largely remain invisible, are poorly networked and isolated, and either lack recognition or become the focus of negative attention (they are hated or disdained, for instance).

On the level of *spatial structures*, the current popularity of metropolitan areas is characteristic of late modernity. Appealing cities attract new businesses, workers, and visitors, and a trans-regional competition is now taking place between cities vying to offer the best quality of life. The reverse side is that this has given rise to "left-behind" areas, which are now in a downward spiral of depopulation and waning attractiveness.

In the end, it is only logical that the singularism of late-modern society has also led to polarization in the sphere of *politics*. Since the 1980s, the dominant form of politics has been a new type of liberalism that is radically based on competition and difference, dynamism, and the removal of social, economic, and cultural boundaries on a global scale. What has recently emerged as a reaction to this liberalism is an aggressive form of populism that propagates the social isolation of nation states. It is supported above all by those segments of the population that were either ignored or threatened by the liberal program of modernization. Populism is thus an articulation of the disgruntled reverse side of the society of singularities.

* * *

In the first chapter – "Cultural Conflicts as a Struggle over Culture: Hyperculture and Cultural Essentialism" – I discuss the ways in which late-modern societies are defined by conflicts over culture and identity. Contrary to Samuel Huntington's prominent thesis that we are dealing with a struggle *between* cultural spheres, I show that, across the globe, there are now two fundamentally oppositional ways of dealing *with* culture. One approach – that of hyperculture – allows for individual self-development and provides space for diversity on global markets, while the other approach – that of cultural essentialism – understands culture as a fixed entity or as the medium of a given community's collective identity. Here I examine the relationship between these two forms of "culturalization" and ask whether there might be an alternative to both of them.

The second chapter – "From the Leveled Middle-Class Society to the Three-Class Society: The New Middle Class, the Old Middle Class, and the Precarious Class" – investigates the new differentiation that presently characterizes the social structure in Western nations. Over the course of post-industrialization and the expansion of education, the formerly all-encompassing middle class of industrial modernity gave way to a new, tripartite class structure. On one end, a highly educated and urban new middle class has risen to the fore – the new leading milieu of late modernity – while on the other end, there is a new precarious class comprised primarily of working-class employees in the service industry. Between these two, there remains the traditional middle class, which is oriented toward order and sedentariness. It will be shown that the relationship among these classes cannot be reduced to material inequalities but is, rather, fundamentally defined by the cultural factor of symbolic valuation and devaluation.

"Beyond Industrial Society: Polarized Post-Industrialism and Cognitive-Cultural Capitalism," the third chapter, is devoted to the structural transformation of Western capitalism. In the West, the industrial economy has lost its structural and formational significance. But what does it mean to say that we live in a post-industrial society? This chapter explains the transformation from the industrial to the post-industrial economy as a response to a dual crisis of saturation and productivity. Here I identify the features of cognitive capitalism, which is based on intangible assets, knowledge, and scalability, and I also examine the mechanisms of cultural capitalism, whose markets depend on the variable reputation that its symbolic goods happen to acquire in the eyes of consumers. Cognitive-cultural capitalism turns out to be a capitalism of extremes that has also paved the way for the widespread economization of the social.

In the fourth chapter – "The Weariness of Self-Actualization: The Late-Modern Individual and the Paradoxes of Emotional Culture" – I examine the culturally dominant lifestyle of the late-modern self, and particularly its everyday practices and psychological dynamics. What does it mean to lead a life that aims to combine the "Romantic" aspiration of self-development with the "bourgeois" goal of social success? This chapter identifies the dilemmas of a late-modern way of life in which subjective experience and psychological contentment have become fragile measures of a success. It is characterized by a paradoxical emotional culture that, on the one hand (and to an extreme extent), is based on positive feelings as a goal in life, and yet, on the other hand, it offers no way of dealing with the negative feelings – such as disappointment and frustration – that it systematically generates.

The final chapter – "The Crisis of Liberalism and the Search for the New Political Paradigm: From Apertistic to Regulatory Liberalism" – is concerned with the current political crisis, in which liberalism and populism stand in opposition to one another. Here, I present an alternative interpretation of political developments since 1945. Rather than being defined by mere shifts between the left and the right, these developments have been shaped above all by a transformation of the overarching political paradigms of social regulation and dynamization. The current crisis of liberalism – which has been dominant since the 1980s as a synthesis of neoliberalism and progressive liberalism – can thus be interpreted as a "crisis of excessive dynamization." Finally, I ask what would be needed to establish a form of "regulatory liberalism," which could replace the present paradigm and also offer an alternative to the rising wave of populism.

Four of the five chapters were written specifically for this book, the exception being the first chapter, which has already appeared in two earlier versions.[12] I have composed them in such a way that they can be read and understood independently. Thus, they do not have to be read in any particular order. Readers should simply go where their curiosity takes them!

1

Cultural Conflicts as a Struggle over Culture: Hyperculture and Cultural Essentialism

In his much-discussed book *The Clash of Civilizations*, which was published shortly after the fall of the Iron Curtain, the American political scientist Samuel Huntington formulated an unsettling thesis.[1] According to Huntington, the end of the conflict between the East and the West would not lead to everlasting peace. Instead, a new, more complex, and threatening conflict would emerge: a global struggle between cultures – between the West, Russia, China, India, the Arab world, and other parts of the globe. Huntington's thesis was rejected at first. During the 1990s, the prevailing wind was one of unlimited liberal optimism and globalization, and most observers assumed that modernization (of a Western sort) would triumph worldwide. In fact, things turned out differently. What we see today is clearly an intensification of new cultural conflicts: terrorist attacks by Islamic fundamentalists, nationalistic tendencies in Eastern and Southern Europe, China's and India's self-confident defensiveness regarding their cultures, and finally the centrifugal forces of right-wing populism in the West itself (even in two of its core nations, France and the United States).

In light of the complexity of this conflict situation, it is easy at first to fall back on Samuel Huntington's thesis about the clash of cultures. His thesis is seductive, but ultimately it is far too simple. Of course, both within national societies and on the global level, these conflicts are often and undoubtedly about *culture*, and the question of culture is closely tied to that of *identity*. Moreover, it is also the case that, in today's late-modern societies, culture is attributed a level of significance that can hardly be overestimated. It is astonishing how often and intensively questions of culture – from the issue of "parallel cultures" to that of the "dominant culture" – become heated topics in public debates. Contrary to Huntington's thesis, however, these conflicts should be seen not as a simple clash of cultures but as something different: a conflict *about* culture – that is, a debate over what should be understood by culture and what place it should take. Instead of an antagonistic struggle between diverse cultures and their cultural patterns, what we are witnessing in late modernity – and this is my opening thesis – is a far more fundamental conflict between two opposed *regimes of culturalization*, as I would like to call them. This is not a matter of various cultural patterns facing one another; rather – and on an even more fundamental level – there are two oppositional understandings of what culture *means* in general, and, accordingly, there are two contrary formats in which culture is *organized*.

In late modernity, the culturalization of the social is taking place on a broad front, and this process has assumed two different forms. On one side – and here I am speaking of "Culturalization I" – we observe a culturalization of lifestyles in which individuals striving for self-development surround themselves with cultural set pieces from a mobile global market. This is a cosmopolitan understanding of culture that can be called *hyperculture*. On the other side, we are witness to a form of culturalization that is directed toward collectives and constructs them as moral, identity-based communities. This process – "Culturalization II" – operates on the basis of an inside–outside dualism, and it follows the model of homogeneous communities, which are created as "imagined communities." The corresponding model of culture is that of *cultural essentialism*, and it can be found in many forms. Late modernity is characterized by an elementary conflict between these two regimes of culturalization.

The Culturalization of the Social

"Culturalization" may at first sound like a strange term. In sociology, we are familiar with a whole series of such terms that contain the ending *-ization* or *-iation* and thus suggest that something is increasing or intensifying: modern*ization*, rational*ization*, individual*ization*, different*iation*, and so on. In a comparable way, the term "culturalization" would then have to denote an extension of culture into areas where it had hitherto not existed. Yet what can that possibly mean in light of the apparent consensus that, to some extent, everything "is" culture, insofar as every human act can only become what it is against the backdrop of contexts and worlds of meaning? Despite this initial consideration, it is possible to furnish the concept of culturalization with social-theoretical significance so long as two important distinctions are kept in mind: first, the distinction between culture in a broad but weak sense, and culture in a narrow but strong sense; second, the distinction between rationalization and culturalization.

How is culture generally understood? And what is its place in modern society? Culture is certainly one of the most controversial and vibrant concepts in the humanities and social sciences. At the same time, the British sociologist Raymond Williams regarded it as a key concept of modernity that began to spread, not coincidentally, at the end of the eighteenth century – that is, with the rise of modernity itself.[2] Culture has been defined in a number of entirely different ways.[3] In early modernity, culture was understood as an eminent and especially distinguished individual way of life; only a few people, then, were thought to have culture – the nobility, the bourgeoisie, the ecclesiastical elite – whereas everyone else (the great majority of people) presumably lacked it. During the era of German Romanticism, alternatively, Herder defined culture as the way of life practiced by an entire people: "German culture" was thus conceived as being different from, say, Chinese culture. This understanding of culture as a group feature also seems to have been shared by Huntington. In contrast, culture can also be understood in a very narrow sense; such is the case, for instance, at ministries of culture, which tend to identify culture with the high culture of education, the arts, and perhaps also religion. Compared with the latter understanding, the cultural theorists of the twentieth century radically expanded the concept of culture. Ernst Cassirer, for instance, associated culture with the way in which the world is perceived – how it is interpreted in worldviews and everyday ideas – and with the meaning that is attributed to it.[4]

This latter, broad cultural-theoretical understanding of culture is in many respects sensible and useful. Every praxis can thus be understood as culture by determining the definitions, concepts, distinctions, and interpretive presuppositions that are contained in it. Culture is not restricted to art and religion. Nature, gender, or technology also have a cultural dimension to the extent that they depend on social worlds of meaning that *define* and *interpret* nature, gender, or technology in a particular way. Nevertheless, in order to understand the role of culture in modernity, we also need, in addition to this broad and yet *weak* concept of the cultural, a narrow but *strong* concept of culture. In the broad cultural-theoretical understanding, everything is to some extent culture because meaning is everywhere at play. The narrow understanding, in contrast, sees culture only where *value* is at stake.[5] This is my point of departure: culture and value are inextricably linked. In the sphere of culture, certain things are attributed *value* – they are laden with value, while other things are denied value. The sphere of culture is thus the dynamic social sphere in which one "valorizes" (assigns value) or "de-valorizes" (denies value). That which is valuable stands on one side, while that which is without value stands on the other. It is important to note that this is not a matter of individuals "having" values, such as those that are asked about in opinion surveys. The issue is rather that, in social processes, elements of the world are attributed or denied value; I am concerned here, in other words, with the highly dynamic and often controversial process of "doing value." In this process, any number of things can become valuable, including works of art or certain individuals, gods or an ethical code, pop music or apartments in an old building, fashion, YouTube videos, or a nation's legal constitution.

Every human society has its own sphere of culture, which means that they all have their own processes for assigning (or not assigning) value to certain things, spaces, events, groups, or subjects. This is also true of modern society, which emerged in the wake of the Enlightenment, industrialization, and the democratic revolutions at the end of the eighteenth century. For a long time, however, it seemed as though modernity's cultural sphere played no more than a marginal role, and that it was far subordinate to the sphere of utility, functionality, and efficiency. This is because culture has a formidable adversary: (formal) rationality. If culture is the sphere of valorization and de-valorization, rationality is the sphere of practicality, neutral procedures, laws, and cognitive processes. This bifurcation is redolent of Émile Durkheim's classical distinction between the sacred and the profane.[6] The sphere of culture is concerned with large and small forms of the sacred, from God to objects of consumption, whereas the sphere of rationality is home to the profane – to objectivity, dispassion, and disenchantment. The positive and negative valorizations of culture involve strong emotions and affects, whereas rationality remains, in comparison, emotionally impoverished.

From its beginning, modernity developed extreme systems of rationalization. As Max Weber insightfully argued, modernity is firmly based on formal rationalization and on the increased efficiency of technology, commerce, government, and science.[7] Classical modernity (that is, the bourgeois modernity of the nineteenth century and the industrial modernity of the first two-thirds of the twentieth century) were thus broadly objectified and secularized. Here, culture existed only in the margins, where, at best, it survived in art and the vestiges of religion. During this phase, traditional bourgeois-oriented cultural institutions such as the theatre, concert halls, and museums formed islands of culture that offered, to a relatively limited audience, temporary refuge from or an alternative to the otherwise dominant logic of industrial, instrumental rationality. At least since the 1970s, however, this insular existence of culture has been a thing of the past, for from then on – and this, in my view, marks the transition from classical modernity to late modernity (or postmodernity) – Western societies began to *culturalize* themselves.[8] Gradually, the sphere of culture expanded, while that of rationality contracted. Of course, powerful forces of rationalization continued to exist (and still exist today), but culture as a dynamic sphere of valorization has expanded in late modernity because more and more things – beyond the question of their utility, interest, and function – have been sucked into the cultural game of valuation and devaluation. More and more, the social in late modernity participates in a logic of assigning value, identity, and affectivity, and this logic has left behind the profane sphere of functionality. This culturalization, however, has been realized in two oppositional forms: as hyperculture or as cultural essentialism.

Culturalization I: Hyperculture

Hyperculture's form of culturalization has been setting the pace of late modernity since the 1980s. It is supported by a new cosmopolitan middle class that prefers to cluster in the urban centers of Western societies, but is increasingly taking over the aspiring cities of the global South as well. In the context of hyperculture, "culture" no longer denotes the high culture of the educated bourgeoisie, and neither does it denote the conformist and homogeneous mass culture of the postwar period. Instead, culture now refers to the *plurality* of cultural goods that circulate on global *markets* and are available to individuals as *resources* for their *self-development*. In other words, hyperculture understands global culture as a single, gigantic reservoir from which to draw diverse resources for self-actualization – the Japanese martial art Aikido or Indian yoga; Scandinavian design, French films, or American video games; Creole or southern German cuisine; city trips, active vacations, or thematic travel; world music or the art museum, and so on and so forth.[9]

Hyperculture is literally *über*-culture; it is a sort of overarching dynamic principle that creates a sphere in which potentially *everything*, in a highly variable way, *can* become an object of value – but, of course, not everything *is* of equal value. Two entities are decisive for hyperculture's form of culturalization: on the one hand, the goods that circulate on cultural markets; on the other hand, the subjects who encounter these goods with a desire for self-development. In this global hyperculture, culture always takes place in cultural markets in which cultural goods compete with one another.[10] In the background of commercial competition, there is a fundamental competition between goods for scarce amounts of attention and valorization. In a sense, the cultural sphere of hyperculture forms a market in which there is a competition to be perceived as valuable – a competition, that is, for visibility, attractiveness, and ennoblement. This market is highly dynamic and unpredictable. It is frequently oriented toward what is new, innovative, and creative (and therefore surprising); however, it also values cultural goods that, over time, have acquired the status of classics.

The central pillar of hyperculture's markets is global cultural capitalism: the constantly growing creative economy, which ranges from computer and internet companies to design, architecture, and tourism.[11] This economy forms the basis of post-industrial society, in whose cities cultural objects and spaces, such as styles, fashions, or scenes, are in immediate contact with one another and thus stand readily available as the aforementioned reservoir of hyperculture. Interestingly, the trans-regional system of cities itself has increasingly transformed into a cultural market in which, nationally and even globally, there is competition for residents, investors, and visitors. Individual cities have become cultural goods that fight for attention and value. This is indeed something new. In industrial society, cities were essentially expected to provide work and housing; in late modernity, on the contrary, cities such as Berlin and Seattle, Amsterdam and Singapore, Sao Paulo and Melbourne, Cape Town and Freiburg are thought about in cultural terms – that is, they are evaluated in terms of features such as their attractiveness, authenticity, and quality of life. They no longer compete to be recognized simply for their functionality but also for their value.[12]

In addition to cultural markets, the second entity that is decisive for the development of hyperculture is, as I mentioned above, individuals with a desire for self-development or self-actualization. Hyperculture is oriented not toward the collective, but rather toward the individual: its anchor is not the group, but rather the individual with his or her own interests and wishes. At the same time, it is singularistic: individuals are intent on getting to know and appropriating cultural elements in all of their uniqueness, particularity, and *singularity* – the uniqueness of a city, landscape, event, brand, object, religious belief, or body culture, to name just a few examples. For these late-modern subjects, cultural goods thus acquire the significance of resources that are meant to help them to develop their *own* uniqueness as individuals. As early as 1900, Georg Simmel spoke about modernity's individualism of particularity, noting that the modern individual strives to cultivate his or her "subjective culture."[13] Yet, in fact, it was not until the 1970s and 1980s that the motif of self-actualization became broadly established throughout society at large, and nearly ubiquitous among its new middle class – that is, within the group of urban and highly qualified people who often work in the knowledge economy.[14] In the meantime, this development has also reached the aspiring societies of the global South.

For such individuals, who strive for self-development, global hyperculture is a paradise of possibilities waiting to be appropriated. Between art and cuisine, travel and spirituality, education and body culture, they can assemble any combination of their choice – an entire lifestyle and identity all of their own – and acquire in this way, both in their own eyes and in the eyes of others, the value of uniqueness. Hyperculture and the search for identity are thus closely related. If identity denotes the way in which individuals or groups interpret themselves – that is, the way in which they understand themselves to be something unique and different from others – then, for the late-modern individual, hyperculture is the medium of this identity formation. The late-modern individual acquires his or her personal identity as a unique individual by processing and combining what global culture has to offer.

Because hyperculture enables potentially everything to become culture, the boundaries that once defined "legitimate culture" have dissolved. In particular, the boundaries between high and popular culture, between the culture of the present and the past, and between one's own culture and foreign cultures (the latter understood as that which exists outside of one's national culture) have now become porous to the point of disappearing. Unlike the classical culture of the bourgeoisie, hyperculture no longer devalues what is popular in favor of education-based high culture. Rather, it is now the case that everyday practices such as cooking or playing football, and formats such as pop music and tattoos, can also potentially become culturally valuable. At the same time, however, the formats of high culture have also maintained their prestige. Think of the great appeal that concert halls and museums have managed to gain since the 1990s: the Guggenheim Museum in Bilbao, the Elbphilharmonie in Hamburg, the MOCAA in Cape Town, etc. Without any inhibitions, moreover, hyperculture also admits both present and historical entities into its circulation: Netflix series, art installations, or photos on Instagram accounts, as well as old stucco apartment buildings, vintage fashion, or revitalized historical city districts. Finally, hyperculture has burst open the fixation on national traditions in favor of a balance between one's own culture and that of others. Here, what is foreign – from the Western perspective, for instance, Asian body cultures or spirituality, or, from the German perspective, Scandinavian or Italian design – potentially seems like something interesting, attractive, and valuable to discover and appropriate.[15]

It is no surprise that diversity and cosmopolitanism are the guiding principles of hyperculture. In hyperculture, diversity is good in itself.[16] A multiplicity of cultural practices from various national, regional, ethnic, historical, social, or religious origins is considered an enrichment, because it enormously expands the field of cultural resources for individual self-actualization. Conversely, a reduction of cultural diversity, or a monoculture, would mean that there are fewer cultural resources and therefore fewer options for self-actualization. Within today's hyperculture, diversity goes hand in hand with the model of hybridity.[17] Hybridity means that cultural features should not exist in isolation from one another but should, rather, be freely combined with one another. It is this that gives rise to what can be called cultural cosmopolitanism. In this sense, cosmopolitanism means having an essentially open attitude toward the diversity of cultural practices and goods, regardless of their origin. Not coincidentally, cosmopolitanism typically overlaps with globalism: it welcomes and promotes the global flow of goods, ideas, and people.

Culture as hyperculture thus designates not only a specific understanding of culture but also, and above all, a particular way in which cultural entities are produced, circulated, and appropriated in society. The fact that culture as hyperculture has been able to become so significant and powerful over the last few decades is due to several aspects of the structural transformation of society that have systematically promoted and favored it. First, the transnational new middle class of highly qualified individuals – which is endowed with extraordinary cultural, economic, and social capital – has sought and discovered its identity in the medium of hyperculture, which defines its lifestyle of self-development and singularity-based prestige. Second, cultural capitalism – which is not focused on industrial functional goods, but rather on goods and services with symbolic and experiential value – fuels hyperculture by constantly introducing new cultural goods into the world and making existing local cultures useful to its own ends. Third, liberal cultural politics, which endorses diversity and globalism, has bolstered the tendencies of hyperculture (especially in large cities), while – fourth – global processes of migration have steadily been feeding new elements into the global sphere of cultural circulation.

Culturalization II: Cultural Essentialism

Along with globalization, hyperculture has spread both within and beyond the old Western world. Over the course of its ascent since the 1980s and 1990s, however, a countermovement has developed that could be called "the International of cultural essentialism." It has been startling to observe how this movement, too, invokes culture, even though its understanding of culture's game of valuation and devaluation is entirely different from that of hyperculture. This cultural-essentialist countermovement includes the diverse forms of fundamentalism within the three monotheistic religions, the numerous and powerful proponents of heightened cultural nationalism (in Russia, China, or India, for instance), and the right-wing populist and identitarian movements in Europe and North America. Though situated somewhat differently, North American identity politics, and regional movements in places such as Scotland and Catalonia, are at least related to these variants of cultural essentialism. At first glance, all of these tendencies can hardly be reduced to a common denominator; viewed from a greater distance, however, one sees that they are all opposed to cosmopolitan hyperculture and that, oddly enough, this opposition is itself waged through the medium of culture and identity.

Keep in mind that cultural essentialism exists in a number of different varieties, which range from regional identities to fundamentalist terrorism and which, at first glance, hardly seem to be related at all. Nevertheless, it is possible to recognize certain common structures. Central to this understanding of culture is the following point of departure: the collective identity of a community. Whereas the keystone of liberal hyperculture is individual self-development, cultural essentialism is based on the collective, the community, the locus of culture. Here, culture (as the sphere of what is valuable) is that which holds a community together and defines its common identity.[18] The individuals involved have accordingly integrated themselves into the collective, where they earn self-evident recognition without competing for it, simply by being part of the group. Cultural essentialism is thus a form of communitarianism. This basic structure applies just as much to religious groups as it does to cultural nationalists or self-conscious ethnic communities. Here, the collective is not a general and anonymous global society but is itself something unique, with its own particular history, beliefs, and origin. In short, the locus of singularity in hyperculture is the individual person, whereas, in cultural essentialism, the community as a whole becomes singular, somewhat like a nation: it distinguishes itself from others and has a complexity "entirely its own".

Cultural essentialism constructs a rigid boundary: between one's own group and others, between ingroup and outgroup. Whereas, in hyperculture, culture and its valuable goods are mobile, dynamic, and unpredictable – and transgressing boundaries is the rule – the central objective of cultural essentialism is to stabilize the symbolic boundary between the internal world and the external world. Here, the internal world of one's own culture is attributed a stable and seemingly unassailable value. In Benedict Anderson's terms, these are "imagined communities," communities that exist in the collective imagination and cultivate their own self-image, history, and moral code.[19] The ideal of cultural essentialism is, therefore, the homogeneity of the community, its unambiguity, and its uniformity, which absorb the differences that exist between its individuals. Of course, a rather strong distinction is draw between the inside and the outside: in contrast to the sacred nature of the inside, the external world seems profane, or even worthless. The context of cultural essentialism thus gives rise to "neo-communities." The prefix "neo-" is necessary here because, unlike the case of traditional communities, neo-communities are not collectives into which people are simply born; instead, they are communities that people consciously choose to join.[20] Cultural neo-communities can coexist with friendly indifference toward one another – according to the manner of ethno-pluralism – but they can also aggressively distance their own culture from the outside and even, in extreme cases, wish to eliminate it. For religious fundamentalists, the outside consists of nonbelievers; for aggressive nationalists, it consists of other, inferior nations; and for right-wing populists, the outgroup consists of immigrants and the cosmopolitan elite.

In cultural essentialism, one's own culture is therefore not a matter of negotiation; it is rather the ineluctable point of departure. Culture seems to have an essence of its own, and time and space – that is, its history and place of origin – are the two important pillars upon which this culture is based. There is no praise for the present or the future; at its core, cultural essentialism is rather a retreat into the past, into the history and traditions from which a given religion, nation, or people supposedly emerged. It is often a common homeland that lends such groups their identity, and thus cultural essentialism is typically critical of globalization: the circulation of goods and people is here perceived as a potential threat to one's own identity.

As mentioned above, cultural-essentialist currents largely take the form of movements that oppose the developmental trends of hyper-culture that are systematically favored, and have become dominant, in Western societies. Of course, instantiations of cultural essentialism have historical precursors – such as the nationalist movements in the nineteenth century, with their discovery of the "people" (and even of "race") – but in late modernity they have a different social significance: they can be interpreted as a *mobilization of peripheries against society's center*, and this is true both within national societies and on the global level. This mobilization of peripheries does not take the form of class conflicts in the traditional (social-material) sense; instead, it adopts the form of *identity conflicts*.[21]

As diverse as the individual forms of cultural essentialism may be – ethnic communities, religious fundamentalisms, nationalism, right-wing populism – they all share in common the fact that they are overwhelmingly represented by population groups that, over the course of the transformation from industrial modernity to the post-industrial society of singularities, perceive themselves as losers of modernization. In terms of social structure, we are dealing here with members of the new underclass and the old middle class.[22] For the latter, hyperculture and its cosmopolitanism are the domain of "elites," whereas their collective identity movements are the medium in which the disgruntled, devalued, and aggrieved have come together to oppose what they perceive to be their unjust loss of social status and cultural influence. In this late-modern iteration of cultural essentialism, feelings of superiority and inferiority form an unusual alliance: those who feel inferior attempt to establish their own superiority via a collective identity.

At the same time, cultural essentialism can also be interpreted on the global level – that is, in the relationships between national societies – as a mobilization of the peripheries against the center. In this case, the "center" is a real or imagined West from which forms of cultural essentialism in Russia, Turkey, Hungary, China, or India – in countries, that is, that perceive themselves as victims of Western hegemony – are attempting to distance themselves.[23] Here, too, it is the case that discrimination and perceived affronts from the privileged – that is, from "the West" (in the form of the British as former colonizers, the United States as a superpower, the European Union under German and French leadership, etc.) – have been transformed into self-ascriptions of presumed superiority, which are meant to secure the identity of the slighted nations in question. If cultural essentialism exerts any influence beyond the social groups that have been left behind by modernization, it does so on the level of the state – for instance, through government-supported cultural, educational, and immigration policies.

Hyperculture and Cultural Essentialism: Between Coexistence and Conflict

What we have witnessed in many areas of late modernity is a polarization between two regimes of culturalization: between hyperculture and cultural essentialism. Only by adopting this abstract perspective does it become clear that, in fact, mutually hostile groups – such as the Salafists or Marine Le Pen's National Rally, Evangelicals or Russian nationalists – follow the same pattern, namely that of Culturalization II. They may fill cultural essentialism with different content, but they employ one and the same schema of culturalization, which they mobilize in fundamental opposition to the other schema – that is, against Culturalization I. This is where my interpretation differs most explicitly from Samuel Huntington's. In Huntington's view, the various national varieties of religious fundamentalism, right-wing populism, and nationalism each formed their own *distinct* "cultures," whereas now it is clear that they all follow the *same* pattern. Conversely, "the West" does not simply constitute an additional culture, as Huntington suggested; rather, in its late-modern instantiation, it enables a form of culturalization that is structured in a fundamentally *different* manner: Culturalization I (hyperculture). That said, it would be too simple a dramatization to characterize the relationship between these two regimes as one of "the West against the rest." As I have already mentioned, the historical roots of hyperculture may lie in Europe and North

America, but it has long since globalized beyond these trans-Atlantic confines. Conversely, moreover, cultural essentialism is by no means restricted to just Asia or Eastern Europe but is, rather, prevalent in Western Europe and the United States as well. "The West" is not a spatial, geographical concept; it is a symbolic concept.

What happens when hyperculture encounters cultural essentialism?[24] Many of today's global and intra-societal conflicts can be deciphered as part of the conflict between these two regimes of culturalization. In this conflict, there are always two possible ways for each side to deal with the other: a strategy of coexistence *qua* assimilation, and a strategy of rejection as an absolute enemy. Assimilation entails making attempts to integrate *phenomena* of the other cultural regime into one's own *perspective* and thus to make them manageable and coexist with them. Rejection as an absolute enemy entails perceiving the radical otherness of the different cultural regime and, accordingly, dramatizing this relation in the form of a friend–enemy schema. In all, there are thus four possible strategies for dealing with one another, and there are plenty of empirical examples of each one (see Table 1.1).

During the 1980s and 1990s, one formula for coexistence between hyperculture and cultural essentialism was multiculturalism.[25] The multiculturalism of Western liberals proceeded from the idea that diverse ways of life represent a fundamental enrichment, so that ethnic or religious communities, for instance, were tolerated even if they were relatively closed off. Essentially, multiculturalism looked at cultural communities through a pair of cosmopolitan-diversity glasses, and what it saw was groups cultivating different lifestyles in which people chose to participate. The result, in short, was that orthodox Islam, veganism, and teenage subcultures were all regarded as being on the same level. From the perspective of multiculturalism, different sorts of groups are embodiments, as it were, of cultural options and styles, and they make no claim to absoluteness. Cultural capitalism, too, is ultimately based on economically applied multiculturalism: cultural communities with local roots thus appear as welcome contexts or reservoirs from which "authentic" cultural goods can be drawn, and these goods can then be commodified and appropriated (the tattoos of sailors, Middle Eastern cooking, the meditation of Buddhist monks, and so on).

Table 1.1 Relations between Culturalization I and Culturalization II

	Culturalization I in relation to Culturalization II	**Culturalization II in relation to Culturalization I**
Coexistence	Multiculturalism	Theory of cultural spheres
Antagonism	"Open society and its enemies"	"Decadence of the West"

Conversely, cultural essentialism has also produced its share of strategies for coexisting with liberal hyperculture. One common strategy consists in viewing cosmopolitanism itself as the worldview of a foreign cultural community that, though peculiar, is not threatening. This attitude is apparent, for instance, in the behavior of non-Western governments that, in response to accusations of violating human rights, insist on the value of their native traditions. From this viewpoint, liberal cosmopolitanism appears, in a sense, as a special feature of the Western cultural community and its history: Westerners may indeed support hyperculture, and they are free to do so – but only on their own turf! From this perspective, which is based on a political *theory of cultural spheres*, different cultures are ultimately thought of as being distinct from one another, and cosmopolitan hyperculture represents just one of these varieties: the sphere of Western (that is, North American and Western European) culture.

Hyperculture and cultural essentialism can thus interact in a state of peaceful coexistence. However, a coexistence of this sort only seems possible if both sides systematically misunderstand one another. In other words, this can only happen if, from the perspective of market-based and self-actualization-based culturalization, identitarian movements embody just another style or another chosen identity among many others, and if, from the perspective of cultural essentialism, hyperculture is merely a particular aspect of Western societies. However, as soon as these two regimes of culturalization begin to perceive one another as contrary ways of dealing with culture – which, from a sociological perspective, they in fact *are* – they see themselves as being fundamentally threatened. What follows is a culture war: a struggle over culture itself.

We have thus come to the third and fourth possible modes of interaction. If cosmopolitan hyperculture recognizes the cultural-essentialist aspects of identitarian culture, then it switches over into a mode that is based on a struggle between the *open society and its enemies*. This is frequently the case today. Now, liberal cosmopolitans perceive cultural essentialism as totalitarian: proponents of hyperculture become aware of the fact that cultural essentialism – with its antagonism between believers and nonbelievers (between "us" and "them") – hopes to put an end to the pluralistic game of hypercultural differences, and they are accordingly forced to revise their model of multiculturalism. Religious fundamentalism, for instance, is no longer regarded today as just another cultural lifestyle that can be freely chosen among others (and thus as a "colorful" enrichment of society); instead, it is perceived as an attack on the foundations of cosmopolitanism. Likewise, a nationalistic claim of "white supremacy" is not regarded as a welcome new option but is, rather, seen as an inimical position, and this is because it undermines, instead of supports, the ideal of equal rights and hybrid ways of life. The result is the line of conflict that divides, in Karl Popper's terms, "the open society and its enemies."[26]

A complementary course of confrontation is pursued by the other side. In the attacks waged by various forms of cultural essentialism against cosmopolitan hyperculture, the latter is made to seem like nothing more than an expression of Western liberal decadence, which has paved the way for the permissive triumph of consumption-based individualism and has corroded national and religious communities. Hyperculture's ever-shifting ascriptions of value, which dissolve fixed distinctions between ingroups and outgroups, and its prioritization of the individual over the collective, now seem like a threat to the collective morality that cultural-essentialist communities claim for themselves. From this perspective, the West – or the liberal cosmopolitans in one's own country – thus become a symbol of cultural decay. Hyperculture, cosmopolitanism, and hybridity have become the preferred counterexamples from which to distance oneself. In this process, as mentioned above, former enemies within the cultural-essentialist camp repeatedly end up being surprising allies in their common cultural struggle against hyperculture: Evangelical Christian and orthodox Muslim communities will join forces in the fight against gay marriage, or diverse groups of European populists will come together in opposition to the American "cultural imperialism" of Google and CNN.

"Doing Universality" – The Culture of the General as an Alternative?

Is the juxtaposition of hyperculture and cultural essentialism inevitable? Are there other possible models of culture in today's society? These questions are urgent, and not only because cultural essentialism is obviously problematic and dangerous – which, from the perspective of Western liberals, is easy enough to see – but also because the model of hyperculture has deficiencies of its own and thus beckons, beyond the attacks from the International of cultural essentialists, justifiable critique.[27]

The two main deficiencies of hyperculture are the absence of a collective (in the strong sense), and the absence of any binding and normative notion of common cultural praxis. Hyperculture is built on an unlimited dynamic of the cultural, and the place where this dynamic is processed and appropriated is the self-actualizing individual with his or her "subjective culture." At its extreme, this cultural model has no room for anything socially common or shared whose validity might transcend the boundaries between individuals (or the boundaries of self-selected lifestyle groups). One's beliefs or convictions seem to be a private matter of "subjective culture," and late-modern society as a whole should not interfere with that. Late-modern society cannot offer anything that is valuable in a binding way. It operates exclusively with abstract mechanisms: aside from general legal rules, which protect personal rights, it is in effect mostly governed by market mechanisms. On a case-by-case basis, negotiations over what is culturally valuable are ultimately handed over to market processes in the broad sense, which determine whether one element of culture or another deserves attention, status, and prestige.[28]

Acknowledging the inadequacies of Culturalization I is a necessary precondition for better understanding why Culturalization II has become so attractive. Of course, every version of cultural essentialism contains the incurable problem of demarcating the boundaries of collective identity in such a way that, in extreme cases, individuality is suppressed on the inside, and outsiders are devalued and excluded in order artificially to homogenize one's "own" culture. And, of course, such cultural essentialism attracts followers because it provides an effective weapon to those who feel left behind by hypercultural late modernity. At the same time, however, things are more complicated. Cultural communitarianism can be interpreted as an understandable response to hyperculture's lack of collectives and norms. By resisting norms and refusing to promote any common values and goals, hyperculture runs the risk of culminating in a social structure that amounts to nothing more than consumption-based individualism. Cultural communitarianism has responded to this by reestablishing cultural communities, which attempt to fill the normative vacuum of hyperculture by reviving the old model of homogeneous collectives.

How do things currently stand with an alternative, third form of culturalization? With a type of culturalization that is oriented toward collectives and yet, *at the same time*, is non-essentialistic (a type of culturalization addressing a collective that does not, in other words, necessitate the existence of a homogeneous community)? Both the British cultural theorist Terry Eagleton and the French sinologist and philosopher François Jullien have pointed to just such a third model of culture, which one could call the model of cultural universality or *culture as the general*.[29] This model has been present throughout Western modernity, but it is now on the defensive; under different conditions, however, a reappropriation of this tradition could be promising. Even if, at first glance, cultural universalism may seem obsolete or naïve, it could perhaps gain renewed currency in today's radically pluralized late-modern societies.

If one contrasts cultural essentialism and hyperculture with cultural universality – which, again, is oriented toward collectives but is not essentialistic – a *common* feature of the first two models, which is otherwise easy to overlook, becomes especially apparent. In both models, what is considered culturally valuable is related to the particular and the unique – to the *singular*: on the one side, the particularity of communities, and on the other side, the uniqueness of cultural goods and the emphatic individuality of those seeking self-actualization. In a sense, cultural essentialism and hyperculture thus share a common Romantic heritage: the legacy of a culture of particularity and uniqueness, as it has developed since the time of Herder, Rousseau, and Schlegel. Both the hypercultural, individualistic model of culture and the essentialistic, collectivistic model can indeed be traced back to the discourses of Romanticism. The latter movement favored the self-development of the individual and the uniqueness of places, moments, and things. At the same time, it also "discovered" the idea of the *Volk* and the nation as cultural communities with unique values of their own. In both domains, culture was clearly associated with the particular and not with the general, for, in their critique of modern rationalism, the Romantics regarded the general as a deficiency.[30]

One should not forget, however, that the discourse of Romanticism was a countercurrent against the powerful river of the Enlightenment. The latter had formulated, especially during its early stages, a concept of culture that was largely based on the general. If culture denotes that which is regarded as valuable, then the concept espoused by European idealism was based on a common human culture, a "humane" culture. In this concept of culture, which is epitomized in Friedrich Schiller's disquisition *On the Aesthetic Education of Man*, not only are aesthetics and ethics closely intertwined – beyond that, culture and civilization were not (yet) pitted against one another.[31] The goal was to achieve a synthesis between the value of culture and the norms of sociality. During the past few decades, this cultural universalism has been discredited in political and cultural debates – and, at first, justifiably so. Among other things, it was shown to be elitist and ethnocentric. The universalism of culture was regarded as a *conceited* idea, in a dual sense. In short, the cultural standards and goods of a small group – the European bourgeoisie – had been exalted as the generally binding measure of things, and thus everything that deviated from it was classified as something inferior. The result was high culture's arrogant disdain of popular culture, and the European or Western feeling of superiority over non-Western cultures.

Today, for good reason, such cultural universalism hardly has any institutional support. Like Eagleton and Jullien, however, I would like to propose that a critically applied and advanced orientation toward cultural universality might in fact represent a desideratum within the framework of a society of singularities. The transformation of the postwar era's culturally homogeneous and socially egalitarian societies into multi-ethnic and multi-religious societies – not to mention their differentiation into socio-cultural classes – raises the question of what is, and should be, culturally valid for *everyone*. Over the course of this social transformation, it has become an urgent matter to ask what might serve as common reference points of value – whether in a city or a region, within a nation state or within supra-national contexts such as the European Union, and ultimately in global society as a whole. The question of what is culturally valuable for all people, regardless of their ethnic, religious, or socio-cultural affiliations and regardless of their individual lifestyle preferences, is, however, a question of the *general*.

It goes without saying that, even on the theoretical level, it is not exactly easy to model such a culture of the general within the framework of late-modern society. To do so, it would be necessary to reconcile the *universal* with the *heterogeneous*, and to regard the general not as something prescribed but rather as a *process* of *working toward* generality. Contrary to the bourgeois notion of cultural universalism, there "is" no *a priori* universal of culture; within the framework of a national society – in France, Great Britain, or Germany, for instance – there is, rather, a dynamic and open process of negotiating what should be recognized as commonly shared and binding for everyone in the country. The universal is not a given; instead, it consists of cultural practices and norms that are always in a state of change. It does not necessarily have to be negotiated on the level of global society. For the time being, it is more likely the case that smaller units such as nation states, or even individual cities and neighborhoods, will take the initiative to determine what should be culturally universal for their own residents. Here, the universal is limited to those who live in such places, for whom it should be equally valid.

Such a general understanding of culture could apply just as much to the value of personal development, gender equality, family, and solidarity as it could to professional achievement, historical awareness, and certain practices of education, technology, and sports. It could apply to the way that we deal with nature, as well as to the way that we interact in public or digital space. The value of art, books, architecture, and other cultural artifacts could also be universalized in this sense. In principle, this will always involve an unending effort of working toward the universal – an incessant act of "doing universality," which will always require revisions. Unlike cultural essentialism, such a culture of the general is not based on the (existing or desired) homogeneity of a *community* but, rather, on the inescapable cultural heterogeneity of late-modern *society*, which provides the reservoir for negotiating the general.[32] Here, the heterogeneity of the cultural is simply a fact that has to be dealt with and not, as in the case of diversity in hyperculture, an occasion for unconditional appreciation. The culture of the general therefore does not follow a market logic; it fosters neither antagonism between collectives nor apathy about their differences. Instead, it follows a logic of universal *participation*, though at the same time it requires that all sides make an effort toward *enculturation*.

This raises the question of the extent to which "doing universality" (on the part of a culture of the general) can go beyond being a theoretical construct and achieve actual relevance. Even under late-modern conditions, one central medium of working toward cultural generality is the sphere of the law – and especially constitutional law – given that it is concerned not only with neutral procedures but also with the matrix of value itself. Another potential medium could be the media-based and political public sphere, even though the digital revolution has done much to place its legitimacy under question. Finally, and above all, educational and cultural institutions – schools, universities, museums, the theatre, etc. – can also play a role in achieving this end.

The practical challenges of working toward cultural generality become especially clear in the case of museums. Museums represent a booming nodal point of the global creative economy, with its markets, its selective cultural consumers, and its celebration of diversity. At the same time, they have also, in certain places, become the focus of cultural essentialists and their identity politics. Could they become a locus of cultural generality that encourages critical reflection about the common features within heterogeneity – about the commonalities within global society, the commonalities within Europe, or the commonalities within a political nation?[33] Here, working toward what is collectively shared in common concerns the past and its vestiges, as well as the present and the future. Of course, museums can fixate on propagating a homogeneous group identity, or they can celebrate cultural diversity and things of individual interest. Yet they can just as well participate in working toward the general by acknowledging the heterogeneity of culture while simultaneously reflecting the common reference points of social praxis by focusing on commemorative culture, the shape of the future, and aesthetic shortcomings, or by thematizing current problems. The educational system, too, faces the challenge of promoting a culture of the general. Since the 2000s, schools have become the venue of numerous cultural conflicts, especially in Europe and North America. Steered by the model of hyperculture, they have had to foster values such as individual talent and cultural diversity, and yet cultural essentialism has demanded that they bolster the formation of national identities. In contrast to this, schools could work toward cultural generality by respecting the heterogeneity of their pupils and functioning as commonly shared places of learning in which everyone – regardless of his or her ethnic, religious, or social background – is taught the same norms and practices that are educationally valuable, socially valuable, and conducive to peaceful coexistence.[34]

In late-modern society, a third form of culturalization – Culturalization III (oriented toward cultural universality) – will certainly not be able to replace the powerful and dominant Culturalization I of hyperculture or the strongly identity-based Culturalization II of cultural essentialism. However, it could function as a critical counterforce that constructively engages with both the cultural reservoir of hyperculture and that of cultural communities. It remains an open question, however, whether the culture of the general will be able, within the framework of the society of singularities, to transcend the boundaries of socio-political debate and have an actual effect on social practices and institutions. Until then, it appears as though the conflict between hyperculture and cultural essentialism will continue to dominate our social reality.

2

From the Leveled Middle-Class Society to the Three-Class Society: The New Middle Class, the Old Middle Class, and the Precarious Class

In the intellectual debates held in Western countries over the past few years, one cannot help but notice that people are once again talking about social class. This may seem surprising at first. For, since the 1980s, sociologists (especially in Germany) had accepted the idea that the advance of social individualization – as Ulrich Beck understood it – would ultimately lead to a mobile society "beyond status and class."[1] For a long time, "class" seemed like a hopelessly obsolete category that the nineteenth century had conjured up, with its antagonism between the bourgeoisie and the proletariat. Contemporary society, on the contrary, seemed as though it was dissolving such social groups: individuals, or so one thought, would take fate into their own hands and choose to live upwardly mobile lifestyles. The question of polarization between social groups was not raised.

The contrast to today's debate could not be greater. In the United States, for instance, the economist Branko Milanović has demonstrated, in his thoroughly researched book *Global Inequality*, that social inequality is on the rise within Western societies, and also on a global level.[2] In his book *Our Kids: The American Dream in Crisis*, the prominent political scientist Robert Putnam investigated the conditions in which American children and teenagers grow up, and he vividly shows how diametrically opposed lifeworlds developed at the beginning of the twenty-first century, with the educated and privileged milieu on the one side, and the milieu of those who have been socially "left behind" on the other.[3] In her compelling case study *Strangers in Their Own Land*, the sociologist Arlie Russell Hochschild investigated families in Louisiana and concluded that there is now a widespread feeling of alienation among the traditional American middle class.[4]

Things look no different in Europe. In Great Britain, where class analysis has a robust tradition, the journalist David Goodhart has recently examined, in his book *The Road to Somewhere*, the new socio-structural and political polarization between mobile, urban, highly qualified people (the "anywheres," as he calls them) and the sedentary, declining middle class (the "somewheres").[5] In France, the social geographer Christoph Guilluy reached comparable conclusions in his 2015 book *La France périphérique*.[6] And in Germany? Here the debate was long more reserved, and it is telling that the most important impulse for reviving the relevance of sociocultural differences was provided by the German translation of a French book: Didier Eribon's bestseller *Returning to Reims*, which, from the autobiographical perspective of a social climber, explicates the antagonistic nature of contemporary class realities and demonstrates how today's social classes feel toward one another.[7] The immediate popularity of these books is largely due to the fact that they are often read as attempts to explain the political upheavals of the present, and especially the rise of right-wing populism and its skepticism toward globalization. Beyond these current political ramifications, however, we are dealing with a more fundamental question: How, over the last few decades (and especially since 1990), has the social structure changed in Western countries? In what ways has the societal and cultural structure of large social groups been transformed, and how have these transformations affected their ways of life, their opportunities in life, and their feelings toward life?

In order to answer this question in an informative way, however, much depends on how it is asked. One classical formulation of the question focuses on material inequality in society: How are income and assets distributed? Is there a great discrepancy between the rich and the poor? Research into this sort of inequality is undoubtedly important, and it provides an abundance of revealing data. On its own, however, it is incapable of answering the question of how large social groups have changed. The "life conduct" (*Lebensführung*) and "lifestyle" (*Lebensstil*) of these groups – to use the traditional terms employed by Max Weber and Georg Simmel – are not merely a matter of material wealth. Rather, the values, interpretive models, and everyday practices with which individuals lead and shape their lives – the *culture* of social classes – form a more complex reality of their own, and material resources represent just one conditional factor among several others.

Over the past few years, moreover, the field of traditional inequality research has popularized a diagnosis that has electrified the political public sphere and yet, at the same time, swept certain essential matters under the rug: the diagnosis of the rise of the so-called "super-rich." By now, this is a well-known fact of life: in Western societies (and beyond), a small group of millionaires and billionaires has formed – the upper 1 percent (or even just the 0.1 percent) – which has accumulated an obscenely high proportion of society's wealth. Thomas Piketty has systematically analyzed this transformation of financial conditions, and the Occupy Wall Street movement gave us the politically effective slogan "We are the 99%."[8] As politically important as the phenomenon of the super-rich undoubtedly is, fixating on this tiny minority leads to the neglect of 99 percent of the population and suggests that the latter constitutes a uniform group. The decisive issue – and this is my point of departure – is that the social structures and ways of life *within* this 99 percent of the population have fundamentally transformed, and this transformation involves far more than just a change in income structures.

Despite my comments above, contemporary sociology certainly offers alternatives to traditional inequality research – approaches, that is, which take into account the everyday logic of life conduct and its transformation. This was and remains the case with so-called lifestyle and milieu research, with its focus on forms of consumption, images of society, and everyday life practices. At its center lies the structure of everyday praxis and how this structure has changed over time; since the 1980s, it has discovered a "pluralization of lifestyles." In Germany, pioneering contributions to this branch of research include Gerhard Schulze's book *Die Erlebnisgesellschaft* ("The Experience Society") and the studies conducted by the SINUS Institute, which continue to be updated today.[9] This tradition of milieu studies is undoubtedly commendable and of lasting value, but it is also not free of one-sided assumptions. One of these is its inclination to prefer the polychrome "colorfulness" of different social milieus with their various lifestyles, consumer preferences, and values. Such research thus tends to proceed from the presumption that, in society, these different lifestyles exist alongside one another on an equal footing. Not only does this presumption underestimate the relevance of the unequal distribution of resources; it also presents the game of lifestyles as a system of cultural differences that is somehow outside of social mechanisms of power and domination. In reality, however, all cultural ways of life are *not* treated equally; rather, they differ radically from one another in terms of their life opportunities, their attitudes toward life, and their social prestige. The fact that ways of life are "cultural" does not at all mean that we are dealing with an inconsequential game of ideas and practices. Here there are hegemonies and hierarchies – and thus inevitably also conflicts *about* hegemony, valuation, and devaluation.

Precisely for this reason, I would like to discuss "classes."[10] Classes are more than just social-statistical income levels, and they are also more than just everyday lifestyles. Classes are cultural, economic, and political *configurations* at the same time. As a class, a group of individuals share a common lifestyle, which includes

a corresponding set of life maxims, everyday expectations, and
practices. This is the cultural dimension of class that makes it a way
of life. Against the popular diagnosis of the "end of work-oriented
society," I proceed from the idea that, even in our late-modern
present, professional activity – one's form of *work* (or lack thereof)
– is still at the center of these various ways of life. Besides labor
practices, there are additional factors that constitute the culture of
a given way of life: forms of consumption and of spending leisure
time, gender roles and family life, geographical restrictions (urban or
national), education and upbringing, media engagement, and finally
also political orientations. This complex of practices also forms an
outwardly perceptible "style" of life. Interaction and communication between individuals typically take place among like-minded
people from the same class. Such ways of life are also characterized
by the emotional states that they tend to produce – by the feelings
that their representatives have about everyday life and their own
self-confidence: one's own existence is "felt" in a particular way, and
this spectrum of emotions ranges from pride and contentment to
alienation and hopelessness.

Within the framework of a social class, a way of life will have
certain resources at its disposal that make such a life possible, and
a different life impossible. These resources thus form the second
dimension of class reality. On the one hand, they are undoubtedly
of a material and economic sort – income and assets – but, on
the other hand, they also encompass what Pierre Bourdieu called
"cultural capital" (one's formal education or other acquired skills)
and "social capital" (one's social relationships and contacts).[11]
Finally, within society as a whole, the classes form an entire socio-
structural and cultural system that involves its own struggles for
position and culture. This is the third – and, in the broadest sense,
political – dimension of the classes, in which questions of power,
domination, and hegemony are negotiated. Over the long term,
certain classes rise while others decline. The classes differ from one
another in their status, prestige, possibilities for satisfaction, and
influence. They can arouse mutual feelings of appreciation, indifference, or resentment. Whereas some classes seem to lead desirable
and worthwhile lifestyles, others seem deficient and shameful. Entire
social groups are subjected to symbolic processes of valuation and
devaluation, and these processes are driven in more or less subtle
ways by the media, the state, and the economy.

The Global and Historical Context

In order to understand the shift that has taken place in the social
structure of late-modern Western societies, it is first necessary to

consider the *historical* development of classes and lifestyles in the twentieth century. At the same time, it is also necessary to view this shift within the context of the socio-structural transformation that has taken place over the last 30 years on the *global* level.

For those living in the West, it is easy to overlook the fact that the profound transformation of today's social structure first occurred in the global South.[12] Whereas, from 1945 to 1980, the industrial societies of the West and the so-called developing nations were – like two different worlds, one rich and the other poor – diametrically opposed to one another in terms of their living conditions, the emerging countries of the global South have since caught up. Since 1990, China and other Asian countries, such as India, Indonesia, South Korea, and Thailand – but also some Latin American countries – have become integrated in the global market and have quickly transformed from agrarian societies into industrial societies with rapidly growing GDPs. Over the course of a few decades, accordingly, the disposable income of large parts of the population has increased dramatically, above all in urban centers. As a result, a large and ambitious global middle class, which is striving for a comfortable standard of living, has arisen in cities such as Shanghai, Seoul, Bangkok, and Mumbai – but also in Sao Paulo or Cape Town. By now, this middle class constitutes approximately a fifth of the global population.

In matters of education and professions, partner selection and family life, consumption and leisure time, this *ascent-oriented middle class of the global South* has developed its own patterns, which are partially influenced by the model of past and present Western middle-class life and are partially shaped by the specific cultural styles of the region in question. The fact that emerging nations have been experiencing the rise of an aspiring middle class since 1990 – the likes of which could be seen in Western Europe and the United States since 1945 – has had a consequence that many observers, who still believe that a polarity exists between the "rich North" and the "poor South," tend to overlook: since 1990, as Branko Milanović has shown, social inequality on the *global* scale (in terms of disposable income) has been *reduced*.[13] In that the large median populations of emerging countries (in China especially) have steadily become more prosperous, the living conditions in these countries have gradually come to approximate those in the West. Today, the social structure of global society is thus considerably different from how it was during industrial modernity (roughly from 1945 to 1980/90). The former economic dualism between industrial countries and developing countries has given way to a *global tripartite division*. On one side, there are the up-and-coming emerging nations with their expanding economies and middle classes: this is the *aspiring global South*. A second segment of the global South, in contrast, has hardly participated (or has yet to participate) in this economic and social dynamic. This segment – that of the *precarious global South* – extends to the places that political scientists describe as "failed states." Third, and finally, there is the *global North*. These are the societies of Europe and North America (plus Japan and Australia) – the countries, in other words, that constituted the core of industrial modernity from the beginning of the twentieth century to the 1980s. In late modernity, these countries have undergone contradictory socio-structural developments.

Whereas regional and national differences exist between, say, the United States and Germany, Great Britain and Scandinavia, or France and Japan, an overarching pattern has emerged in the transformation of the social structure in Western societies. In basic terms: whereas, up until the 1980s, industrial modernity in such countries essentially adopted the structure of a *leveled middle-class society*, late modernity in these places has increasingly been defined by a *three-class society*. It consists of three extensive groups: an ascendant and highly qualified *new middle class*, a stagnating *old* or *traditional middle class*, and a declining new underclass or *precarious class*.[14] These classes clearly differ from one another in their cultural lifestyles, their resources, and their place within today's power structures – to the point of polarization. The class structure reflects an essential feature of late-modern societies in the global North: it is defined by simultaneous processes of social ascent and descent, as well as by simultaneous processes of cultural valuation and devaluation. Late-modern society as a whole is therefore not entirely "in social decline" (in Oliver Nachtwey's terms),[15] and neither is it the society of the upward "elevator effect" (in Ulrich Beck's terms) that it once was. Instead, it is both at the same time: depending on the social group that one is examining, it is either a society of upward mobility or a society in decline. It is this *paternoster-elevator effect* that makes its structure contradictory and controversial.

A brief historical overview is necessary to appreciate how the situation has changed. To what extent is this structure new? In retrospect, of course, one should beware of downplaying the social inequalities during the three decades from the end of the Second World War to the 1970s – the (economically speaking) *trente glorieuses*, as Fourastié called them.[16] There have always been, after all, social and cultural differences in modern societies. That said, the lifestyles practiced during this developed stage of industrial modernity are distinguished by their relatively high degrees of social equality and cultural homogeneity. This becomes especially apparent when one compares this era to what came before: the heated class conflicts between the bourgeoisie and the proletariat during the nineteenth century and the first half of the twentieth century. The society of industrial modernity was indeed a "society of equals" (as Rosanvallon called it); or, to use Helmut Schelky's term, it was a "leveled middle-class society."[17] This was especially true of West Germany and the United States, with their nearly all-encompassing middle class. Two concepts proposed by West German sociologists summarized the important features of this social structure quite well: Karl Martin Bolte's "onion model" and Ulrich Beck's "elevator effect."[18] The "onion model" suggests that the vast majority of society is part of the large middle class, with the exception of small groups at the very top and very bottom of the social structure. The "elevator effect," in turn, suggests that just about every member of society, regardless of differences in income and education, can always expect to become increasingly prosperous.

On the one hand, industrial modernity's leveled middle-class society was characterized as a whole by its relatively egalitarian distribution of wealth (controlled, in large part, by the state and by labor unions). On the other hand, it was also characterized by continuous gains in prosperity (owing to dependable engines of economic growth).[19] After 1945, both the workforce and the rural population were largely able to join the all-encompassing middle class. Its economic basis was industrial production, primarily in the form of Fordist mass production. In fact, during the 1950s in countries such as West Germany or the United States, nearly half of the working population was employed in the industrial sector. A developed industrial economy and an egalitarian middle-class society thus proved to be two sides of the same coin. Interestingly in this context, levels of formal education did not turn out to be decisive factors in the prosperity of the middle class – even having minimal formal qualifications was no impediment to achieving a middle-class life, because Fordist mass production had no urgent need for lofty qualifications.[20] Society's middle ground thus equally included skilled workers, low-level employees, independent contractors, and uneducated members of the workforce. Ralf Dahrendorf's so-called "house model" from 1965 – the third suggestive model of industrial modernity's social structure beside the "onion model" and the "elevator effect" – represents this broadly middle-class society, the bulk of which consists of the middle class in the strict sense together with the socially ascendant ("petit-bourgeois") working class, in an impressive graphical form (see Figure 2.1).

One should not forget, however, that the leveled middle-class society was based not only on a relatively egalitarian distribution of resources but also on a particular everyday culture. This culture can be described as petit bourgeois. The middle *class* can be understood as a middle *status* with corresponding "status-appropriate" manners of behavior, and after 1945 this way of being gradually included the working class as well. Work ethic and family values were highly regarded, while gaining financial security and improving

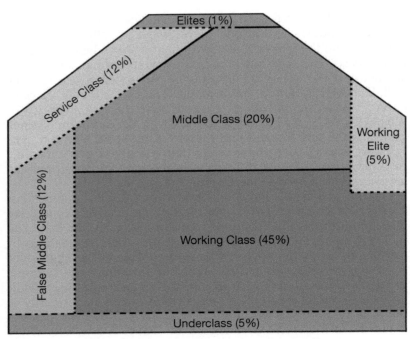

Figure 2.1 The social structure of West Germany in 1965.[21]

social status were central goals. There was a great deal of "status investment," which means systematically working toward improving the conditions of one's own status (by securing a home loan, for instance, or by being promoted at work).[22] The idea of one's "standard of living" was not just an economic concept but also an everyday cultural model: one strove to lead the comfortable life of those "who have made it." In his book *The Organization Man*, which is still worth reading today, William Whyte thus characterized this 1950s attitude of gradual social and economic climbing with the now-famous phrase "keeping up with the Joneses."[23] He also emphasized the importance of norms and normality, which was typical of this old middle class. People were, he wrote, "determined to be as normal as anyone else, or a little more so."[24] This pursuit of social normality pervaded all areas of life: consumption and leisure, work and careers, family and gender relations. The leveled middle-class society was a patriarchal society that was based on the traditional model of the immediate family, with the husband playing the role of the provider and the wife that of the housewife. Raising children, too, was typically oriented toward quiet conformity – expressions of emotionality or deviant and eccentric behavior were frowned upon. The *leveling* effect of this middle-class society thus also extended to individuals and their personalities. This broad middle was not just a social and material entity; it was a cultural phenomenon as well. It lionized the moderation, restraint, order, and rules to which individuals – in their families, jobs, and neighborhoods – felt compelled to conform.

This leveled middle-class society no longer exists, and yet it remains surprisingly alive: as a nostalgic memory and even as a normative model invoked by the left and the right alike, as in the current German debate over the "crisis of the middle class." Apparently, it is easier to imagine what is happening today in terms of what has been lost, and is "no longer," than it is to see it as something new. How, then, did this new situation come about?

Underlying Conditions: Post-Industrialization, the Expansion of Education, a Shift in Values

Three interrelated factors are central to the gradual transformation from the leveled middle-class society to late modernity's three-class society – a transformation that began in Western countries in the 1970s and has gained momentum since the 1990s. All three are related to long-term processes of economic, social, and cultural history in the twentieth and twenty-first centuries: *first*, the post-industrialization of the economy; *second*, the expansion of education; and *third*, the process of liberalization that has led to a shift in values.

Over the last quarter-century, the economic basis of Western countries has fundamentally transformed. Essentially, industrial economies have increasingly become *post-industrial economies*.[25] This transformation is immediately reflected in the structural shift that has taken place in the nature of gainful employment.[26] Whereas the first two-thirds of the twentieth century were defined by a drastic reallocation of the workforce from the agrarian to the industrial sector, a similarly drastic shift has since taken place from the industrial to service sector. Thus, in the United States, the share of the workforce employed in the industrial sector shrank from 50% in 1960 to 26% in 2015, while in (West) Germany it fell from 45% in 1950 to 24% in 2017.[27] Certain regions have experienced outright deindustrialization, as in the American Midwest, northern England, northern France, and the Ruhr area in Germany. In the twenty-first century, the industrial employee – with his socially valued and physical "hard work," and with his government-supported and union-backed middle-class standard of living – has nearly become an extinct species.[28] In the late-modern economy, there are far fewer middle-class jobs than were once available during industrial modernity.

Parallel to the reduced employment in the industrial sector, there has been an enormous expansion of employment in the tertiary sector.

In the United States, the share of employees working in the service industry grew from 47% in 1960 to 73% in 2015, and in Germany this same share increased from 33% in 1950 to 75% in 2017.[29] At the beginning of the twenty-first century, the tertiary sector thus became a more dominant sphere of employment than the industrial sector itself ever was during the peak of industrial society. Two additional features complete the picture of the post-industrial working world. First: it includes more women. Whereas the economy of industrial society was defined by male employees, the participation of women in the workforce has clearly affected the tertiary sector and contributed to its expansion. Second: in contrast to the full employment (of men) during the economic miracle of the postwar decades, the late-modern economy since the 1980s has produced, in many Western countries, a wide base of unemployed or under-employed people who never appear in official unemployment statistics.

If we take a closer look, however, at the tertiary sector that dominates the late-modern working world, we see that it is by no means homogeneous. The "service industry," as an umbrella term, is entirely misleading, for post-industrialization has in fact resulted in two very different and oppositional forms of employment. On the one hand, there has been a clear increase in the types of work available to highly qualified individuals, who can be called *knowledge workers*. Such work includes demanding jobs in research and development, in business-related services (consulting, marketing, etc.), in education and medicine, in the creative branches, in law and finance, in the media, and now in the digital economy. These branches of the post-industrial economy have the features of a knowledge economy. On the other hand, there has been a considerable increase in so-called *simple services*, which require minimal formal qualifications. Examples include working as a security guard, cleaner, cook, bus driver, or landscaper. As a whole, this has given rise to *polarized post-industrialism*. It is characterized by what the sociologists Maarten Goos and Alan Manning have referred to as the opposition between "lovely jobs" and "lousy jobs."[30] The knowledge-based careers of the professional class – which involve intellectual, communicative, and (in part) creative and innovative activity – typically require a high level of education. The activity of the service class, on the contrary, consists overwhelmingly of routine physical tasks that are performed by so-called "low-qualified" workers. Labor of this sort is often conducted outside of normal working conditions (under-the-table jobs, temp work, small jobs, limited-term appointments, and so on).

The second factor that has contributed greatly to the late-modern social structure is the expansion of education. In the global North, there has been a considerable increase in (male and female) college graduates since the 1970s.[31] In 1950, for instance, only 5% of all

Americans had a college degree, whereas today that figure is 30% (see Figure 2.2). In Germany, the percentage of secondary school graduates entering college or university rose from 6% in 1960 to 51% in the year 2012, and by the year 2017 almost a third of the population aged 30 to 35 held a post-secondary degree.[32]

In historical terms, this expansion of education has to be regarded as a revolutionary change. For the first time in social and cultural history, those who have attained more than a basic education – a process that takes at least 15 and often 20 years, and extends well into post-adolescence – no longer form a small and elite sector of society, but rather constitute a sizable group with access to a high degree of cultural capital. The expansion of education and academization thus provides the post-industrial knowledge economy with its educated workforce. It should not be overlooked, however, that this also has consequences for the value of non-academic education. The term "expansion of education" suggests that there is only one process at play and that everyone benefits from it. The opposite, however, happens to be the case: the expansion of education is not an "elevator effect"! In this regard, of course, there are differences between individual countries; some, for instance, provide more vocational training than others (this is a major difference between, say, Germany and the United States). In general, however, it can be

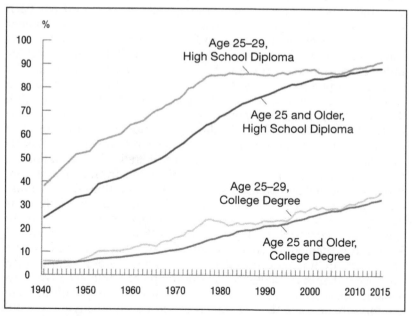

Figure 2.2 Percentage of the US population older than 25 who completed high school or college (by age group).[33]

said that the rise of academization has caused lower levels of educational attainment – for example, a high school diploma in the United States or a vocational degree in Germany, which, in the leveled middle-class society, represented the "normal standard" of formal qualifications – to lose this value and the social prestige that was once associated with it. Over the past three decades, the expansion of education has thus led to educational polarization: between those who possess coveted academic degrees and those who do not.[34]

Finally, we now come to the cultural *shift in values*, which was the third main factor that induced the transformation to our late-modern social structure and its lifestyles. Decisive in this respect, again, were the 1970s, which gave rise to a "silent revolution" (to borrow a term from Ronald Inglehart). Abstractly speaking, this revolution consisted of a gradual transition away from values of duty and acceptance toward values of self-development – and, overall, toward comprehensive cultural liberalization.[35]

In its broad middle, the life conduct of industrial modernity was based on values of social duty and self-discipline. Social service (in the working world, in one's family life, and as a citizen) was highly regarded, as was fitting in with social expectations of normality. Achievement and social status were ends in themselves, and one was expected to persevere in the face of adversity, to the point of self-denial. In the decades after 1970, this "disciplinary" complex of values has lost its legitimacy and attractiveness, and it has been supplanted by the guiding value of individual self-development (whose historical roots go back to Romanticism). The result of this "silent revolution" is that, now, it seems worthwhile and natural for individuals to live according to their personal needs, to cultivate the desires and potential of the ego, and to shape their lives in such a way that it is emotionally satisfying and subjectively meaningful. The values of self-development are thus closely related to those of creativity, individuality/singularity, emotionality, and subjective experience. One could say that there has been a shift toward "post-materialistic" values. It is reflected in the liberalization of parenting and in the increased pleasure that people derive from consumption; it is also reflected in increased demands or expectations for satisfying employment. This post-materialistic orientation is especially clear among those who entered adulthood at any point from 1970 to the present day – that is, approximately a third of the population.[36] Within this segment of society itself, one sees that post-materialistic values are in turn concentrated more highly among people with advanced degrees. Values of self-development influence Western societies on a broad front; in large portions of the population, there is a mixture between the new values of self-development and the old values of duty. That said, the main impetus behind social liberalization was and remains the educated class.

Without a doubt, the international student movement of 1968 and its reverberations throughout the subsequent decade played a decisive role in this liberalization of values. In a different way, however, it was also fueled by an economic shift – by the rise, that is, of consumer capitalism within the framework of an affluent society. It remains a matter of debate whether the post-materialization of lifestyles is purely a result of the wealth effect. The psychologist Abraham Maslow seemed to support this interpretation by arguing that values of self-development can only emerge when the basic human needs for security and material subsistence have been met.[37] Regardless, this shift in values – whether it was primarily caused by the inherent dynamics of culture, by economic factors, or by a combination of the two – has contributed a great deal to the way in which lifestyles and conduct have been restructured in post-industrial society.

In the Paternoster Elevator of the Three-Class Society

In all Western societies, the post-industrial economy, the expansion of education, and the liberalization of values led to the erosion of the leveled middle-class society. The latter has since been replaced by a tripartite social structure consisting of a *new middle class*, a *new underclass*, and – between them – the *old middle class*, which is a vestige of the leveled middle-class society. In addition, and on the very top, there is a small *upper class*: the super-rich. The dynamics of the late-modern social structure thus move in two directions: an *upwardly mobile* new middle class has risen from the traditional middle class, and a *downwardly mobile* precarious class has fallen away from it. This is the paternoster elevator of late modernity (see Figure 2.3).

The new middle class, which is an educated class, is at the center of *all three* of the economic and cultural processes of transformation mentioned above, and thus it represents the driving force behind the social developments of the last three decades. It has been the main supporter of educational expansion and post-industrialization, in whose knowledge economy its members are typically employed. At the same time, it is also the most significant proponent of the process of liberalization associated with society's shift in values. Furthermore, the new middle class is still the *middle* class; that is, it differs fundamentally from the upper class – which can live off its (ever-growing) wealth – in that its members depend on having gainful employment. At the same time, however, the new middle class has shifted the social standard of what constitutes an "average" way of life.

Conversely, however, these processes of transformation have had a negative effect on the two other large classes. An underclass, in

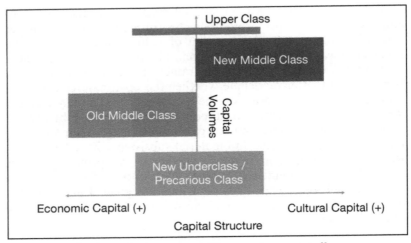

Figure 2.3 The three-class structure of late-modern society.[38]

the strict sense, hardly existed in developed industrial society. It was brought about by the structural shift from the industrial to the post-industrial economy, with its service class, low-wage sector, and underemployment. This precarious class is also a group with lower levels of educational attainment. This has resulted in a dual effect: whereas the dynamics of post-industrialization and the expansion of education have elevated the new middle above the old middle class, these *same* mechanisms of post-industrialization and the expansion of education have pushed the precarious class beneath the old middle class. While one class profits from the end of industrial society in many respects, the other suffers from it.

And the old middle class? Only at first glance does it seem to be unchanged. It cannot remain stable, however, given that the system of classes has changed around it. In industrial modernity, this middle class was to some extent the only social and cultural option; it was the undisputed social hegemon. Now, however, it occupies a sort of sandwich position; it is "clamped" between the two new classes. As a result of the restructuring of employment and education, it has fallen behind the new middle class in subtle, rather than drastic, ways. Moreover, the values of duty and acceptance espoused by this class have lost legitimacy over the course of cultural liberalization. On the other hand, the emergence of the new middle class has demonstrated to the old middle class that social decline represents a real possibility in late modernity.

On one level, as I already remarked at the beginning of this chapter, these socio-structural transformations undoubtedly have a material component. In addition to cultural matters, that is, they are *also* about social inequality in the strict sense of income and asset disparities. In most Western societies, as is well known, this inequality has been growing since 1980, and not only due to the rise of the super-rich. Between the two middle classes and the underclass there is a clear difference in incomes, with that of the underclass approaching the poverty line. The difference between the new and old middle class also has a material component: even though its members are for the most part gainfully employed, the old middle class forms a segment of society whose income is stagnating, while the new middle class is the relative winner of recent income trends. The data show that the median income of the educated class is higher than that of employees with average educational qualifications.[39]

What is central, however, is this: both the difference between the middle class and the underclass and, even more so, the difference between the new and the old middle class are primarily *cultural*. The new middle class fundamentally differs from the old middle class on account of the high cultural capital – and especially formal educational capital – that it has at its disposal. With respect to cultural patterns of lifestyle, life principles, and everyday practices and values, the three classes have developed in different ways. Finally, they clearly differ from one another in terms of their respective cultural influence, symbolic status, and prestige. Beyond rising and falling material conditions, the late-modern social structure is also – and especially – characterized by a symbolic *valorization and de-valorization* of different lifeworlds. Cultural differences can thus transform into a model of polarization.

In this regard, the contrast between the new and the old middle class has turned out to be particularly consequential. Although sociology and the political discourse have been well aware of the problems facing the new underclass for at least a decade, the internal divide within the former middle class has only recently come to light. Whereas public debate in the United States, Great Britain, and France has increasingly focused on this divide, the trend in Germany has been to tiptoe around this fragmentation and uphold the myth that there is a comprehensive middle class and that it is simply undergoing a crisis. There is, however, no "crisis of the middle class," and this is because *the* middle class no longer exists. All undifferentiated discussion of "the middle class" should be abandoned, and the discourse should instead focus on the *division of the middle class* into the two segments, or new classes, outlined above: into the new middle class and the old middle class! Although the latter two classes continue to share a few formal characteristics – such as their lower income in relation to the upper class and their common desire to invest in status – the realities of their lives are very different.

The New Middle Class: Successful Self-Actualization and Urban Cosmopolitanism

Culturally, economically, and politically, the new middle class is the most influential group in late modernity. It is the class of highly qualified individuals – of those, that is, who typically hold an advanced degree and are employed in the knowledge economy in its broadest sense. To this extent, it is an educated class. Without understanding the new middle class, it is impossible to understand the economic, cultural, and political dynamics of the post-industrial social structure. In its scope and orientation, it is a historically new class.[40]

The essential characteristic of this class is – to borrow a term from Pierre Bourdieu – its high cultural capital, especially in the form of formal education but also in the form of its informal skills. The economic capital of this class (its income and assets) is average to above average. Basically, this educated class has profited from the income trend of the late-modern economy, but *within* this class there is a considerable spectrum between those with clearly above-average income and assets (especially in certain international sectors such as computer science, medicine, or law), those with an average middle-class income (especially in the educational sector), and those with below-average incomes (as is the case, for instance, in certain creative jobs). Despite this broad range of incomes, however, it is mainly the quantity and quality of cultural capital that lend a specific form to the life conduct of the new middle class. On the one hand, its high cultural capital is reflected in the professional positions and activities that are characteristic within this group. This "immaterial labor" (in Lazzarato's terms) is something that its practitioners can identify with emotionally, and it is also a source of ever new and changing performance requirements. At the same time, the competencies associated with such cultural capital also affect the new middle class's entire way of life – from its parenting style and physical fitness to its leisure activities and political cosmopolitanism. This holds true for men and women alike: gender equality charac-terizes the new middle class more than the other classes.

Finally, its spatial structure is also important. The new middle class is an urban class concentrated in metropolitan regions and in a few select smaller cities (university towns, above all). It does not, therefore, live exclusively in global cities in the broad sense (such as Los Angeles, Paris, Berlin, Sydney, etc.), but also in medium-sized cities such as Seattle, Atlanta, Glasgow, Lyon, Stuttgart, Helsinki, Milan, Perth, and so on. It is in such places that the new middle class conglomerates and where it shapes social space to a considerable degree. It is less strongly represented in small cities and rural areas.

Overall, the new middle class is distinguished by its mobility, which has also become one of its important lifestyle values. It is typical for members of this class to leave home in order to study elsewhere, to leave a city or even a country for professional reasons, and to choose where they want to live in general.

The new middle class conducts its life according to the formula of striving for "successful self-development," and this formula is fraught with tension.[41] Here, the central maxim is to develop one's desires and talents in order to live a life that is satisfying, meaningful, and substantial. At the same time, this life should also be successful and bring with it a high degree of social status and social recognition. This dual formula for successful self-development thus synthesizes two cultural and historical motifs that were originally oppositional to one another. On the one hand, the idea that individuals should actualize themselves through their uniqueness and pursue satisfying and meaningful experiences stems from Romanticism. The post-materialist shift in values has adopted this tradition. On the other hand, the maxim that one should achieve high social status via education and achievement stems from the traditional bourgeoisie. Late modernity's new middle class is thus an amalgamation of the Romantic ideal of self-actualization and the bourgeois infatuation with education and achievement.

The pursuit of self-development defines the entire everyday life of the new middle class. Here, one is not content with the material standard of living that characterized the leveled middle-class society; instead, one strives to achieve a *quality of life* and to live the "good life." Working toward this quality of life pervades every aspect of this lifestyle: nothing should be merely average; everything, if possible, should have value in itself. One's job, for example, should not simply be a means of putting bread on the table; rather, it should be fulfilling and intrinsically motivating. Marriages are not merely a matter of convention, but should rather be satisfying and stimulating. It is not enough for food to satiate one's hunger; it also must be ethically good or aesthetically pleasing. Children are not simply there; rather, they provide parents with experiences that can't be missed. Growing up is not about fitting in, but rather about fostering one's own talents and needs. Where one lives should not be like everywhere else but rather an attractive place with a unique set of cultural, educational, and leisure opportunities. And so on and so forth.

The new middle class's way of life is thus defined by the impera-tives of *singularization* and *valorization*. Singularization means: that which constitutes one's life should not be standardized or "off the rack" but, rather, unique, special, and authentic – and this includes everything from one's apartment and circle of friends to one's career, travel destinations, and the schools attended by one's children.

Valorization means: that which constitutes one's life should not be a means to an end but should rather be valuable in itself – from food and marriage to yoga classes and political engagement. By singularizing and valorizing the everyday world, individuals perceive themselves to be singular and valuable – "I am worth it" – and they make culture the central sphere of everyday life. In this regard, "culture" does not mean the high culture of the bourgeoisie. Instead, the new middle class adheres to a broader understanding of culture that includes all possible aspects of everyday life (cooking, cycling, traveling, for example), which means that it aims to "cultivate" such things and enjoy them with a certain level of expertise. The new middle class is therefore also the most important pillar of global hyperculture.[42] It celebrates a sort of cultural cosmopolitanism that is no longer restricted to national cultures: we are all "at home" in the whole world.

In the new middle class, the culture of self-development, quality of life, and valorizing everyday matters is synthesized with an interest in success and status. Here, this class proves to be a *neo-bourgeoisie*. Typically, its interest in status and success does not demonstrably stand in the foreground of its lifestyle, but it is constantly there in the background. The new middle class thus invests actively in its social status, and it does so by investing in various forms of capital: it certainly invests in economic capital, but also in social capital (characteristic in this regard is its cultivation of trans-regional networks), in the capital of body and mind (fitness, coaching, mindfulness), and last but not least in cultural capital. Raising and educating children have therefore also transformed into an essential task. The new middle class has embraced the parenting style that the American sociologist Annette Lareau describes as "concerted cultivation" and "intensive parenting."[43] Children's talents are comprehensively fostered via a cluster of multifaceted activities, and parents are ambitious in selecting their children's schools and universities. Beyond investing in status, the new middle class is interested in self-development as a sign of social prestige. The more or less subtle demonstration of one's own uniqueness, interestingness, worldliness, and curated lifestyle has supplanted the leveled middle-class society's desire to demonstrate its normality and decent standard of living. The status of normality has thus been replaced by the *prestige of singularity*, by the demonstration of one's own authentic ego and one's own attractive life.

Overall, the new middle class is a progressive class in the sense that, minor critical details aside, it views itself as being in favor of social progress. This is no surprise, for it is ultimately this class that benefited most from the transformational processes of post-industrialization, the expansion of education, and liberalization. This orientation toward progress also defines its political position.

Political scientists have shown that, since the 1990s, a new line of conflict has developed across the traditional left–right divide, and that this line now separates "cosmopolitans" from "communitarians" (a term that is not unproblematic).[44] The former is based on social openness – from economic globalization to the pluralization of identities and the idea that migration is beneficial. The latter favors regulation and the creation of order, above all within a national framework – from social and economic policy to the preservation of national culture. In this regard, the new middle class is now the standard bearer of political cosmopolitanism. It endorses a "new liberalism" that combines economically liberal and social-liberal elements: a high appreciation for educational and professional achievement, free trade, and economic liberalization, but also a high regard for personal rights, equal rights, and ecology. Therefore, the attitude of the new middle class toward globalization – with its deregulation, cultural hybridization, and mobility (both geographical and social) – is basically positive.[45]

This political attitude is indicative of the social position of the new middle class. Within a broader historical framework, this professional class is a large social group that is "on the rise," and especially with respect to its cultural prestige. Its members have highly respected jobs and live in flourishing city centers. They fully enjoy all the consumer options and self-development opportunities offered by global cultural capitalism. Since the 1980s, they have actualized and fully participated in the lifestyle and maxims that have served as the guiding principles and dominant discourses of many social institutions, and they have done so in distinction to those who have been unable or unwilling to pursue this way of life, which is characterized by flexibility, mobility, entrepreneurship, creativity, lifelong learning, internationality, health consciousness, stylistic confidence, personal pleasure, emotional competence, tolerance, diversity, emancipation, ecological awareness, etc., etc. Within the global context, the relative loss of significance of Western societies has hardly affected the new middle class. That said, its lifestyle of successful self-actualization is paradoxical and highly prone to disappointment.[46]

The Old Middle Class: Sedentariness, Order, and Cultural Defensiveness

In its life principles, everyday activity, employment, and resources, the old (or, one could say, traditional) middle class is the immediate heir of the formerly comprehensive stratum of society that dominated industrial modernity. When described in this way, its difficult position in the late-modern class landscape becomes clear: this class was once the "measure of all things"; it embodied the "standard" of what was normal and generally valid. In the meantime, however, it has lost this culturally dominant position. Simply put, while society and the world have changed around it in extreme ways, its members have hardly changed at all. In the wake of the rising new middle class, the old middle class no longer represents the standard, but rather embodies the "average," and it is at risk of retreating into the social background and becoming invisible in culture, politics, and the media.[47]

The old middle class includes, above all, people in mid-range professional positions with mid-level academic qualifications: skilled workers and employees with vocational degrees who perform traditional office and service activities, mid-level civil servants, and independent craftsmen. Rather than having a university degree, its members typically have a high school diploma, an occupation-specific *baccalauréat*, or professional training from a vocational school. Unlike the new middle class, this class has not profited from the post-industrialization of the economy, but it has also not suffered from it as clearly as the new underclass has – at least not yet. Materially, its members are well situated or fairly compensated; their income and assets are usually above average or average (with exceptions at the high and low ends). One important parameter of the old middle class is its social-geographical location: unlike the new middle class, which is concentrated in metropolitan regions, it is concentrated in small towns, mid-sized cities, and rural areas. Usually, these places are also where the members of this class grew up. The old middle class is a *sedentary* milieu – a milieu that (in negative terms) can be called geographically immobile or (in positive terms) can be said to have strong local roots.

The guiding principle behind the lifestyle of the old middle class is not that of successful self-actualization. Its members have largely not participated in the late-modern transition from focusing on one's standard of living to focusing on one's quality of life (which includes the singularization of all aspects of life); here, the question of status is essentially still one of material wealth. This way of life is therefore characterized by investments in status, and especially by the development of economic resources. However, the old middle class is not concerned with materialism alone. The cultural framework of this lifestyle is formed from values of self-discipline, *order*, and geographical and social rootedness. Its individual members demand discipline of themselves and others: orderly conditions – in one's own life, in parenting, in one's place of residence, and in society at large – are regarded as indispensable and valuable. Their own self-perception depends on social connections and obligations to people and places with whom and which their relationship is rather circumstantial (and not actively chosen): to their immediate and extended families, and to the places and regions where they live, which are typically the places and regions where they were born (as is true of their neighbors, colleagues, school friends, etc.). The members of the old middle class have largely remained loyal to these people and places. In Arlie Hochschild's terms, the old middle class is characterized by the concept of the "rooted self."[48]

For the traditional middle class, an ethos of work, family, and region are therefore central. Having work to do furnishes the individual with a moral quality. Here, work has little to do with self-development and creativity; rather, it is related to an ethos of necessity. It is what "has to be done" in order to provide material security. One has a sense of pride in "hard" work (and in part, too, in "good" work), which lends shape to one's life. There is thus a rather dismissive view of those who do not work for a living but are, rather, dependent – for instance, on state support. The family ethos of the old middle class is often based on the model of a traditional division of labor between genders and on actively supporting one's family members. The strong sense of regional and local rootedness felt by this class means that its social contacts typically remain restricted to where they live, and that this context – "home" – is often a significant aspect of its members' personal identity ("I come from Franconia/Normandy/Minnesota"). Regarding the political line of conflict mentioned above between cosmopolitans and communitarians, the old middle class – not surprisingly – represents the latter, communitarian side (which can in turn lean either conservatively or social-democratically). Its political preference is for maintaining order: for sticking to traditional economic and social policies and for preserving national cultures. Its members are often skeptical of globalization.

Materially, as I mentioned above, the old middle class is (still) in a fairly good position, though in this regard there are considerable differences from one country to the next. Nowhere, however, is the material welfare of this class still on the rise. Even more important than its material status is the fact that, *culturally*, the old middle class is on the *defensive*: its life principles have lost their former dominance in society and its lifeworlds have been displaced from the center to the periphery. This shift has involved multiple dimensions of *cultural devaluation*, some more subtle than others. The members of the old middle class do not necessarily suffer from an objectively bad situation, but rather from a situation that, in comparison to the past and to the rising new middle class, has become relatively worse. They suffer, in other words, from what sociologists have called "*relative* deprivation."[49]

A matter that should not be underestimated is the extent to which certain geographical areas have become déclassé. In Western societies, many rural and provincial regions, in which the old middle class often live, have lost their economic viability and cultural attractiveness. They have been drained of jobs, young residents, and investment; some regions and cities are in a state of decay. In contrast to the economic and cultural appeal of metropolitan regions, provincial areas are at risk of becoming "flyover country" occupied by people who have been "left behind." The rooted existence of the old middle class is at odds with the geographical mobility that late-modern society demands. Among the residents of small cities and provincial areas that are still prospering, there is often a sense that they represent a bulwark against urban decadence and the cosmopolitan elite.

No less significant is the erosion of recognition that the old middle class's careers and educations have experienced. In a society in which a university degree has increasingly become the entrance ticket to a middle-class life, those with lower levels of educational attainment (and who can still be proud of such achievements) are at risk of losing prestige. In the meantime, while internationally educated computer scientists or lawyers from the big city have since come to represent the *true* middle class (and they perceive themselves and are publicly perceived as such), how should shopkeepers or expert craftsmen from the "provinces" understand their position in society? In light of the new culture of "attractive" (that is, interesting, multi-faceted, and flexible) jobs, the work life and work ethic of the old middle class also seem to be second rate. It is thus no surprise that, in Germany, it has become more attractive for younger people to go to university than to enter the workforce right after finishing school.[50] In light of the social ideal of emancipated and professional women, the family model of the old middle class (housewives, traditional gender roles) has also lost prestige. Conversely, the modernization of gender relations has meant that the once secure role of men as "breadwinners," which was the norm in industrial modernity, is no longer a fact of life.

In general, the old middle class's way of life is no longer as socially influential as that of the new middle class. The ideals of order, sedentariness, and discipline, which were dominant during indus-trial modernity, have taken a back seat to the ideals of autonomy, mobility, and openness, which characterize late modernity and its new middle class. In a society that favors singularity and difference in so many respects, the culture of the old middle class seems lackluster, limiting, and deficiently innovative and attractive. From the perspective of the old middle class, the culture of the new middle class seems narcissistic and rootless: members of the old middle class perceive themselves as champions of the common good, while "others" indulge in self-development, which in their estimation is merely an empty and egotistical façade. The social transformation that the new middle class has largely perceived as an opportunity is understood by the old middle class as a threat to its cultural influence and social status. In extreme cases, members of the old middle class believe that they have been unfairly compensated for their efforts. Those who were once well established feel as though they have been pushed to the periphery, and one possible reaction to this is political and cultural resentment. It is therefore no surprise that some of the staunchest supporters of right-wing populism – with its critique of elites, metropolitan areas, and globalization – are members of the old middle class.

The Precarious Class: Muddling Through and Losing Status

It has often been observed that, since the 1980s, a considerable segment of the population has fallen out of the leveled middle-class society and formed a new underclass.[51] The size of this class and its social implications vary from country to country, but its features are similar everywhere. It can be said that this is a precarious class, a class with structurally uncertain living conditions. A portion of this class exists outside of the labor market; such people live off government or family support, and thus number among those whom sociologists have labeled "excluded" or "superfluous." This group can be found primarily in deindustrialized and structurally weak regions, whether in Northern France, the American Midwest, or in parts of Eastern Germany. Another important portion of the precarious class is the so-called service class. The latter is concentrated in the metropolitan regions that provide such jobs in large numbers. Finally, the precarious class also includes certain employees engaged in unskilled or generally insecure work within the industrial or agricultural sector.[52]

In the underclass, income is generally below average, often near minimum wage. Its members are offered little support from the social system, and they often hold no assets. With respect to their economic capital, they are no longer part of the middle class. The cultural capital of the precarious class is likewise minimal; it largely consists of so-called "low-qualified" individuals. The precarious class has suffered from the structural transition to post-industrialism, and the expansion of education has had paradoxically negative effects on it, given that those who have not benefited from this expansion have become "educational losers" (*Bildungsverlierer*). Historically speaking, today's precarious class descended from yesterday's working class – that is, from the formerly enormous group of people who earned a living from manual labor. Thanks in part to the successful efforts of social democracy and labor unions, the leveled middle-class society had included the working class, whereas the post-industrial society of late modernity has expelled this (meanwhile reduced) group from middle-class life and taken away its status, income, and security.

The new underclass, too, is defined by its own sort of lifestyle. Here, the long-term investments in status made by the middle class are unrealistic, and the educated class's devotion to successful self-actualization seems just as eccentric. Although parts of this class still adhere to the values of the old middle class (self-discipline and order), overall it is characterized by a different lifestyle pattern that is indicative of its precariousness: the pattern of muddling through from one day to the next. The primary feature of this precarious lifestyle is thus the motif of dealing with the incessant difficulties of life – with the multitude of daily struggles that might unfold into existential threats (illness, divorce, unemployment, excessive debt, housing problems, difficulties at school, and so on). The temporal horizon of this lifestyle is necessarily short-term; long-term planning seems impossible. In a sense, the art of living in the precarious class consists of tenacious and wily perseverance. Endemic to this class is the idea that life is a "struggle" and that merely surviving this struggle is a central achievement in itself. Given such low expectations, the modest ideal would be to lead a somewhat predictable life without any major disasters.

In comparison to industrial society's working class, the new underclass of late modernity is experiencing social decline and cultural devaluation at the same time. Its members have fallen down the class ladder because, in post-industrial late modernity, what could be called industrial modernity's *instrumentality deal of labor* no longer exists. According to this informal pact, someone who did hard, laborious, and not terribly satisfying work would receive in exchange an acceptable degree of social status (a middle-class income, social security). This deal is no longer in place, and thus the new underclass is at a dual disadvantage. Over the course of post-industrialization and the expansion of education, primarily "physical" jobs moved outside of the classical industrial sector; they are no longer well paid, and they are no longer socially secure. Thus, the exchange of "sweat for status" no longer functions on the material level. In addition, the rise of the knowledge economy and the shift in values have turned "attractive work" into a leading social ideal, and by no means is this ideal met by the mainly repetitive types of jobs performed by the service class. The idea of work as "drudgery" no longer has any social credit. In late modernity, the heroes of manual labor – they can still be found, for instance, in monuments in eastern Berlin (relics from the workers' and farmers' state) or in old phrases such as *Ich bin Bergmann, wer ist mehr?* ("I am a miner, who is anything more?") – are a thing of the past.[53]

Thus, the new underclass has not only fallen in material terms; it is also culturally devalued. Manual labor is clearly less respected than work in the knowledge sector. Laborious routine activity is less respected than intellectual innovation. In light of the massive academization of society, a mere high school diploma is a handicap. Moreover, even seemingly trivial aspects of life – such as the eating habits of the underclass or its physical fitness – are frowned upon in today's social discourses, which are dominated by the new middle class. Here, unhealthy eating and unfit bodies are targets of critique. Finally, the gender ideal that has been cultivated in parts of the underclass – particularly the ideal of "real" and authentic masculinity and femininity – are widely scorned in late-modern society, which is increasingly dissolving the rigid distinction between masculine and feminine behavior.

It is therefore no surprise that the new underclass, which has fallen out of the old middle class, has a decidedly pessimistic or fatalistic view of its own place in history and society. In this regard, its difference from the proud old working class could not be more blatant. Although the latter was admittedly a socially subordinate class until the first half of the twentieth century, it was nevertheless able to develop a positive class consciousness, regard itself as a fundamental part of society, and work politically to increase its welfare via reform or revolution. In today's precarious class, in contrast, the prevailing class consciousness is negative: its members perceive themselves as having been "left behind" by society. The strategies for dealing with this situation have been varied: political indifference and social isolation are one way; hoping to rise from nothing on account of one's own talent – in sports or showbusiness, for instance (especially among teenagers and young adults) – is another. A further possibility is to withdraw to local communities – to "parallel societies" of people who were born in a certain place or immigrated there – that cultivate their collective identity. Members of this class can also, however, become reawakened politically, and this can take place within the framework of the neo-socialist left (as in the case of Jean-Luc Mélanchon's movement La France Insoumise) or it can also lead to the espousal of right-wing populism, which is already supported by portions of the old middle class. Both politically and in matters of lifestyle, the social-liberal or economically liberal cosmopolitanism of the new middle class is far from the minds of the new underclass.

The Upper Class: Distance due to Assets

The upper class hovers above things. The place of the "super-rich" – the top 1 percent (or less) of society – is easy to define in formal terms. Whereas the two middle classes depend on income from employment, the upper class can live off (inherited or earned) assets. Since the 1980s, as authors such as Thomas Piketty have shown, the people at the peak of the economic hierarchy in Western societies – but also, since then, in countries such as Russia or China – have experienced an exorbitant increase in their private assets.[54] Therefore, that which clearly distinguishes the upper class from the middle class (the new middle class included) is the extent of its *economic* capital, not the scope of its cultural capital. In this regard, a conversion from quantity to quality has taken place: here, assets – whether in the form of financial capital or real estate – are so great that, strictly speaking, it would no longer be necessary for members of this class to work. However, unlike the traditional type of the rentier (the *old* upper class, which of course still exists), it is characteristic of the *new* upper class that its members *nevertheless* work and remain active: they sit on corporate boards and work in the uppermost echelon of finance or law. The new upper class also includes the publicly influential stars in the media, in professional sports, art, and architecture, as well as the top earners in the leading companies of the digital economy. Some of the wealth of the new upper class may have been inherited, but it is largely the result of skillfully increasing one's exorbitantly high employment income. Here, one profits from the winner-take-all markets of the late-modern knowledge and creative economy, which excessively rewards those who are especially successful.

Whereas the *old* upper class was and remains relatively sedentary – and in this respect resembles the traditional middle class – the *new* upper class is distinguished by its global mobility. Given that its members so often have international biographies, it could be called, in Ralf Dahrendorf's terms, the "global class."[55] This cosmopolitan consciousness, which also characterizes the new middle class, thus exists here in an especially pronounced way. The new upper class no longer represents the sort of conservative values espoused by the old upper class, but rather propagates – in addition to political views in line with its own financial interests – an ethos of "improving the world," which is perhaps clearest to see in the gurus of the digital economy (Gates & Co.), the titans of financial market capitalism (Buffett & Co.), and their "solutionism."

Culturally, there are many indications that the new upper class shares, on one level, the formula of self-actualization that is familiar to us from the new middle class, and that it places special emphasis on the aspect of achievement. However, the fundamental difference between the financial resources of the upper class and those of the middle class are reflected in their respective lifestyles: whereas members of the middle class must diligently invest in their status – and can also fail at this – members of the new upper class are exempt from this necessity. In general, they are able to *distance* themselves as far as possible from the exigencies of life. Of course, they also invest (or have others invest for them), but they can maintain their lifestyle without worrying about the future and can thus "play around" in a way that is unthinkable to the new middle class. The lifestyle of the upper class can therefore ascend to luxurious and exclusive heights. International magazines such as *Wallpaper, Monocle,* or *Architectural Digest,* which feature the opulent homes, metropolitan real estate, and the preferred travel destinations, restaurants, and consumer goods of the global upper class thus function as display windows into a lifestyle that seems unachievable to most people and yet enviable to some. Their effect therefore extends far beyond the tight circle of the super-rich.

Cross-Sectional Characteristics: Gender, Migration, Regions, Milieus

So far, the image that I have drawn of the late-modern social structure is necessarily abstract. My goal was to construct a framework or a minimal structure according to the following basic principle: as simple as possible, as differentiated as necessary. In what follows, I would at least like to point out the directions that could be taken by more detailed and sophisticated analyses, which might sharpen the image in some respects but also (and inevitably) make it unmanageably complex in others.

A more finely grained analysis could be achieved, in particular, by examining the three-class structure in light of three other socially relevant distinctions: between men and women, between natives and migrants, and between urban and rural areas. In my view, one should proceed from the presumption that the social position and life of individuals is *primarily* defined by the fact that they belong to the new middle class, the old middle class, or the precarious class. In this light, there is little sense in speaking of the social position of *the* woman or *the* man without referring to classes. The same is true of migrants. It would be absurd to speak in sweeping terms about *the* migrant or about *the* migrant way of life – not only because this label applies to entirely different ethnic groups but also, and above all, because the lifestyles of migrants differ considerably depending on the social class to which they belong.[56]

The situation regarding the urban–rural divide is somewhat different because the social structure of late modernity is *inherently* defined by a particular socio-spatial structure, without which it is impossible understand at all. Finally, I would like to say something about the internal differentiation of the three classes, for none of them is homogeneous upon closer inspection. Each of the three classes is composed of diverse and smaller socio-cultural milieus in which the class-specific logic of lifestyles is manifested in different ways.

Gender The transformation from industrial modernity to late modernity led to a shift in gender relations that is closely related to the aforementioned three main factors of the transformation itself: the post-industrialization of the economy, the expansion of education, and the liberalization of values. The facts are familiar: despite persistent shortcomings in various areas of society, the equal rights of women have been slowly but continuously advancing since the 1970s. The participation of women in the workforce has increased considerably. At the same time, women have benefited inordinately from the expansion of education: women now constitute the majority of university graduates in Western countries.[57] Finally, social values have shifted and traditional gender roles have eroded, in both the professional and the private sphere. Characteristics that are typically associated with men (physical strength, for instance, or courage and military valor, etc.) have increasingly lost significance, whereas presumably "feminine characteristics," such as communication skills and emotional competence, have gained more and more prestige and relevance – for women *and* for men.

As my description already suggests, this change in gender roles is related to matters of class in a decisive way. It would thus be rather meaningless to speak broadly of the "rise of women" in late-modern society, and it would be just as meaningless to speak in sweeping terms about the "crisis of men." Within the three-class social structure of late modernity, there are in fact three different gender structures:

In the new middle class, women have benefited the most from post-industrialization, the expansion of education, and liberalization, and they have actively driven these developments. Here, too, they perceive themselves most strongly as representatives of emancipatory progress. As highly qualified educated women in metropolises, they have gained autonomy and a professional identity, which most women were barred from having in the old industrial society. Moreover, the new middle class attempts to cultivate a model of partnership and family that is based – or at least claims to be based – on equal rights. For men in the new middle class, women are therefore competitors on the job market, and everyday family life has become an object of negotiation. At the same time, the liberal-cosmopolitan men of this class are typically oriented toward values of cooperation, so that their deviation from traditional masculine roles, in both the professional and private sphere, is usually regarded less as a loss than as an expansion of their options, and can occasionally even be seen as liberating. Finally, in many places, the life of the new middle class is based on the neo-bourgeois model of a "successful family" with intensively supported planned children, who in turn provide men (keyword: "new fathers") and women with additional identity resources. In general, the new middle class therefore opens up – for both its male and female members – opportunities for successful self-actualization,[58] but it also introduces the specific risks associated with it (excessive work and stress, above all).

Gender relations in the two other classes look entirely different. The processes of class decline and devaluation, which have affected both the old middle class and the new underclass, have a male *and* female side, and in some ways they define the entire gender hierarchy in these classes. The old middle class is characterized by family-based and traditional gender roles: the classical division of labor between husband and wife, the separation of the private from the public sphere.[59] Of course, these relations have also been thoroughly modernized, given that women in the old middle class, too, have also become more autonomous and more active in the workforce. However, the tendency here is to perceive the social dominance of the new middle class's liberalized gender arrangement as a more or less subtle devaluation of one's own traditional conception of men, women, and family life. This is true not only on the part of men, who have increasingly lost their status as the sole breadwinner and head of the household, but also on the part of women who embrace their traditional identity: in late-modern society, to be "just" a housewife and mother has lost prestige. From this perspective, the successful women of the new middle class can be seen as a threat to one's own identity.[60]

Different still are the prevailing notions of femininity and masculinity in the late-modern underclass. First of all, it should not be overlooked that the urban service class is predominantly female. What might look like emancipation here is typically not a matter of professional fulfillment or *opportunity*, but rather a matter of *needing* a job in order to support oneself and one's family. For men, conversely, it is in the new underclass where, if anywhere, there is indeed a much-discussed crisis. Whereas working-class men in industrial society derived their identity from their role as breadwinners and heads of households, from their physical work, and in part also from the model of "authentic" masculinity, such elements of traditional masculinity have since eroded. Especially among young men, the counter-reaction to this can be a form of "masculinism" that involves an especially pronounced staging of one's own gender.[61]

Migration The structural transition from the postwar industrial society to late modernity includes the expansion of migration into the societies of the global North. Of course, there are clear and also historically determined differences between countries – between, for instance, Germany and Scandinavia, former colonial powers such as France and Great Britain, and a classical immigrant country such as the United States. In general, however, it can be said that the industrial societies of the postwar era were (relatively) ethnically homogeneous and that, since the 1980s, the extent of the migrant population has increased. Western nations have become immigrant societies. Thus, in the Federal Republic of Germany, the portion of the population with a migrant background increased from 2 percent in 1964 to 21 percent in 2012.[62] It is thus impossible to make informed statements about the transformation of the modern class structure without taking into account migration processes. How are such processes reflected in today's social structure?

From the outset, it is necessary to avoid a potential misconception: that the structure of a three-class society applies exclusively to "native" German people, British people, French people (etc.), and that migrants should be regarded as a separate block. The exact opposite is true: the migrant population is differentiated into highly diverse milieus and classes. What is essential is that, among people with an international background, there is the same differentiation between a new middle class, an old middle class, and a new underclass that we have already examined. Or, expressed the other way around: the three classes *already include* both migrants and non-migrants. Here, too, the class reality is thus primary; ethnic difference is secondary.

Empirical studies of "migrant milieus" in Germany – to the extent that the latter have been analyzed as independent milieus – demonstrate this social differentiation.[63] Thus, it turns out that here, too, there are milieus that can be interpreted as segments of a new middle class. They consist of highly qualified migrants who typically live in cities, work in the knowledge economy, and possess a high degree of cultural capital.[64] According to the studies, what prevails here is a bicultural self-perception that generally fits in with the cosmopolitan and international orientation of this class. In addition, there are also segments of a less-educated and traditional migrant middle class whose orientation toward self-discipline, achievement, family, and social status does not fundamentally differ from the lifestyle of the "native" old middle class. In this group, one's own ethnic background plays a relatively minimal role; the tendency is to assimilate into the majority society. Finally, there are migrant milieus that belong to the underclass and include people who are unemployed or have precarious jobs. Often, their orientation is highly traditionalistic. This migrant underclass occasionally gives rise to much-discussed "parallel societies," with their tendency to segregate themselves from the native local society (often to the point of ethnic seclusion).

It is now possible to propose the hypothesis that, within the three classes of the late-modern social structure, the *relationship between* locals and migrants is each structured *in its own specific way*. Regarding the new middle class, it would thus be accurate to say that – in light of its cosmopolitan values, the increasingly inter-national constitution of work teams in the knowledge economy, the tendency of its members to cultivate large and trans-regional networks of acquaintances, and the geographic mobility and "inter-nationality" of the urban educated workforce – the relationship between migrants and non-migrants is here one of *social mixture*. Although this mixture exists largely *within* this class (supplemented by "contacts" with the migrant service class), it contributes to the fact that native or local constituents of the new middle class have a predominantly positive attitude toward migration.

The constellation is different within the old middle class. Because this way of life is strongly family-oriented and because the typical jobs held by members of this class are less reliant on projects and networks, locals and migrants here exist *side by side* but have minimal social contact with one another. This sort of parallel existence is enhanced by the fact that the native old middle class is primarily located in small cities, whereas migrants are concentrated in the metropolises. At the same time, the non-migrant members of this class often have a critical attitude toward migration. Regarding the underclass, finally, there are many indications that here the segre-gation between locals and migrants is most pronounced, and that it often takes the form of a *status competition*. Native and migrant members of this class compete for the same simple jobs as well as for state services, subsidized housing, and generally for "respect" in light their own precarious situation. Consequently, both sides also employ strategies of cultural identity formation (in youth groups, for instance).

Finally, migration processes create a further complication in the structure of the three-class society. The question is whether the devaluation experienced by the old middle class and the new under-class affects the migrant components of these classes in the same way. Evidence suggests that the situation here is more complex. For, in the migrant portion of the old middle class and (in part) the new underclass, it is possible to observe what the social anthropologist Boris Nieswand has called the "status paradox of migration."[65] The social status of migrants may be limited – mid-level or below average – in their adopted country (and according to its standards), but it can be high or even very high according to the standards of their place of origin. This is perceived not only by the migrants themselves, but also by their families back in their homeland. This difference in self-perception between migrants and non-migrants is especially striking in the old middle class: whereas the native members of this class generally perceive themselves to be devalued because they have lost their former central position in society, the migrant members of the old middle class view themselves as something like the aspiring and ambitious middle class in developing countries. To the extent that they use not a nation but a global and transnational measure of comparison, migrants in this position generally regard themselves not as part of a downward dynamic but, on the contrary, as part of an *upward* dynamic. To a lesser extent, this status paradox can also be seen in parts of the migrant underclass. Here, however, the status paradox is especially strong among migrants of the first generation, who still have an immediate connection with their homeland, and it is weaker among those in subsequent generations, who tend to use the common standards of comparison of their adopted country.

The urban–rural divide The late-modern social structure has an *a priori* spatial dimension; it is tightly intertwined with the social geography of post-industrial capitalism. Economic polarization and its attendant logic of valuation and devaluation, which characterizes this social structure, go hand in hand with *spatial* polarization and its consequent *spatial logic of valuation and devaluation*, which operates on the macro-level of regions as well as on the micro-level of neighborhoods.

Even in industrial society, of course, there was never a complete leveling between regions that were more affluent or less affluent. However, with the post-industrialization of the economy, the expansion of education, and the liberal shift in values, the economies and residents of richer and poorer regions have since grown further apart from one another socially. Post-industrialization, the expansion of education, and the shift in values all have a socio-spatial aspect. I have already mentioned what post-industrialization means in terms of social geography: globally networked metropolitan regions – Toulouse and Atlanta, Munich and Melbourne, Kyoto and Milan, etc. – attract the branches of the knowledge economy that value the innovative environment of these cities, with their educated populations and networks of businesses. As a consequence, the number of service jobs has also expanded there. On the other side, many old industrial cities and regions lost their status as economic engines over the course of deindustrialization. The expansion of education likewise has a spatial dimension: the growing segment of the population pursuing higher education has streamed into university cities. If they are not already city dwellers, the members of this segment leave their home region and, for professional reasons, seldom return. There has thus been a brain drain away from rural regions. The shift in values has also had socio-spatial effects: for the educated class, which is oriented toward self-development, where one lives is not a matter of destiny; rather, one's place of residence is consciously chosen on the basis of how attractive it is to live there. Cities therefore compete for residents with "high potential," and large metropolitan regions, with their more enticing job opportunities and leisure activities, have in turn profited from this competition.

As the social geographers Allen Scott and Christophe Guilluy have shown in their detailed studies of the United States and France, the result of these developments is a characteristically late-modern spatial structure that has taken the form of self-reinforcing polarization between metropolitan regions and small-town or rural areas.[66] Of course, there are also prosperous small-city regions – in southern England or southern Germany, for instance – and many former industrial metropolises – in the Ruhr area, for example – are also economically disadvantaged. Fundamentally, however, what has emerged is a pattern of asymmetry between centers and peripheries. On one side, there are urban centers, which attract the knowledge economy and the new middle class; on the other side, there are non-urban regions whose economic basis has shrunk over the course of deindustrialization, whose educated young have departed, and whose sedentary old middle class (and in part their underclass, too) have remained. The concrete socioeconomic rise and fall of regions corresponds to a symbolic valuation and devaluation that has further intensified this asymmetry. In the perception of society, metropolises seem "attractive." They embody the new middle class's values of cosmopolitanism and diversity. To the extent that they are not desirable vacation destinations for urbanites, rural and small-town regions, in contrast, have lost prestige. The result is that there is now a dynamic defined by an attractiveness competition *between* cities themselves, to an extent that would have been unthinkable during industrial modernity. Metropolitan regions compete for investment, highly qualified residents, and tourists. Urban planners have reacted to this by promoting their respective city's creative economic clusters, cultural and leisure-time offerings, educational and healthcare facilities, and spectacular architecture. That which was already attractive to begin with – the metropolis – has become even more attractive.

As is probably clear by now, the classes of late-modern society are closely tied to this geographical segregation. The new middle class predominantly lives and works in metropolitan regions and influences them, while the (native) old middle class and the (native) new underclass are concentrated in rural and small-city regions. This pattern is complicated somewhat by the migrant population. By definition, migrants are geographically mobile, and they move to places where there are already migrant milieus and/or where they can find employment. This means that metropolitan regions are home not only to the migrant new middle class but also to the majority of migrants in the old middle class and the new underclass. The economies and social structures of metropolitan regions are therefore characterized by a *dual structure*: highly educated people (national and international) *and* a largely migrant old middle class and new underclass (the service class in particular) are all concentrated in cities such as Los Angeles, London, Paris, Berlin, and Frankfurt.[67] Here, in turn, these groups themselves are usually segregated. More so than in the cities of industrial society, late modernity's metropolitan regions are defined by a spatial separation between the "desirable," attractive neighborhoods of the new middle class (plus the upper class) and the "plain" neighborhoods of the precarious class, many of which are regarded as places of "social unrest."[68]

The differentiation of milieus None of the three classes is socially, culturally, and politically homogeneous. The sociological distinction between classes is necessarily stricter and more abstract than social reality – with its many peculiarities, mixtures, and asynchronicities – could ever be. The model of the three-plus-one-class society is able to illustrate the transformation and basic structure of Western society today, but a closer look at individual ways of life reveals internal heterogeneities. In other words: within the new middle class, the old middle class, and the new underclass, there are smaller socio-cultural *milieus* that reflect a given class's basic way of life in different ways.

Regarding the structure of society, "class" and "milieu" thus designate two different levels of abstraction. There can even be important lifestyle differences between the milieus within a single class, but these differences are less fundamental than those between the classes themselves. At this point, it is possible to draw a connection between the theory of the three-class society and socio-logical studies of milieus, which shed light on the variety of different lifestyle groups in today's society. Especially enlightening are the studies conducted by the SINUS Institute, which have resulted in so-called SINUS milieus.[69] According to the current version of the SINUS study, German society can be divided into ten different milieus, some of which can be further differentiated into sub-milieus.

Decisive for our context is this: this highly differentiated map of milieus can be translated into the more abstract model of the three-class society, and vice versa (see Figure 2.4). That is, if the lifestyles and everyday values of these milieus (and the social positions that are reflected in them) are viewed from a more abstract perspective, what emerges are the three classes outlined above. It becomes clear that the *new middle class* can be divided into four smaller milieus: the "liberal-intellectual milieu," the "socio-ecological milieu," the "milieu of performers," and the milieu of "cosmopolitan avant-gardes," which are all milieus with high levels of cultural (and, in large part, also economic) capital, and that follow the guiding principles of successful actualization and cosmopolitanism in various, and

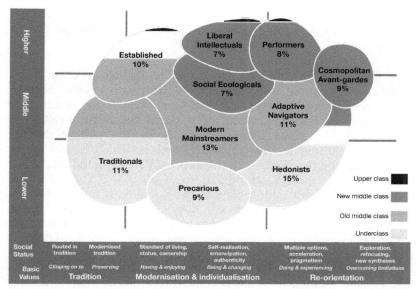

Figure 2.4 Socio-cultural milieus according to the SINUS studies and their "translation" into the three-class model (pertaining to Germany in 2018).[70]

sometimes conflicting, ways. In the first of these new-middle-class milieus, the prevalent feature is a close bond to education and high culture ("liberal intellectual"); in the second, it is a strong post-materialist orientation ("socio-ecological"); in the third, the focus is on combining high social status and geographical mobility with entrepreneurship, and with providing experiences ("performers"); and the fourth, finally, includes urban creatives and the young generation and thus is the trend-setting milieu for the development of the new middle class ("cosmopolitan avant-gardes").

Within the *old middle class*, too, various factions are apparent in the milieu studies: an older milieu that values order and duty and, at the same time, is culturally insecure ("modern mainstreamers"); a younger, more pragmatic, more hedonistic, and slightly less bitter segment ("adaptive navigators"); and a conservative milieu that is strongly oriented toward achievement and status ("established").[71] Finally, the internal structure of the *new underclass* also becomes clear. The latter includes the "precarious" milieu in the strict sense, along with parts of the "traditional" and the "hedonist" milieus (namely those who are hedonistic with respect to consumption). With the help of the milieu studies, it is thus possible to make finer differentiations within the broader three-class model, and they also provide quantitative information about the sizes of the classes themselves. Now we see (from a comparative historical perspective as well) that late-modern society has developed into a three-thirds society.[72]

A Trend toward Political Polarization and Future Social Scenarios

The social structure of late modernity is distinguished by being highly dynamic and prone to conflict, and this is evident both in Western societies and on the global level. This is the result of a complex constellation in which social ascent and cultural valuation have been taking place alongside social decline and cultural devaluation. In addition to the global upper class, which hovers above everything, the two winners in this process have been the ascendant middle class in the developing nations of the global South and the highly qualified new middle class of the global North. In the former case, this is a traditional success story; that is, there has been a measurable quantitative improvement in living standards and life options. The latter case is characterized above all by a qualitative improvement, for the new middle class has moved beyond the issue of living standards and is focused instead on quality of life. In the West – so far, at least – it has become the culturally dominant class whose values and goals are the most socially influential. The losers of these late-modern transformations have been, for one, the inhabitants of the precarious global South, who have to live without any prospects for improvement and yet are aware of the rising middle class in developing nations and of Western prosperity. But there are losers in Western countries as well. For the new underclass and the old middle class, the transition from industrial modernity to late modernity has been a story of loss. It has meant social decline in the case of the new underclass, and (subtle) cultural devaluation in the case of the old middle class. In that the leveled middle-class society has given way to a rising new middle class, a declining precarious class, and a stagnating old middle class, late modernity in the West has been characterized by a juxtaposition of disparate lifeworlds, and thus also by disparate self-perceptions, life opportunities, and feelings toward life – by disparities, that is, that did not exist to such a great extent in developed industrial society. Since 2010, this juxtaposition of positive and negative experiences in the late-modern social structure, which translates into optimistic or pessimistic feelings about the future, has also been reflected in the political landscape of many Western countries. Of course, the dissolution of the leveled middle-class society has been affecting the political system since the 1980s, during which it began to be influenced more and more by the new middle class. Since 2010, however, the establishment of right-wing populism has formed a countermovement that has completely restructured the political landscape in many countries. This political development can be explained quite well in light of the three-class model.

The dominance of people's parties went hand in hand with the leveled middle-class society. The main political divide here was between the conservatives / Christian democrats and the social democrats / socialists, who governed most Western nations from the 1950s to the 1970s. Following Dahrendorf's "house model" (see Figure 2.1), one could say that the social democrats represented a large portion of the working class during this phase, while the conservatives were supported by the traditional middle class, the professions, and by a smaller portion of the working class.

With the erosion of the leveled middle-class society, this overarching structure has splintered more and more. Since the 1980s, the slow but steady rise of the new middle class has considerably influenced the political agenda of both the social democrats and the conservatives. The cosmopolitanism and globalism of the politically engaged and culturally influential educated class, which can be motivated by both progressive liberalism or neoliberalism, have had huge effects on these two large sets of political parties. The center-left has distanced itself increasingly from the union-supporting statism of the old school (in Germany, for instance, the Social Democratic Party under Gerhard Schröder), while the center-right has taken a step away from classical conservatism (such as the Christian Democratic Union under Angela Merkel). At the same time, the rise of the new middle class has led, in many places, to the establishment of new parties that represent its values. In Germany, such values are expressed most clearly by the Green Party. In France, Emmanuel Macron's La République en Marche is now the new party of the urban educated class; in an almost textbook way, it embodies the dual set of values of progressive liberalism and neoliberalism.

How has the rise of the educated middle class politically affected the other two classes? At first, the shrinking old middle class remained faithful to the conservatives and the social democrats, even though both blocks had increasingly distanced themselves from the "communitarian" values and interests of the traditional middle class, and even though the members of this class played an increasingly smaller role in their internal party structures. Since 2010, the members of this class who have felt devalued and alienated have become supporters of right-wing populist parties such as the Alternative for Germany and the Rassemblement National in France, which present themselves as aggressive antipodes to liberal cosmopolitanism. Finally, the new precarious class is in large part politically indifferent. Otherwise, its members tend to support the right-wing populists or the neo-socialist left (the Left Party in Germany or, in France, Jean-Luc Mélanchon's party La France Insoumise).

In most Western countries, the effect of the three-class paternoster elevator has become obvious. Wherever there is not a cemented two-party system (as in the United States), the landscape of political parties has fragmented. The main polarity is no longer between social democrats and conservatives, but rather between the liberal cosmopolitanism of the new middle class, which is embodied by new parties such as the Greens or La République en Marche, and right-wing populism, which represents the aggrieved members of the old middle class (and the precarious class).[73] Meanwhile, the former people's parties have been falling apart.

Throughout all of Western Europe, the causes of the erosion of social-democratic and conservative parties are the same, and they all derive from the altered social structure. First, the core voting group of the traditional middle class has shrunk. Second, the new middle class, which the people's parties have largely ignored and yet thought they could win over, has since moved on to more liberal-cosmopolitan alternatives. Third, the right-wing populists and the neo-socialist left have attracted former centrist sympathizers, who now feel alienated, to the far right or the far left. Social democrats and conservatives are thus performing a political balancing act that is difficult to sustain. If the former party moves too much toward liberal cosmopolitanism, it will lose core voters from the traditional middle class. If the latter party shifts drastically toward nationalist and communitarian policies, it will risk losing voters from the new middle class entirely. The way in which the party system might transform is already visible in France. There, the political landscape is defined by the new polarity between the new middle class's liberal cosmopolitanism (La République en Marche) and the old middle class's right-wing populism (the Rassemblement National), while the traditional socialists and conservatives have been marginalized. The French party system has thus clearly adjusted to the new social structure.[74]

How will the development of the class structure proceed in Western societies? As a sociologist, I am hesitant to make any bold predictions, but it at least seems possible to outline possible future scenarios. As to which of these scenarios will emerge, this depends on how transformations in the economy (especially in light of digitalization and demographic developments), politics, and culture will unfold. Three scenarios are conceivable: an intensified socio-structural dualism between high- and low-qualified people and a corresponding "disappearance of the (old) middle class"; a general social decline of large portions of society, resulting in pervasive precariousness; and, finally, an "upward alignment," with the reconstitution of a new middle-class society.

In the first scenario, the process of the last few decades is sustained. The old middle class continues to shrink, while both the new middle class (the highly qualified employees in the knowledge economy) and the new precarious underclass (the service class) continue to grow and gain importance, with the result being a pronounced "hourglass structure" with two large segments on the top and bottom and a nearly empty middle. The central mechanism of this development would be that one portion of the old middle class would, via education, rise and join the new middle class, whereas another portion would not do this and would thus be forced, given the decrease in traditional routine jobs, to join the service class. In this scenario, professional polarization – and thus also socio-structural, cultural, and political polarization – would escalate.

In the second scenario, large segments of the new middle class join the old middle class in a downward spiral. This would mean that Western countries – perhaps in contrast to ascending societies in Asia – are in fact becoming "societies in decline." The mechanism of such widespread precarious employment has already been discussed in the pessimistic diagnoses of labor sociologists: a drastic loss of jobs on account of digitalization. In the event that employees in both the old and new middle class were widely affected by a shift toward technological automation, and in the event that new jobs were not being created in other sectors, the result would be a "downward alignment" for large portions of society. Under these circumstances, moreover, the liberal-cosmopolitan culture of highly qualified individuals would become unsustainable for all but a select few. This process of precarization could be exacerbated by the effects of inflated education: the expansion of education reduces the value of advanced degrees, and thus more members of the educated class than is presently the case would find themselves on the losing end of an economic downturn. The political effects of a society declining in this way would be highly uncertain.

The third scenario would be the result of precisely the opposite development: a shrinking precarious class and the stabilization of the old middle class via the creation of a more expansive new middle class. This scenario would involve integrating the former underclass, and it would also involve a new historical compromise between the two middle classes. One driving force behind such a process could be demographic developments, especially in Europe. Projected labor shortages (owing to declining birth rates) could make many of the jobs performed by the service class and the traditional middle class seem more valuable than was previously the case. This might lead not only to material gains but also to a gain in prestige. Such a development might also be propelled by a corresponding paradigm shift in national politics, which could attempt to "de-precarize" the underclass and – as a response to right-wing populism – create a balance between the cosmopolitans of the new middle class and the communitarians of the old middle class. Regardless of whether its leanings are somewhat more progressive or somewhat more conservative, this paradigm shift would require a form of "regulatory liberalism" that leaves behind the symbiosis of neoliberalism and progressive liberalism.[75] In this possible path ahead, both the conservatives and the social democrats could once again play an important role.

It is fairly certain that these three extreme scenarios do not represent mutually exclusive alternatives, and that entirely different varieties of them could unfold in different Western societies. Of course, it is even more difficult to assess the cultural factor than it is to foresee the economic, technological, and political developments that will influence the social structure. How much value will be placed on individual self-actualization in the future, and how much on ecological sustainability? How important will living standards and material income be? Will there be even more intense symbolic struggles between liberals and populists? Will urban life continue to seem more appealing than rural life? Will a culture of resentment (from above and below) become permanently established, or will experiences of devaluation disappear from one generation to the next? The postindustrial social structure is highly sensitive to shifts in social values, and so much depends on which way of life will seem attractive, desirable, and worthwhile. It is largely impossible to control or predict how these values will look in the future and which will become culturally dominant.

3

Beyond Industrial Society: Polarized Post-Industrialism and Cognitive-Cultural Capitalism

What are the foundations of the economy in late modernity? In what respect has Western (and global) capitalism undergone a profound structural transformation since the 1980s? And what are the causes and effects of this shift? We do not need to resort to a simple basis–superstructure model to realize that it is impossible to understand major changes in Western societies without a fundamental understanding of the transformation of goods, labor, consumption, and capitalism at large.

In order to understand the *post-industrial economy* in which we presently live, however, it will be necessary to abandon certain deep-seated presumptions and clichés. This is especially true of sociology, which emerged in the early twentieth century as a science of industrial modernity – as a discipline meant to answer the "social question" posed by industrialization – and often struggles today to free itself from the obsolete categories of industrial society. It is true of the media, in which it is still common to hear talk of Western "industrial nations" and to read coverage of traditional industrial firms. And this is also true of political debate, in which social democrats frequently evoke the ideal of unionized labor, and conservatives pine for the ideal of the old middle-class way of life (often, in both cases, with a heavy dose of nostalgia). As it seems, the images and concepts of industrial modernity are deeply embedded in the cultural and political subconscious of the West – a subconscious that Donald Trump suggestively addressed when, after his election, he announced his intention to revive the rust belt and thereby restore the American economy to its former glory.

There is a clear reason why certain ideas and images of industrial modernity have remained so stubbornly entrenched, and this lies in the history of modernity itself. For two whole centuries, *modernization* was synonymous with *industrialization*. That which we call "modern society," which emerged in the eighteenth century in Europe and North America, is inseparably tied to the Industrial Revolution, which pushed the agrarian economy into the background. In his book *The Wealth of Nations* (1776), Adam Smith was the first economist to outline this profound change.[1] Enabled by technological inventions, the liberation of the rural population, and the efficient organization of new factories, industrial production gradually became the heartbeat of the modernizing societies of Europe and North America. Its most important features were the standardization of production, the division of labor, urbanization, and novel political struggles, which were initiated above all by the socialist movements. It is easy to forget today that the process by which industrial society replaced agrarian society lasted 150 years. While in exile in London during the middle of the nineteenth century, Karl Marx, who was a great theorist of capitalist industrial society,[2] was repeatedly told that he was focusing his attention on a marginal phenomenon – for at that time, in fact, most Britons were still working in the agrarian economy or as domestic servants, whereas the industrial proletariat in Manchester and elsewhere formed no more than a small minority.

The industrial economy did not become fully dominant until after 1945. This was when the era of the developed industrial society really began. The labor unions achieved their peak influence, mass production corresponded to mass consumption, and employment arrangements were "normalized" – that is, they were full-time, indefinite, and usually permanent at the same company. It is not a historical coincidence that this very phase in capitalist economies – the *trente glorieuses*, as Jean Fourastié called it[3] – happened to overlap with the socialist planned economies of Eastern Europe (and that they both disappeared around the same time). Despite the competition between these political systems, the truth of the matter was that they were in fact just two versions of a mature industrial economy. This social reality of industrial modernity also corresponded to cultural conceptions that continue to be influential today, from images of hard, physical, "honest" work (done mostly by men), cities based around industrial facilities, work as a routine activity performed by the masses in giant corporations – all the way to the assembly lines and large office spaces memorialized by Charlie Chaplin in *Modern Times* and Billy Wilder in *The Apartment*: an economy that efficiently produces, by hand and in large numbers, everything from machinery to toothbrushes.

These times, however, are long gone. Classical industrial society began to erode as early as the 1970s, and this decay has been accelerating since the 1990s. The German historian Lutz Raphael has described this process in clear terms in his recent book *Jenseits von Kohle und Stahl* ("Beyond Coal and Steel").[4] The departure of the industrial economy has transformed the entire structure of society, cities, politics, and identities – but this new transformation unfolded within a single generation, and thus far more quickly than the transformation that took place in the nineteenth century. The numbers are clear: today, only a small portion of the Western workforce is still active in the industrial sector (that is, in the production and processing of material goods), and the contribution of this sector to wealth creation has diminished considerably. Of course, this has been a challenge for society. The 200 years of industrial society (of which only 30 were of the glorious ideal type) are just a blink of the eye in the history of human civilization, and yet people have oddly come to believe that industrial modernity represents the zenith of social progress. By now, however, this phase has already reached its end – and, so far, it seems undecided for whom, and to what extent, post-industrial modernity represents a story of progress or loss.

What sort of economic structure has come in the wake of the formerly dominant industrial economy? What does the term "post-industrialism" really imply? This remains a difficult question to answer, even though, since the 1980s, social scientists and economists have worked out a number of insightful approaches to understanding aspects of the post-industrial economy. The concept of *post-Fordism* concentrates on today's more flexible means of production; theories of the *service economy* and the *knowledge economy*, such as those developed by Peter Drucker and Daniel Bell, and theories of the *experience economy* emphasize other aspects of the post-industrial economic structure.[5] Authors such as Yann Moulier-Boutang have drawn attention to *cognitive capitalism*,[6] while others, including Nigel Thrift and Luc Boltanski, have analyzed elements of *cultural capitalism*.[7] After the financial crisis of 2008, much has been written about late-modern *finance capitalism*, and, in recent years, authors such as Nick Srnicek have identified the main features of *digital capitalism*.[8] Moreover, the evaluations of this post-industrial transformation have often been contradictory. The first book to consider this transformation was Jean Fourastié's *Le Grand Espoir du XXe siècle* ("The Great Hope of the Twentieth Century"), and it was given that title with good reason.[9] In his eyes, this would be a transformation to a society that has left behind toil and physical labor, and promises a high quality of life thanks to knowledge-based work and automation. Alongside such optimistic interpretations, however, there are also authors who are highly skeptical of the late-modern economy. Their keywords are deindustrialization, precarization, and rampant unemployment.

In my view, as convincing as many of these analyses and theories regarding the post-industrial economy may be, none of them tells the whole story. Without a doubt, late modernity's global economy remains essentially a capitalist economy, and it follows the formal structural principles that have defined capitalism from the beginning – that is, even during the era of industrial modernity. Two things are new in late-modern capitalism and in the late-modern economy as a whole: *polarized post-industrialism*, on the one hand, and *cognitive-cultural capitalism*, on the other. In what follows, I would like to examine these two features more closely. In contrast to the sweeping optimism of theses in favor of the knowledge economy, and in contrast to the sweeping pessimism of arguments about deindustrialization and precarization, it seems important to acknowledge the Janus-faced nature of the post-industrial economy. What we are dealing with is polarized post-industrialism, which is clearly reflected in the structure of employment. While the relevance of the industrial workforce and traditional white-collar careers has declined, the sector of highly qualified knowledge-based work and the sector of low-qualified work performed by the service class have grown.

This image of the post-industrial economy is made more complicated, however, by the structural transformation of goods and commodities that has taken place within its framework. At its core, the post-industrial economy can be understood as a dual economy fueled by cognitive and cultural capitalism. The cognitive *and* cultural character of goods constitutes the *immaterial* nature of the late-modern economy – a sort of immateriality that is paradoxically characterized by tangible goods such as tablets, high-tech medical treatment, sneakers, or kitchen tables.[10] This economy is *cognitive* because, since the 1990s, the bulk of its investment and its capital has not been directed toward machines but rather toward what economists call "intangible assets" – that is, immaterial capital: patents, copyrights, human capital, networks, and data. Most of the labor that directly or indirectly goes into these goods is, accordingly, knowledge-based: from education and research and development to design and marketing. Whether tangible or not, goods produced in this way thus have the character of *cognitive goods*. This iteration of capitalism is *cultural* because, among such cognitive goods, those that are regarded as especially valuable are not the goods that are functionally useful but, rather, those that consumers consider culturally valuable and culturally unique or singular: from Netflix programs and brand-name clothing to organic food and apartments in desirable locations. In order to be successful in cultural capitalism, a good has to have symbolic value beyond its mere function (in the form of originality, exclusivity, trustworthiness, etc.) In other words, it has to be a *cultural good*.

This means that the markets for goods in cognitive-cultural capitalism have a different structure from those in the old industrial economy. It is worth taking a closer look at this structure. The monetary gains that cognitive-cultural goods bring – and which make them so lucrative for late-modern capitalism – depend on their immaterial capital and the features of knowledge work, on their scalability (that is, on the ability to reproduce them at low costs), and on the cultural, "imaginary" value that consumers see in them. What is central is that cognitive-cultural capitalism is inclined to form so-called winner-take-all (or winner-take-the-most) markets, with extremely profitable goods at one end – whether in the pharmaceutical industry, the property market, the digital economy, the market for art, or the food industry – and with the many goods, at the other, that do not come close to achieving such success. In cognitive-cultural capitalism, the conditions of wealth production are therefore extreme. That capitalism in late modernity has become immaterial – that it has become cognitive and cultural – by no means implies that it has become "softer." On the contrary, it is harder, more competitive, and more expansive than its predecessor, and to a great extent it culminates in constellations of market winners and market losers. In the end, it promotes a profound economization of the social that has increasingly come to define the late-modern lifeworld, even in non-commercial areas of life.

The Rise and Fall of Industrial Fordism

In order to understand the genesis of cognitive-cultural capitalism, it is necessary to take a historical step back; otherwise, it is easy to lapse into short-sighted diagnoses and explanations. For instance, rising and falling markets (with their booms and crises), inflating and popping financial bubbles, and the effects of automation enabled by new technologies have characterized modern capitalism since its beginning. Knee-jerk references to recessions, financial crises, or the unemployment caused by digitalization are insufficient for explaining long-term transformations.

The economic history of Europe as the birthplace of capitalism can roughly be divided into three phases: a long phase of coexistence between a static agricultural economy and merchant capitalism, a second phase of industrial modernity, and finally the third and most recent phase of post-industrial, cognitive-cultural capitalism.[11] From the Middle Ages to the eighteenth century, the European economy was predominantly that of a static agrarian society. Thus, in European countries around the year 1800, between 70 and 95 percent of the working population worked in the agricultural sector. The agrarian economy was dominated by the problem of scarcity, and it was in large part a subsistence economy with minimal growth. Since the late Middle Ages, however, there existed alongside it a parallel economic universe in the form of merchant capitalism. Concentrated in certain European cities, intensive trans-regional or global long-distance trading was taking place (of luxury goods, above all), and this gave rise to the dense and ramified logistics of trade companies, joint-stock corporations, banks, credit institutions, and (later on) stock markets as well.

At the end of the eighteenth century, the Industrial Revolution catapulted the agrarian society into industrial modernity – this is true of Europe and, shortly thereafter, North America. Technological developments enabled a rapid rationalization of agriculture and the development of factories (organized according to divisions of labor) for the production of consumer and capital goods; new transportation technologies and the harnessing of electricity further increased growth in productivity and the production of goods. As Nikolai Kondratieff and Joseph Schumpeter demonstrated (each in his own way), a series of technological surges repeatedly fueled the expansion of industrial capitalism between 1790 and 1950 – from the mechanization of textile factories and the invention of the steam engine to trains, telegraphs, electrical engineering, and heavy industry, all the way to the industry of mass consumer goods, the paradigmatic example of which being the automobile industry.[12] Industrial capitalism thus developed into a dynamic, self-enhancing system for the production of material goods. Unlike merchant capitalism, it was based on factories, rising productivity, and the rationalization of the workforce. Urbanization and the number of industrial workers therefore increased exponentially in the nineteenth century.

From the beginning of the twentieth century, industrial modernity found its mature economic form in a system that can broadly be described as *Fordism*.[13] After 1945 in the West, this system was politically framed by the Keynesian welfare state. Fordism, which is named after Henry Ford, is based on the dual structure of mass production and mass consumption. Here, the production of large numbers of standardized goods required, in addition to advanced machinery, an extreme division of labor (typically labor of a manual, physical sort). The Taylorism of organization that prevailed in this context (named after Frederick Taylor, the inventor of scientific management) led to an extreme specialization of production steps based on measures of efficiency, so that even unqualified workers could accomplish the tasks in question. A typical feature of Fordism was large, hierarchically organized corporations with high capital investments, often in the form of publicly listed companies. What is central is that, since the 1920s in North America and since 1945 in Western Europe – unlike the early phase of industrialization, with its impoverishment of workers – the broad masses enjoyed a degree of prosperity within the framework of Fordism. The industrial economy was supported by mass consumption; the workers who produced the goods were also their primary buyers, and mass production, of course, required such mass consumption. The latter, too, had a standardized form and was oriented toward the functional goods that were so characteristic of Western middle-class life from the 1950s to the 1970s: homes, cars, yearly vacations, etc.

Economic growth and the extent of mass prosperity were high during the *trente glorieuses*. On average, the West German economy grew nearly 6% every year from 1950 to 1973, and the value of all produced goods and services tripled. The share of the workforce employed in industry – that is, in the secondary sector – reached its peak in 1960 at nearly 50%, and full employment was the norm. Moreover, the contribution of the industrial sector to the wealth of society as a whole was immense during this phase: it was around 53% (see Figure 3.1). This industrial capitalism was framed by active economic and social policies – driven in part by the macroeconomic principles of John Maynard Keynes – as well as by strong national labor unions. After the Bretton Woods conference in 1944, the relationship between nations and their currencies was regulated according to fixed exchange rates based on the US dollar and gold, and the International Monetary Fund and the World Bank were created.

In the early 1970s, this industry-driven economy fell into a fundamental structural crisis that had repercussions beyond the recession of 1973 (the oil crisis, rising unemployment).[14] Within a matter of a few decades, the industrial economy transformed into a post-industrial economy. Only today has the full extent of this structural shift become clear (see Figure 3.1). Since the 1970s, the share of workers in the industrial sector has drastically shrunk in all Western societies. In the Federal Republic of Germany, it has sunk from 48% (1960) to 24% (2017), and in the United States it has sunk from 50% (1960) to 26% (2015).[15] The same is true of the portion that industry contributes to the GDP, which in 2017 in Germany was only 31% (down from 51% in 1961), and in that same year was just 17% in the United States (down from 41% in 1942).[16] In many regions of the Western world – the Midwest in the United States, northern England, northern France, Wallonia, the Ruhr area, broad swaths of eastern Germany – outright deindustrialization has taken place. In parallel to this, the share of the tertiary sector – that is, the broad and heterogeneous service sector – has grown rapidly. In 2017, 75% of working Germans were employed in this sector, which accounted for 68% of the GDP. In 2015 in the United States, 73% of the labor force were employed in the service sector, and it accounted for a striking 82% of the GDP.

Regarding this textbook development of the Western economy – from the agrarian economy to the industrial economy and, finally, to the new, tertiary-sector economy – it should be pointed out that this is one of the few cases in which the prognoses of social scientists

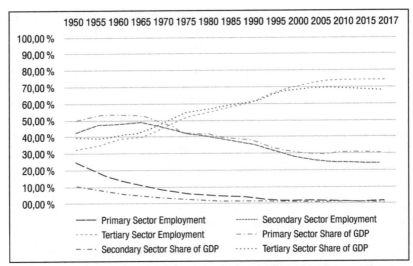

Figure 3.1 The development of employment and GDP in the Federal Republic of Germany, 1950–2017.[17]

turned out to be correct. As early as 1949, Jean Fourastié predicted this pattern of development (regarding the most recent transformation), and in 1973 Daniel Bell confirmed this prognosis while the development in question was already under way.[18] However, neither Fourastié nor Bell was in a position to recognize the *contradictory* structure of this post-industrialism. This has only become possible in retrospect; only in hindsight is it possible to identify the causes, mechanisms, and conditioning factors of a transformation. Why, then, did the system of industrial Fordism erode?

The Saturation Crisis

As is well known, the capitalist economic system is driven by a logic of growth that essentially consists of three elements: the pursuit of profitability, the reinvestment of these profits, and the expansion of economic activity enabled by this reinvestment. Within this system, there are several possible ways to ensure and increase profitability. These include the rationalization of production (by means of automation, for instance), increasing workloads, wage reductions or the introduction of new incentive structures, outsourcing production to "low-wage" nations (or regions), promoting innovation, searching for new markets on the global level, developing new goods to create new demand, securing certain price structures through monopolies or brand development, and the creation of corporate growth via financing. Even though all of these strategies were in play during the structural shift from the industrial to the post-industrial economy, the structural crisis that arose in the 1970s can be understood as the convergence of a *saturation crisis* and a *productivity crisis*. In hindsight, moreover, it can be seen why and to what extent post-industrial, cognitive-cultural capitalism emerged as a way out of this twofold impasse.

First, the saturation crisis. This concerns the demand and consumer side of the economy. At the end of the *trente glorieuses*, the needs of the leveled middle-class society for standardized, functional goods with specific utility functions – that is, the basic comforts that industrial modernity provided (well-equipped houses and apartments, cars, electronic devices, basic healthcare, mass tourism, etc.) – had largely been met. What does a growth-oriented economy do, however, when it has satisfied these basic needs and therefore saturated the demand for functional goods? If it wants to expand further, it has to move *beyond* the realm of established, functional, mass consumer goods. This is exactly what has been happening since the 1970s.

We have therefore arrived at a place where we are surrounded by the more complex and differentiated goods of a cognitive and cultural economy. As mentioned above, this is about goods that promise to do *more* than merely satisfy basic needs, and they do so by addressing culture and the psyche, our experience, our cognitive capabilities, emotions, identities, and our heightened interest in symbolic status. In contrast to the functional goods of mass consumption, the desire for such "immaterial" goods has no saturation point; rather, this desire can be expanded indefinitely, so that such goods can be "economized" far more extensively than was the case with functional goods. Moreover, the companies that produce cognitive and cultural goods *themselves* require – beyond raw materials or machines – the increasingly complex activities performed by other companies: IT consulting, design, marketing, legal services, organizational consulting, etc. The expansion of cognitive-cultural goods has thus established a new demand chain in which, beyond private consumers, companies themselves also participate as customers.

The spread of these complex cognitive and cultural goods has required a corresponding change in consumer desires (which, of course, are further fueled by capitalism itself). This *consumer revolution* has in fact been taking place since the 1970s. The demand for comfortable, functional, standardized goods that promise the same utility (and status) for everyone has increasingly been super-seded (supplemented or replaced) by the desire for goods that seem immaterial in the sense outlined above – by creating memorable lived experiences, for instance, or by telling good stories, imparting individual or collective identity, enabling education or wellbeing, radiating an aura of aesthetic or ethical value, or promising rarity and exclusivity.[19] The goal of achieving a certain *standard* of living through consumption has been surpassed by the more ambitious wish for the goods that we consume to contribute to our *quality* of life. Media and entertainment, sectors such as education and healthcare, differentiated consumer goods, consumable services, and events (in the tourism sector, for instance) are now in high demand. The revolution of self-actualization, which has likewise been in motion since the 1970s, turns out to have been an important precondition of this consumer revolution. Over the course of the revolution of self-actualization, the petit-bourgeois values of duty and social acceptance, which prevailed in the leveled middle-class society of the 1950s and 1960s and which tolerated no more than a moderate level of consumption, have increasingly been replaced by values that favor quality of life, the development of the self, the enjoyment of life, the development of opportunities for lived experiences, the pursuit of unusual experiences, and an aesthetically (and, in part, ethically) conscious lifestyle. The primary impetus behind this shift in values has been the rising, highly educated, urban, and well-off new middle class, though the effects of this shift can now be felt beyond the boundaries of this one social group.[20] The simple consumer society of the 1950s and 1960s, with its standardized and functional mass products, seems to have been no more than an intermezzo along the way toward a fully *developed consumer society* whose consumers count on having differentiated and singularized goods. They are also frequently associated with an advanced interest in symbolic status. In the high-income new middle class (and all the more in the free-spending upper class), the model of "keeping up with the Joneses" has been replaced by the desire for exclusivity and rarity.

At the same time, the companies and organizations that make complex cognitive and cultural goods available promote, in a sense, their own version of the "consumer revolution," which concerns their own "consumption" of goods and services. Post-Fordist companies are not the large-scale, "blue chip" hierarchical corporations of old, which aimed to generate the greatest possible output in the most standardized and efficient possible way; rather, they increasingly operate in extremely dynamic and unpredictable global markets. Post-Fordist companies depend on qualified employees, on networks with other companies or with the public, and on being constantly aware of the desires of private consumers. To a considerable extent, they therefore require *cognitive expertise*, which they themselves demand on the market. Whereas industrial-Fordist corporations had their own standardized "needs" – affordable raw materials, functioning transport routes, and a predictable workforce – the companies of the late-modern economy have themselves developed expansive "needs" for cognitive achievements, which are satisfied by so-called business-related services, from marketing and employee training to legal counseling.[21]

The Production Crisis and Polarized Post-Industrialism

The crisis of classical industrial capitalism was not, however, just a saturation crisis on the demand side; it was also a stagnation crisis on the side of productivity, innovation, and the organization of labor. Productivity growth was also restrained by the fact that the technical and organizational possibilities of Fordism had been exhausted. Since the 1970s – and especially since the 1990s – the response to this has been a number of transformations that have moved the apparatus of production in the direction of post-Fordist capitalism. This shift involves multiple dimensions, although computer and internet technology have played a central role throughout. In fact, after the first four technological revolutions diagnosed by Kontratieff and Schumpeter, which defined several stages of the modern economy since the eighteenth century, a fifth technological upheaval is now taking place in the form of the digital revolution (see Figure 3.2). The digital revolution has done more, however, than simply further perfect industrial production, which has been growing more efficient for over two centuries; rather, it has been an

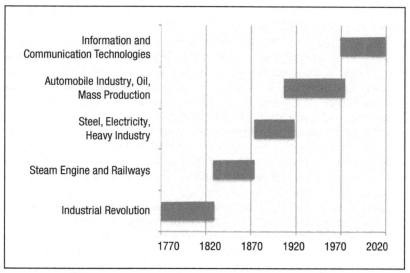

Figure 3.2 Technological revolutions since 1770 (a graph based on the work of Carlota Perez).[22]

important driving force behind its fundamental transformation into post-industrialism.

On one level – a level that remains highly significant even in the early twenty-first century – computerization and digitalization mean *automation*: that is, replacing routine jobs with the activities of intelligent machines. In this respect (and this confirms Jean Fourastié's thesis about post-industrialism), deindustrialization is also the result of an advanced form of automation. To the extent that they still exist, industrial companies are now clearly less reliant on human labor. Certain traditional services – administrative and secretarial work, for instance – are also feeling the pressure of automation. At the same time, however, new information technologies have also made it easier for companies to coordinate labor across broad geographical distances. They have therefore provided the infrastructure for the *spread of global production networks*, which, especially since the collapse of communism and the opening of markets in the global South, has been driven by Western companies. These global production networks represent a means of increasing profitability that is no less important than automation. Production facilities are transferred from their original locations to countries and regions with far lower wages and site costs, thus setting in motion a process of industrialization there. At the same time, cognitive tasks (innovation research, product design, marketing, and sales), which are closely interconnected with production via digital communication media, continue to be performed in the global North. In broad terms, it can be said deindustrialization and post-industrialization in the global North are results of the industrialization of the global South.[23]

The transition of many Western companies toward *knowledge work* and ongoing innovation, which has been observable since the 1980s, is another response to the productivity crisis. In this regard, too, digital information technologies have provided an infrastructure, particularly in their capacity as technologies of creativity and innovation. As Michael Piore and Charles Sabel have pointed out, we are no longer dealing with a Fordist "economy of scale" – that is, with an economy oriented toward producing large numbers of identical goods over long periods of time – but rather with an "economy of speed," whose pace is set by the need to produce ever more new goods for special segments of consumers.[24] In post-Fordist companies, *permanent innovation* has thus become a central objective, and not only with respect to material goods. The development of new services, new media formats, new events, and innovative ways to use things are part of this as well, as is the creation of (product-related) stories, aesthetic atmospheres, and even entire brand worlds. The primacy of innovation also applies to forms of labor and organization. As Maurizio Lazzarato has put it, post-industrial labor is based entirely on the "power of invention."[25] This economy therefore has very little need anymore for (physically) strong workers; instead, it depends on those who are cognitively skilled. The expansion of knowledge work has called for a significantly large group of highly qualified employees, who have been able to provide the innovation required; it has also necessitated a reorganization of career paths away from rigid hierarchies and extreme divisions of labor toward project work and cooperative networks (of companies, employees, etc.).[26]

There is yet another development, however, that can be interpreted as a response to Fordism's growth crisis. It is contrary to the innovative knowledge economy described above, and yet it has taken place exclusively in the tertiary sector. What I mean is the expansion of so-called *simple services*, for instance in the areas of transportation, building maintenance, logistics, housekeeping, public safety, healthcare, and the hospitality industry. This segment, in which the vast majority of low-qualified workers is employed, has likewise grown exponentially in the post-industrial economy, and there are two reasons for this. First, the consumer revolution and the rise of knowledge work have generated increased demand for these services. To be more precise, the core branches of cognitive-cultural capitalism – tourism, for instance – require simple services (cooks, hotel workers, etc.), as do today's more flexible consumer habits (delivery services). In addition, there is the desire of professionally stressed and well-paid participants in the knowledge economy to delegate, in their private lives, household-related activities such as care work (childcare, elderly care, etc.), and this has likewise created increased demand for services. At the same time, the simple services have been rationalized in a neo-Fordist way *without*, however, offering the negotiated salaries and social benefits that labor unions and government regulations had provided in the era of Fordism. Within the framework of the capitalist system, with its logic of growth, the simple services have thus represented since the 1990s an additional profitable (because "cheap") way for the economy to expand into new areas. Although labor productivity in the sector of simple services may admittedly be limited, this can be compensated for by cost reductions – low pay, cuts in social benefits, increased working hours made possible by more "flexible" labor laws and the threat of unemployment – all of which lead to profitability. Alongside knowledge work, the establishment of the simple-services sector, which in terms of manual labor has replaced industrial employment, thus represents the second pillar – one could also say: the underbelly – of the post-industrial economy.[27]

This is what I mean by the term "polarized post-industrialism": on the one hand, there has been a clear increase in highly qualified employment (that is, in knowledge work); on the other hand, there has also been an increase in the number of employees who are regarded as low-qualified and who perform so-called simple services, often in the low-wage sector. In contrast, there has been a contraction of jobs that require mid-level qualifications – for instance in traditional service sectors (such as administration and retail), and especially in industry. Framing this issue in terms of "lousy jobs and lovely jobs," the sociologists Maarten Goos and Alan Manning have conducted a thorough analysis of this polarization, which has been clear to see in Western societies since the 1980s. The data show that the sector of the workforce engaged in highly qualified activities, which in 1979 constituted the upper 20 percent of the population, grew considerably over the next 20 years, while the number of those engaged in simple activities, who made up the lower 20 percent of the working population, increased as well (though not as drastically). In contrast, the group of employees engaged in activities requiring mid-level qualifications, which once formed 60 percent of society, shrank conspicuously (see Figure 3.3).

As I have already stressed in a different context above, it would be misleadingly shortsighted to associate the post-industrial working reality with the idea of "services" alone.[29] Rather, it is now the case that two diametrically opposed working worlds exist side by side. They follow different logics of post-industrial labor, both of which have been thoroughly examined by economic and labor sociologists.

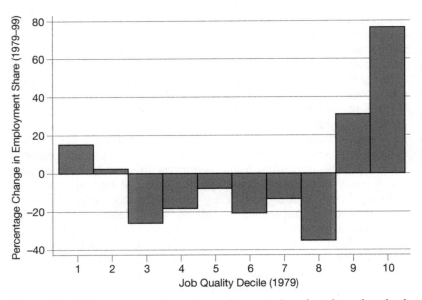

Figure 3.3 The percentage change in employment share by job-quality decile in OECD countries, 1979–1999.[28]

Knowledge work is a subjectivized type of labor, and those who do it are highly likely to identify with it. It is based on the "intrinsic" motivation of employees (and therefore frequently, too, on their self-exploitation), and its projects and networks often involve the "whole person" of the employees in question, including their communicative and emotional competencies (which means, at the same time, that such competencies are economically valued).[30] It requires complex cognitive capabilities and often innovative thinking and teamwork. In general, the highly qualified people who do work of this sort can count on a high degree of social recognition, and they are often (but not always) paid accordingly. The labor logic of simple services has a completely different form. As mentioned above, this is largely a matter of physical routine work that could be described as "normalization labor." The goal of such work is to maintain normal conditions (safety, cleanliness, etc.), so that the work itself often remains invisible – or it only becomes visible when it ceases to be done.[31] As a consequence of extreme specialization, what is required in this segment is anything but the "whole person" of the employees in question. Because such work requires low formal qualifications, its social recognition is minimal; and because the power of labor unions is limited and the competition is high (on account of migration, among other things), the compensation is below average.[32]

However, high-qualified and low-qualified jobs share one thing in common: at least parts of both are *transnationally* organized, which is to say that the workers in both sectors circulate beyond national borders. This is true of the "talent wars" in the knowledge economy, and it is also true of the migration processes within the service class. Whereas traditional industrial labor was organized nationally and remained within the confines of respective nation states, both sides of the post-industrial economy's polarized structure are tightly intertwined with globalization. Moreover, both sides of polarized post-industrialism share a common socio-spatial structure. Both the knowledge work of cognitive capitalism and the simple services are concentrated in *metropolitan regions*. The representatives of both sides live in Los Angeles, Amsterdam, Frankfurt am Main, Melbourne (etc.), and they depend on one another.

One consequence of the dual structure of polarized post-industrialism is that two extreme but widely held evaluations of the contemporary economy have to be dismissed. The first – optimistic – diagnosis proceeds from the idea that we are dealing with a fundamental transformation of the industrial economy into a knowledge economy, and assumes, in the sense of a classical narrative of progress, that the entire economic structure and employment structure are rising to a higher level. This assessment of things disregards, however, the expansion of simple services, and the fact

that not every member of the working population has high qualifications and advanced academic degrees. The second – pessimistic
– diagnosis dwells above all on the painful process of deindustrialization, and predicts that the entire working population will soon
find itself in a fundamentally precarious state. This assessment
disregards the fact that the post-industrial age not only has losers
but also a sizable group of winners – namely, the highly qualified
people employed in the knowledge economy, whose job satisfaction,
social status, and standard of living have all benefited from the new
economy.[33]

Globalization, Neoliberalism, Financialization

The consumer revolution and its mobilization – by higher demand
for new immaterial goods, by the increasing needs of companies for
cognitive expertise, by the opportunities of the digital revolution, by
the new shift toward automated production, by the global network
of production sites, and finally by the expansion of simple services
and innovation-oriented knowledge work – are thus the immediate
conditions and characteristics of the transformation from industrial
to post-industrial capitalism. This transformation has required structural parameters that have been mutually supporting one another
since the 1980s: the globalization of capitalism, the paradigm shift
of state economic policy toward neoliberalism, and the growing
financialization of the economy. Such topics have been widely
discussed in recent economic and sociological literature. From my
perspective, however, it is important not to interpret these three
factors as the *core* of the new economy, but rather as its *boundary
conditions*. The core of the new economy is cognitive-cultural
capitalism, which produces new forms of *goods* and which depends
on new forms of *labor* and *consumption*. Without the corresponding
boundary conditions of globalization, neoliberalization, and financialization, however, this would not have been possible, and so here
I would at least like to provide a brief outline of these phenomena.

As already mentioned (and is well known), the late-modern
economy is globally networked to a great extent.[34] Since 1990,
the capitalist economy's shift toward globalization has included
the integration of the former communist countries of Eastern
Europe and the formerly closed economies of the global South
(China's and India's, above all) into the global market. Of course,
Western economies during the *trente glorieuses* were also based
on international cooperation (within the framework, for instance,
of the European Economic Community), but this openness was
primarily restricted to the internal structure of the West. It was
the shift toward globalization after 1990 that first enabled the

new model of the global division of labor discussed above. The post-industrial development of the West has depended on the industrial development of countries in the global South, which made it possible for global production networks to emerge. The new cognitive-cultural capitalism of the West and the new industrial capitalism of the global South are thus complementary phenomena. Both the labor market of highly qualified employees and that of the service class are at least in part organized transnationally.

The globalization of production and trade is related to a readjustment of economic policy on the part of countries in the global North. This new structure is based on neoliberalism, and its effects extend far beyond matters of trade. Since the 1980s, the Keynesian managed economies and welfare states in the West have become Schumpeterian (that is, innovation-oriented) competition states, as Bob Jessop calls them.[35] The goal of government policy is no longer to guarantee the general welfare of citizens by regulating the economy and society within national frameworks; instead, it is to ensure and bolster the competitiveness of national economies (including individual companies and employees) within a global context. The neoliberal competition state promotes future technologies, slashes subsidies for old industries, facilitates global production chains, reduces taxes on incomes and corporations, privatizes social benefits, and enables both the rise of a low-income sector and the accumulation of great wealth. Not least, the neoliberal state also deregulates international financial markets. It has thus contributed to a profound economization of the social – to the commercialization of sectors that were formerly not organized in a market-oriented fashion (infrastructure, cultural institutions, etc.). Overall, this neoliberal paradigm shift has supported and enhanced the structural transformation from the industrial to the post-industrial economy in all of its facets.

Finally, the intensified financialization of the economy since the 1980s has also been a significant condition behind this structural shift.[36] This has involved two elements: financial capitalism and debt. More often than was the case during the Fordist economy, the companies of the post-Fordist economy are typically listed corporations that rely on investment funds. It is no coincidence that the rise of financial capitalism coincided with the rise of neoliberalism. For companies, financialization offers the opportunity to generate capital through stock exchanges, regardless of their creditworthiness with banks. The new, small but – in the most ideal case – easily expandable companies in the IT and digital sectors (but not these companies alone) are capitalized in just this way, at least as long as they enjoy the trust of the financial markets. As in earlier stages of modern capitalism, the financialization here is typical of a new economic phase in which new technologies, new goods, and new companies are appearing on the scene.[37] At the same time, the neoliberal privatization of social benefits (especially the privatization of pension funds), the wealth of the new middle class, the financial strength of the new upper class, and the increasing activity of companies on financial markets have led to a stronger inclination across society to invest in stock markets, and this has in turn resulted in greater demand for investment funds and financial products. For the companies participating in financial capitalism, this has had considerable consequences, especially because – far more than was the case under Fordism – the heads of such companies now have to focus on shareholder value, and thus on maximizing short-term profits. In a sense, financialization has led to the economization of the economy itself, and this has resulted in a competition for the best stock-market performance and in the ongoing pressure to optimize short-term gains.

Since the 1970s, the second consequence of financialization has been growing levels of private and public debt.[38] Whereas the level of debt during the *trente glorieuses* was relatively minimal, it has grown conspicuously since the end of this boom period, on account of sinking growth rates and the attendant drop in state and household incomes. Although states were the first to take on large loads of debt, it was not long before private debt began to increase via short-term loans for consumer goods (think of credit cards) but, above all, through property loans, which have had especially dramatic economic effects in the United States. Despite economically unfavorable conditions, the desire was to maintain the level of both private consumption and government services of the "fat years," and debt seemed to be the only way to avoid painful cutbacks. Even though many countries today have instituted balanced-budget policies, it is nevertheless the case that the post-industrial Western economy as a whole is financed by credit and debt to a considerable extent. This economy is constantly in need of fresh money, which, after the end of the Bretton Woods system, can basically be created from nothing.

Cognitive Capitalism and Immaterial Capital

By this point, I have outlined the crises of the Fordist industrial economy; the ways in which capitalism responded to the crises of saturation and productivity in the 1970s; the new structure of polarized post-industrialism, which is divided between highly qualified and low-qualified employees; and the structural boundary conditions that have supported this transformation (globalization, neoliberalism, financialization). Now we can turn our attention to the *deep structure* of cognitive and cultural capitalism. How does it differ from classical industrial capitalism? Clearly, the statistically demonstrable shift of importance from the industrial sector to the service sector of the economy (in the case of employment, as well as gross domestic product) is an important factor here. But what is truly new and consequential is that, in cognitive-cultural capitalism, the *form of goods*, around which the economy revolves, has changed. The theories of cognitive and cultural capitalism that I will draw upon here are concerned directly with this structural transformation of goods.

I suggested above that the broad concept of the "service society" runs the risk of overlooking the utterly complex and polarized situation that exists within the tertiary sector of the post-industrial economy; an additional danger is that it falsely *reduces* this economy to services of any sort whatsoever. Even the post-industrial economy continues to produce material goods, though – from automobiles and clothing to medicines. Thus Daniel Bell, the very "inventor" of the idea, had quickly set aside the guiding concept of services and instead emphasized the leading function of the knowledge economy when describing the main engine of post-industrial value creation.[39] In fact, one could now say that the central feature of today's new economic structure is that *complex knowledge* has become a genuinely valuable commodity. In this sense, the economist Peter Drucker has also pointed out that the structure of the post-industrial economy is one in which knowledge is produced by knowledge; it is thus an economy of knowledge goods, which for their part require knowledge work – and therefore knowledge (because it leads to innovation) is the most important force of value creation.[40] Thus, the direction in which we have to dig further to understand the deep structure of the post-industrial economy is known in advance. This economy is driven by *cognitive capitalism*, and it has already been studied systematically by the French economist Yann Moulier-Boutang and others.[41]

That said, the impressive theories that have been formulated about the knowledge society and cognitive capitalism often lack awareness of the fact that the types of goods that are important within this system are not only cognitive but also *cultural*, in that they promise consumers symbolic, narrative, aesthetic, or ethical value. Cultural goods are thus knowledge goods *of a particular type*. Their relevance to late-modern capitalism has been recognized in particular by authors who have been in close contact with the transformation of the world of consumption – Luc Boltanski and Arnoud Esquerre, for instance, who recently published a fundamental analysis of one aspect of cultural capitalism.[42] Above, I referred to the post-industrial economy as one defined by *cognitive-cultural capitalism*, and in fact I consider this dual structure to be a true novelty in comparison with the old industrial economy. In its basic structure, the post-industrial economy is one of *cognitive* capitalism. This framework of cognitive goods, however, also includes *cultural* goods, and thus the mechanisms of cultural capitalism have become especially relevant. In order to understand cognitive-cultural capitalism more precisely, it is therefore best to start by examining the goods themselves.

Goods are the simplest elements of the economy. In modern society, they are offered on markets and demanded by consumers. They can also be offered as non-commercial goods, for instance by government authorities (in the case of public education, for instance); in fact, public services constitute a considerable portion of the tertiary sector of the economy, especially in continental Europe.[43] Mostly, however, we are dealing with commercial goods – that is, with *commodities*, which, in addition to their use value for consumers, also possess a monetary value that is realized in their price. Goods exist in a wide variety of forms. Traditional *things* immediately come to mind: from simple groceries (an apple, for instance) to complex technological devices (such as a particle accelerator). However, three additional types of goods, which have likewise always existed, need to be mentioned. First, *services*, in which case buyers do not exchange money for an object, but rather for an activity, to achieve a certain effect; second, *events*, which involve ensembles of things *and* services to be experienced by the consumer at a particular moment (a theatre performance would be a paradigmatic example of this); and, finally, *media formats*, in which case ensembles of things and services are saved as sequences of signs – texts, images, sounds, games, instructions – in a material form that can be accessed at will by consumers.

This simple typology of goods is useful because it plainly showcases a primary difference between the industrial and post-industrial economies. At its heart, the industrial economy was a material economy of things, while the three other types of goods could then be treated as marginal phenomena. This is no longer the case in the post-industrial economy, in which services, events, and media formats have acquired considerably greater economic significance. *Services* in the strict sense have clearly become more relevant, particularly those that are business-related.[44] The paradigmatic branch of the economy that offers *events* is the tourism industry, which accounts directly for 4 percent of the German GDP, and indirectly for 11 percent.[45] And the breadth of available *media formats* has considerably widened on account of the digital revolution. As I have said, this does not mean that material goods have become irrelevant in the late-modern economy; on the contrary, it is important to develop an understanding of the post-industrial economy that includes produced things ("industrially" produced things as well). On an elementary level, it is no longer decisive whether the goods in question are things, services, events, or media formats. What is central is that *all* of these goods can circulate within the framework of cognitive-cultural capitalism *so long as* they are essentially *cognitive goods* (that is, complex knowledge goods), and, beyond that, many of the latter are also *cultural goods* whose cultural value is more important than their material utility. Cognitive and cultural goods are goods of high complexity. In this respect, they differ from functional standardized goods (and also, under late-modern conditions, from simple services). Their cognitive and/or cultural nature depends on the type of *labor* and the type of *capital* that is needed to produce them – *and* on the way that *consumers* perceive the goods in question.

Since the 1970s, the triumph of cognitive capitalism has manifested itself in the rapidly increasing importance of *immaterial capital* – in the rising importance, that is, of what economists call *intangible assets*, a development that Jonathan Haskel and Stian Westlake have investigated in detail.[46] This means that a good becomes a cognitive good through the high significance of the immaterial capital that went into it. Within the framework of industrial modernity, the assets of a company, in which the company itself invested to develop its capital over the long term, were primarily of a material sort: machinery, buildings and facilities, stored raw materials, and the like. This material capital formed the foundation of business productivity. Put another way: in order to tax the assets of a company in industrial modernity, it was more or less sufficient to assess the value of its physical premises.[47] Today, that is no longer the case. As a share of the total economy in Western nations, investment in immaterial capital has increased remarkably (see Figure 3.4). In some countries, in fact, investment in intangible assets has even

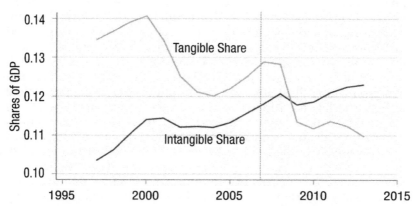

Figure 3.4 The development of investment in tangible and intangible capital relative to GDP in Austria, the Czech Republic, Denmark, Finland, Germany, Italy, the Netherlands, Spain, Sweden, and Great Britain, 1998–2013.[48]

overtaken material investment, as is the case in the United States, Great Britain, Sweden, Finland, and France.

What are intangible assets? In basic terms, immaterial capital is the capital of ideas, knowledge, and social relationships. It involves, first of all, innovative property or intellectual capital: the possession of copyrights, trademarks, and patents.[49] Here, in a sense, the capital consists in owning "blueprints" to knowledge (or the rights to such blueprints), which, once developed, can be used again and again for economic gain. This intellectual capital makes it possible for companies to produce and sell their specific products. Traditionally, immaterial assets in the form of copyrights constituted the capital of companies operating in the culture industry (in the strict sense) – publishing houses with their author rights and backlists, record companies with their artists and titles, etc. – but, more recently, it has become central for all companies engaged in cognitive capitalism to invest constantly in the development of their own intellectual capital. Additional components of a company's immaterial capital include digital databases – databases, for instance, with special information about relevant customers – as well as the competencies of a firm's employees (who are recruited and whose individual abilities are further developed), the economic network in which the company operates locally and beyond, its cooperative relationships, and the organizational routines that it has developed and maintained.

Today, immaterial capital is largely created through knowledge work (cognitive labor).[50] As already mentioned, the decisive feature of such work is its orientation toward innovation and creation. Instead of being engaged in reproducing things, its aim is to develop something new. This ability to innovate alone is what allows new intellectual capital and new cognitive goods to be generated. In this sense, a high-tech good such as a turbofan is, upon closer inspection, no longer a material good but rather – as Paul Mason has suggested in his analysis of the information economy – a cognitive good.[51] Of course, the turbofan itself is a material thing, but only a small fraction of its enormous price is related to the costs of its material and production; the lion's share of this price is due to the intellectual capital that has been invested in it, which for its part depends on knowledge work. However, because this type of work is innovation-oriented, its results – unlike those of manual or administrative jobs – are essentially unpredictable. Whereas, in the case of routine work in a factory or an office, it is more or less clear what "value" such efforts lend to the product in question, in the case of cognitive work it is basically uncertain whether it will succeed in bringing something into the world that is novel and useful, that can find customers, and that can be successfully marketed so that it in fact generates profit and can develop into intellectual capital.

It cannot be stressed enough: cognitive labor and immaterial capital are not only the backdrop to immaterial goods in the strict sense – media formats, events, and services; they are also behind many of late modernity's *material* goods, which continue to be produced "industrially," be it capital goods such as high-tech machines, or consumer goods such as sneakers. At this point, then, it is possible to resolve an apparent contradiction. Even though the post-industrial economy of cognitive-cultural capitalism continues to produce (often in an automated fashion) material things in large numbers and distribute such products worldwide (global production chains and distribution structures!), these superficially material goods have increasingly become cognitive goods on account of the (expensive) knowledge work that has gone into them – from their conceptualization and development to their marketing – and because of the high degree of immaterial capital that they involve.[52] Cognitive-cultural capitalism is not only widespread in the tertiary sector but in the secondary sector as well. In short, large portions of the economy have become "cognitive" in late modernity.

Cultural Goods and Cultural Capitalism

To what extent has *cultural capitalism* developed within the framework of *cognitive capitalism*? To repeat yet again: even in the late-modern economy, cognitive goods continue to exist alongside simple standardized goods, including simple services. At the same time, not all cognitive goods are cultural goods – that is certainly not true of the turbofan, for instance – but every cultural good is a cognitive good. To be more precise, cultural goods are cognitive goods with certain preconditions, and they have a specific relationship to consumers. The sales, prices, and profits that they can attain depend decisively on the cultural value that consumers *ascribe* to them or *perceive* in them.

There is a fundamental distinction between cultural and functional goods. Functional goods are used because of their utility; in a sense, they are "means to an end" – groceries are the means to the end of survival, seeing a doctor is the means to the end of recovery, watching the news is the means to the end of staying informed, etc. Cultural goods also frequently have a means-to-an-end function for consumers, but this is secondary. Their primary aspect, in contrast, is that they possess value in the strict sense. Regardless of their function, they seem valuable in themselves, and thus they have what I would like to call cultural value. Value of this sort exists in a variety of dimensions. Goods with *aesthetic value* address the senses and create experiences – a trip, a piece of music, an item of clothing, a visit to a make-up artist. A good with *narrative value* is associated with symbols, meanings, and stories – the apartment in a desirable location, the designer chair, the elite university, the sneaker by a particular brand, the trendy bar. Goods with *ludic value* involve the pleasure of play – whether such play is enjoyed passively (as when someone attends a live football match) or actively (playing a computer game, for instance). Goods with *creative value* incite people to participate in an activity – a workshop, an active vacation, a yoga group. Finally, goods with *ethical value* possess a moral quality – organic products, sustainable energy sources, fair-trade products, vegan restaurants, and so on. In general, cultural goods are strongly associated with emotions and affects, and they are in a way that functional goods and their practicality are not. In addition, cultural goods can also be linked to high degrees of symbolic prestige – here, rarity and exclusivity can play a role.

Cultural goods are not an invention of the post-industrial age; rather, they have existed since the beginnings of modern capitalism.[53] Many of the luxury goods of merchant capitalism can be regarded as such, as can the work of painters and sculptors that were traded on the art market or acquired by museums. Even during the age of industrial Fordism and mass culture – that is, during the era of the first consumer revolution – goods often acquired a secondary cultural value beyond their functionality, for instance in the form of brands or within the framework of the culture industry. However, it was not until Fordism's saturation crisis and the response to it that cultural goods, fueled by the second consumer revolution, became overwhelmingly relevant. Only then was it possible for cognitive-cultural capitalism to develop on a broad front. Ever since, goods that are culturally symbolic and emotive have infiltrated the economy more and more, and a seemingly unlimited economic space has arisen for cultural–affective goods, which consumers, whose needs for functional goods have been satisfied, increasingly demand. Late-modern consumers have thus developed a special expertise in cultural goods, and the act of "curating" such goods within their own lifestyles has become important. At the same time, the emotional connection to goods and the ability of people to identify with them have also gained significance. In that they are actively acquired and are made a fixed element (and expression) of one's lifestyle – the food that one eats, the trips that one takes, the sports that one plays, the objects used to decorate one's apartment, one's passions or hobbies – these goods are no longer perceived as trivial "consumer goods."

As a whole, the goods circulating in the economy can thus be classified, according to the degree of their complexity, into a "pyramid of goods" (see Figure 3.5). Those with the simplest structure – in terms of both their production and consumption – are functional standard goods. This complexity increases in the case of

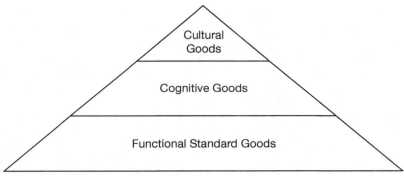

Figure 3.5 The pyramid of goods.

cognitive goods on account of the knowledge work that has gone into them. At the peak of the pyramid, finally, there are cultural goods (which are always *also* cognitive goods), for here there is an increase in complexity not only on the production end but also on the side of consumption.

What is characteristic of cultural capitalism, as it has expanded since the 1980s, is that its cultural goods typically claim to be *unique* (*singular*) and that consumers expect them to be so.[54] In other words, cultural capitalism is *singularity capitalism*, with an extremely diversified form of consumption that revolves around *singularity goods* and their qualitative differences. Singularity is not an objective feature of a good – rather, it depends on the perspective of the consumer and on authoritative evaluations, which certify its aesthetic, ethical, narrative, or ludic uniqueness. A thing, service, event, or media format seems to be singular when something about it seems original to the eye of the beholder. A fashion brand can be singular, as can an apartment in a particular neighborhood, the techniques of a particular therapist, a particular travel destination or event, a certain Netflix series, or even a special exhaust hood in a kitchen. Uniqueness does not necessarily mean that something occurs only once, for many singular goods exist in large numbers or are available to many people – the shoes produced by a certain brand or the television series *Babylon Berlin*, for example. In some cases, however, this originality is enhanced by a good's *rarity*, which means that it is not only unexchangeable but also relatively scarce (limited-edition clothing, certain wines). On the extreme end, goods can exist in only one exemplar (a bespoke pair of shoes, the city of Venice, an irreplaceable work of art); in this segment, the cultural goods also promise symbolic exclusivity. Generally, what consumers expect from the goods of cultural capitalism is that they seem "authentic," which means that they are not simply bought "off the rack" (so to speak).

The process of singularizing goods draws from the entire reservoir of culture: high culture and popular culture, youth cultures and sub-cultures, regional and national cultures, the different features of global culture, as well as past and present culture. The entire world in all its aspects seems to be a potential cultural resource for cultural capitalism – Caribbean cooking and the European Middle Ages, S&M culture and attending the opera, t'ai chi and Scandinavian furniture design, Montessori kindergartens and client-centered talk therapy, the beard fashion of the 1960s and French wines, the experience of nature in Scotland and the history of Paris. Within the framework of the culture economy, the process of singularization has also transformed what was once ineffable, ignored, functional, or even useless into something that possesses cultural value.[55]

For the goods of cultural capitalism, there are two essential features that had little to no effect on the functional goods of industrial modernity: short-term *fashions* and long-term *reputations*. The result of this is thus two oppositional temporal structures: the rapidly shifting nature of novelty on the one hand, and the long-term preservation of value on the other. When they first appear on the market, cultural goods can create short-term buzz; they can attract interest and excitement that leads to success for a certain amount of time but then fades or is redirected toward the latest innovation or attraction. This is the cycle of fashion – of films, travel hotspots, stores, events. Cultural goods can also, however, acquire a long-term reputation that makes them seem singular and valuable over long periods of time and thus guarantees lasting profits. Whether such a status is achieved depends decisively on society's authoritative critical voices. *If* such a status is achieved, then the result is classics: classics of design and music, classic travel destinations and highly reputable services, venerable universities, and prestigious residential areas.[56]

In which areas and branches of the economy is cultural capitalism especially "at home"? The first that come to mind are those branches that have always specialized in cultural goods: the so-called creative industries – media and the internet, design and architecture, publishing, games, music, art, and marketing. In his study of the "experience economy," Jens Christensen has demonstrated the extent to which sports (active and spectator sports) and tourism can also be classified as part of the culture economy.[57] This is similarly true of fashion apparel, for here too the goods have symbolic significance beyond their functionality.[58] However, it is characteristic of the expansion of cultural capitalism not only that the branches traditionally associated with cultural goods expand with it. In addition, the "functional" branches of the economy also increasingly culturalize their goods and claim that the latter are singular.

The reason for this shift from functional to cultural singularity goods has already been mentioned more than once: it is an effort to guarantee economic expansion at a time when basic human needs are already met. In short, since the beginning of the twenty-first century, the *entire consumer goods industry* has tended more and more to culturalize and singularize its goods – even in traditional branches such as the food industry, gastronomy, education, and healthcare. This trend is just as noticeable in the case of food products – which are said to have ethical value (organic groceries) or a particular flavor on account of their special origin – as it is in the case of restaurants, which strive to be extraordinary by adopting a particular culinary style and décor. Within the context of the expansion of education and the pluralization of educational institutions, individual schools have developed special profiles, and it has become essential for them to maintain their long-term reputations as valuable, trustworthy, and prestigious. In the case of healthcare, moreover, traditional basic care in the event of an illness has been supplemented by multiple new opportunities to improve physical and mental wellbeing, or even to enhance one's body and mind.

Once it has begun, the process of culturalizing and singularizing individual goods clearly tends to fuel itself. Competitors come under pressure and must, in order to keep up economically, react to the *singularization advantage* of other businesses by likewise singularizing their own goods. This is just as true of groceries as it is of schools, hotels, and medical facilities. As soon as certain food products enter the sphere of cultural capitalism, the makers of other such products feel pressure to do the same; as soon as certain schools begin to refine their particular profiles, others will feel pressure to offer more than just a standard educational product, and so on. This is not only true because cultural–singular goods, with their emotional attractiveness, are more enticing to consumers; it is also true because they can generate especially high *profits*. This, however, raises the fundamental question of how the *markets* for cognitive-cultural goods are structured, and how they differ from the markets for functional mass-produced goods.

Winner-Take-All Markets: The Scalability and Attractiveness of Cognitive and Cultural Goods

In industrial society, standard goods circulated on standard markets. This was typically a matter of material goods, which competed with one another on the basis of their utility and price. Prices were thus related to material costs, labor costs, and costs associated with the means of production. Function and price were the two components that attracted consumers to a given good: optimal functionality at the lowest possible price was the basic mechanism. This is the classical domain of economic analysis. In cognitive-cultural capitalism, this is no longer the case. The fundamental transformation of goods, labor, and consumption has also changed the form of markets and, with them, the way in which goods are priced. Accordingly, the way that capitalism creates wealth has also changed.[59]

Take the example of a sneaker produced by a global brand – for instance, Nike.[60] The fact that buyers are willing to spend 300 euros on it can only be understood by realizing that the shoe is not a purely material-functional product but, rather, a cognitive-cultural good whose price follows the laws of the immaterial economy. The relatively low material and production costs of the shoe certainly do not justify the price. Rather, the immateriality of the shoe and its price are the result of its "cognitive production" and its "cultural consumption." Regarding production, it can be said that cognitive-cultural work constitutes the lion's share of human labor that went into the shoe, and that the capital invested in it largely consists of intangible assets. Such cognitive-cultural work includes the development of Nike into a brand with a particular aesthetic and narrative appeal, the research and development behind the production of athletic shoes in general, their design, the creation of ever new and slightly different versions, the work involved with issuing limited editions, the sponsorship of prominent athletes for the sake of advertising, keeping a close eye on the interests and ideas of local youth cultures, maintaining the company's homepage, sending tailored messages on social media, sponsoring events, and – with different target groups in mind – cultivating a certain look in smaller stores and in the company's flagship stores (which exist in the best shopping locations in major cities). On top of this, there are the "business-related services" that a company such as Nike has to invest in: personnel development, IT services, legal advice pertaining to patent and copyright law, and organizational development. Far more than its material capital, it is ultimately the company's immaterial capital that has established the brand value of "Nike" over the years, and it goes without saying that this value is not low.

Regarding consumption, it can be said that, from the perspective of the consumer, the shoe is simultaneously a cultural good. The Nike customer does not merely consider the functionality of the shoe but also its cultural attractiveness – as a symbol of certain identity-forming characteristics, as a point of entry into the Nike community. Although it is produced in large numbers, the shoe, as a product made by this brand, is regarded as a singular and non-interchangeable good by its buyers. And this fact also comes with a (culturally motivated) price, which consumers are willing to pay. In this way, cognitive production and cultural consumption have transformed an unspectacular (and, in fact, inexpensive) functional good into a valuable (and thus also expensive) cognitive-cultural good.

The monetary value of cognitive and cultural goods should therefore be understood in relation to a specific form of labor and to a specific form of capital: cognitive labor and immaterial capital.[61] At the same time, cognitive-cultural goods can become so economically lucrative on account of the fact that they possess two particular features that distinguish them from functional goods. In the best-case scenario, cognitive goods are *scalable*. As cultural goods, they can profit in the best case from their *attractiveness capital* and their *reputation capital*. Keep in mind: this is the best-case scenario! As I already mentioned, however, the flip side of this is that it is risky to develop them. Under unfavorable circumstances, the process of researching and developing a new cognitive good might not lead to the desired result, and newly introduced cultural goods can fail by not attracting enough consumer attention (and thus by not gaining a reputation as something attractive). In the market for these goods, there are thus enormous discrepancies between success and failure. This, in fact, is the main characteristic of winner-take-all markets, toward which post-industrial capitalism is inclined.

The scalability of many cognitive goods (and, among them, many cultural goods as well) has frequently been discussed by economists,[62] particularly in contrast to the non-scalability of industrial modernity's functional goods. Scalability means that a good, once it has been developed, can then be endlessly reproduced with minimal effort (in terms of energy, capital, and forms of labor). In the case of scalable goods, most or all the effort involved is devoted to development, while the question of their (re)production is hardly of any importance at all. A pharmaceutical product, for instance, requires enormous amounts of research and development, whereas the costs of mass-producing the medicine itself are relatively low. It takes a great deal of time and energy to write a novel, compose a symphony, or direct a film, while it is a relatively minor affair to reproduce books, records, or film reels on a large scale. Something similar is even true of the more materially demanding serial production of designer furniture (the Eames chair, for instance): here, too, the profit-generating capital of the company in question lies in its intangible assets (in the licensing rights that permit the company to reproduce such a chair, for example). At the extreme end, scalability also accounts for goods that are disseminated via electronic or digital media: an opera or pop concert that can be listened to on a smartphone, a football match between two top teams that is broadcast on television, an app or computer program.

The scalability of many cognitive goods has a serious consequence: if a product is successful, the gap between its initial development costs (cognitive labor) and the profit that it generates will widen more and more. The product will "take off," and if a company owns the product as intellectual property, its high price or high sales will soon cover the initial costs and turn it into a cash cow that yields high profits with just a minimal amount of additional work: an effective cancer treatment, a bestselling novel, a timeless designer chair, a star singer, a classic film, a championship game, or a brand-name shoe. This is the way in which cognitive capitalism often creates wealth. Yet, as I mentioned above, cognitive goods are also highly risky goods. It is demanding and expensive to develop them, and it is highly uncertain whether this effort will succeed at all (think of the development of high-tech products). In fact, it is often a matter of pure *chance* whether a new cognitive good will break through and become a profitable scalable product. This dependence on chance is especially true of *cultural* goods, whose attractiveness is symbolic and emotional. This context of high risk and high reward in cognitive-cultural capitalism can be demonstrated with two examples that, at first glance, might not seem to have much in common: art and urban real-estate markets.

Given the marginal role that the art world seemed to play in the economy of industrial modernity, economic sociologists were long able to ignore it (or, at most, mention it in a footnote). In late modernity, however, the markets for art are in many respects representative of the market structures that govern cultural capitalism as a whole. The French sociologist Pierre-Michel Menger has done pioneering work on this very topic.[63] Markets for artistic goods are characterized above all by what economists call winner-take-all (or, at least, winner-take-the-most) structures.[64] Here, seemingly minimal differences in "achievement" are translated into enormous discrepancies in market success. In the first place, there is generally a high degree of overproduction in this field: of all the pictures that are painted, pieces of music that are composed, and films that are made, only a small fraction ever reach a broad audience. On top of that, it is difficult to predict which new painters, new composers (or singers), and directors (or actors) will be successful and which will not. Here we are dealing with so-called "nobody-knows markets," which involve a high degree of risk and uncertainty. Some of these artists will manage to attract an enormous amount of attention and will ultimately become stars. Among these, some will in turn succeed in establishing a lasting high reputation. The monetary gains to be made in such cases can be exorbitantly high – in visual arts, by the fact that original paintings can fetch a very high price; in music, shown by the fact star musicians can demand very high fees; in the film industry, by the fact so many people around the world go to see movies and by the fact that film stars, for instance, are showered with endorsements. Many other players in this market, however, come away empty-handed, and the middle range of the spectrum is limited. This is the very reason why such a market structure is called winner-take-all (or winner-take-the-most).

How can these enormous discrepancies in success be explained? For anyone who still thinks in terms of the categories of the old industrial economy – that is, in terms of labor input and customers who make cost–benefit calculations – winner-take-all structures must come as a surprise: Gerhard Richter and the unknown (fictitious) painter Klaus Lichter put just as much work, material, and time into their respective paintings, while the Coen brothers and the unknown (fictitious) director Johanna Kuhn put just as much work, material, and time into their respective films. But this is not the decisive factor. In the case of cognitive work (and this is what I am discussing here), the crux of the matter is not effort but innovation – and it is unpredictable whether even this will result in success. As the audience, moreover, consumers are the authority that decides whether a given work is innovative. Clearly, works of art are not purchased because of their utility function but because of their cultural value. They are paradigmatic singularity goods, and thus must seem unique (that is, non-interchangeable) to the eye of the consumer. They have to have "that certain something." Paramount here is the value of otherness or originality. Works of art therefore circulate on attractiveness markets that are simultaneously singularity markets, and attractiveness lies in the eye of the beholder. On the basis of their own cultural and emotional criteria, consumers themselves decide which films, paintings, and songs are fascinating and which are bland and therefore worthless. What is electrifying and memorable? What is uninteresting and thus a mere mass good? It is consumer taste that creates the enormous discrepancies in market success. For interested consumers, it's all or nothing. If something is fascinating, its success will be total; if it leaves us cold, it will fail. This is the apparent "injustice" that is embedded in the markets for cultural goods.

A more mundane example of cultural capitalism's winner-take-all markets can be found in certain segments of the late-modern real-estate market, which Luc Boltanski and Arnaud discuss at length in their study of the enrichment economy.[65] This example is interesting because, here, a type of good that was once overwhelmingly functional has been culturalized. Apartments and houses are primarily utility goods, but things are quite different for those "in the best locations." The latter have acquired a symbolic, aesthetic, and narrative quality, along with the social prestige that is often associated with this cultural value. These apartments and houses have thus also become singularity goods. They are regarded as unique because the place where they are located seems singular in a positive sense, and they themselves *become* a singular place. Therefore, an apartment in Hamburg-Harvestehude with a view of the lake, or in the San Francisco Bay Area or a townhouse in Brooklyn, is bought (or rented) not only on account of its functionality, but also because of its socio-cultural reputation and the singularity value that the property possesses. This high reputation is reflected in its high purchase price or rent, which is entirely unwarranted from a purely functional perspective, and is fundamentally unrelated to construction costs.

Here too, of course, it is true that the monetary value that arises from cultural reputation can fluctuate and is dependent on chance developments. This is to say that it is risky: neighborhoods once regarded as unattractive can become extremely attractive within a few years and thus increase in value (much to the delight of its current residents and to the chagrin of future buyers and renters), but the opposite can occur as well – for instance, if an unforeseen change in circumstances (excess tourism, blocked views) causes the reputation of the area to fall and leads to a drop in prices. In addition to this, there is also the fact that there are only a few places within a given country where real estate can succeed in becoming singularity goods, and correspondingly profitable. Usually, this applies to just a few particular neighborhoods in large cities or to a few limited areas with great natural beauty. In comparison, many other regions and cities are "only" functional living places that are untouched by the nimbus of cultural value and singularity. This is easy enough to see in the real-estate prices in such places, which are considerably lower than those in the few "best locations." In this case as well, what we have is thus a winner-take-all market structure.

The two examples of art and real estate make it clear that, within the framework of cultural capitalism, the price of *all sorts* of goods has to some extent been *uncoupled* from the amount of labor that goes into them – the very thing that political economists from Adam Smith and David Ricardo to Karl Marx considered the fundamental criterion for determining the value of a good – and from additional material factors (raw materials, machines, etc.). Instead, prices can now drastically rise or fall regardless of these factors, so that seemingly similar goods (which involve a similar amount of labor input) can have radically different prices. We have seen that the profitability of goods in cultural capitalism can turn out to be exorbitantly high and also, in the worst case, very low. Seen in this way, cultural capitalism is a capitalism of extremes. And this is not only based on the scalability of goods or the characteristics of cognitive work and immaterial capital; it is also based on the fact that goods circulate as cultural goods on an attractiveness market that is influenced by emotions. Here, they can become popular singularity goods – or not.

Essentially, the consumer is only interested in the result: in the good itself and how it seems valuable and appeals to the emotions.

The consumer, that is, is not really interested in how the good was produced. In addition, there are the characteristic, self-reinforcing mechanisms that cause the attention that certain goods receive and their positive evaluations to snowball. In the sense of the Matthew effect ("For to everyone who has more will be given"), cultural goods that have already managed to attract attention tend to attract even more, and possibly even exorbitant amounts of attention. Cultural goods that have already established a high reputation have an easy time maintaining it or renewing it.[66] As mentioned above, the winner-take-all structure of cultural markets cannot be understood in terms of the traditional cost–benefit calculus of standard markets. According to that measure, they in fact seem irrational. From a sociological perspective, however, cultural capitalism is anything but irrational. It has a logic of its own: a logic that determines how cultural value is assigned and how goods become emotionally attractive. This is the logic of an immaterial economy, and it governs how cultural capitalism produces wealth.

Extreme Capitalism: The Economization of the Social

We have thus reached the final step. Post-industrial, cognitive-cultural capitalism is the most advanced form of capitalism, and for a long time its effects have not been limited to the economy alone. Rather, since the 1980s, what has instead taken place is an expansive economization of the social.[67] This basically means that the patterns and norms that are characteristic of the economic sphere have seeped into and gained validity in social spheres that lie outside of the economy – in cultural and social institutions, in education and metropolitan social life, in religion and politics, in the media, and even in romantic partnerships and personal relationships.

What, exactly, does economization mean in this context? In a narrow sense, it can be understood as commercialization: things, services, or events that previously circulated free of charge now have to be purchased by "customers" and follow the rules of profit maximization and cost reduction. As commercialization, an econo-mization of this sort took place in the 1990s, for instance, when nationwide student fees were imposed at British universities. In a broader and more abstract sense, however, the economization of the social goes beyond this understanding of commercialization. In this sense, economization means *marketization*, which itself means that the logic of the market has encroached upon areas of society that had previously not (or hardly at all) been organized according to a market structure. Markets have a particular form: various entities ("goods" in the broadest sense) compete with one another in matters of price, utility, value (etc.) to win the favor of buyers, customers, recipients (etc.), who for their part exist within a constellation that involves making choices and comparisons.[68] The logic of the market is thus one of competition – a competition that does *not* necessarily have to be organized via the medium of money. The competition between potential partners on a dating platform or that between different schools within a publicly funded educational system illustrate how the logic of the market has also infiltrated non-commercial spheres. Paradoxically, moreover, the economization of the social can also affect the economy itself. During the era of Fordism, the market structure of the economy was clearly limited – for instance by labor law, by the relative paucity of innovative goods, by consumer norms, or by the specific limitations of a given national economy – but now, in the post-industrial era, this structure has shed many of these strictures.

What are the causes of the economization of the social that can be observed in late modernity? Undoubtedly, the three aforementioned parameters of the late-modern economy have played an important role in this: globalization, neoliberal policies, and financialization. The globalization of production and the global circulation of goods have meant that "domestic" goods and labor now have to compete on an international stage. Neoliberal policies have strengthened or introduced market-based structures where, under Fordism, they had hardly existed before – for example, in higher education and cultural institutions, in the transportation sector, or in the energy industry. Finally, financial capitalism has increasingly placed publicly listed companies (especially) in competition with one another by permanently evaluating them in terms of shareholder value. These are not, however, the only factors that have brought about the economization of the social. Even more important in this regard is the transformation from industrial to post-industrial capitalism – to the cognitive-cultural capitalism that I describe above. This form of capitalism has become so expansive that it now directly or indirectly affects broad swaths of society. Often, the economization of the social has turned out to be a massive *cultural* economization of the social – that is, it is a process of economization that transforms more and more aspects of society into commercial or non-commercial markets for cultural goods – for singularity goods in the sense described above.

Only by realizing that the economization of the social is an expansion of the structures of cultural capitalism is it possible to understand that this is not simply the result of social forces "from above." It is not, in other words, solely the result of the pressure to compete that has been imposed and institutionalized by globalization, neoliberalization, and financialization. It is also related to a fairly new type of desire that has developed in late-modern societies and can only be satisfied by a market for singularity goods. The consumer revolution that has been taking place since the 1970s (and is itself a consequence of the revolution of self-actualization) has created subjects who prefer, in every aspect of their daily lives, situations in which they "have a choice" – between goods that satisfy their emotional desires for identification and lived experience and fulfill their cultural desires for something valuable and singular. In the form of the new middle class (as the main group fueling this consumer revolution), the cultural economization of the social thus also has a powerful driving force *from below* – that is, from the lifeworld itself.[69]

Since the 1980s, this cultural economization of the social has affected various areas of life – *education*, for example. Kindergartens, schools, and universities have become cultural singularity goods (or it could be said they provide such goods). Moreover, they operate on local, trans-regional, or even international markets of attractiveness. Increasingly, the market for education has detached itself from the state-regulated educational system. Whereas, up into the 1980s, it was still presupposed that children would attend the school that was closest (or close enough) to their home, now certain other criteria play a role in this decision. Particularly in metropolitan regions, what has in fact developed is a differentiated educational market on which schools, with their particular profiles and reputations, compete with one another to attract selective parents and pupils (mostly from the new middle class). This is no longer just the case for private schools; it is true of public schools as well.

Such a competitive structure has also been established between *cities* and regions. With unprecedented intensity, cities now compete on a regional, national, and global level for residents and employees (taxpayers). For the new middle class, which is characterized by its high degree of geographical mobility, where one lives has become the object of a targeted choice between different possibilities. The cultural and emotional attractiveness of a city – the uniqueness of its atmosphere – has thus become an important selection criterion for (future) residents. However, it is not only for the sake of its residents that cities work toward increasing their attractiveness; the aim of this competition is also to attract tourists, as well as investors, companies, and organizations (especially those involved in cognitive-cultural capitalism), which likewise choose their locations on the basis of a given city's singularity. Sooner or later, highly qualified job opportunities tend to cluster in attractive cities. Accordingly, cities make efforts to refine their "profiles" in order to attract attention and recognition.[70]

A third area that has been infiltrated by singularity markets is that of personal relationships. In this case, the clearest example is the initiation of *partnerships* and marriages (or "merely" sexual encounters) by means of digital dating platforms, which have been expanding since the turn of the millennium. Here, a competition takes place between people and personalities who are striving for (physical) intimacy, but also to be seen and recognized as valuable and unique. Of course, a marriage market already existed in bourgeois culture, but this market structure has a different quality in late modernity. Because we are now dealing with a trans-regional and quantitatively larger partnership market, the competition among individuals for attention and recognition has clearly intensified. In a sense, such individuals present themselves as "cultural singularity goods" with the promise of enhancing another person's value and lived experience.[71]

Beyond the special example of dating platforms, the communicative space of the *internet* as a whole can be interpreted as a sphere in which a (cultural) economization of the social has taken place that affects the daily life of nearly every individual. Although there are also online social networks and communities that are not necessarily market-structured, the internet overall fundamentally has – even independent of its commercial use – the structure of an attractiveness market in which individuals, with their profiles, compete for the attention of other users (a scarce resource) and for their positive evaluation. Here, too, it is the case that only those people who seem to be singular – different, surprising, special – can potentially have success. Individuals attempt to be influential and to attract "followers" in this way; everyone is constantly a consumer – and, at the same time, at least potentially also a producer who is presenting himself or herself as a cultural singularity good. Within the context of the digital attention economy, the winner-take-all constellations are drastic. The few phenomenally successful user profiles – for instance, on YouTube or Twitter or as a blog – stand in contrast to the many that are unsuccessful: extreme visibility on the one hand, social invisibility on the other.

Over the course of the cultural economization of the social, the mechanisms of cultural capitalism have expanded into areas outside of the economy, and therefore the meaning of capitalism itself, given that it now pertains to more than just the economy, has become more abstract. Typically, as we have seen, cultural capitalism's "capital" is not monetary, but this does not mean that it has no monetary consequences. Whereas, in the late-modern economy, *immaterial* singularity capital can immediately be converted into *monetary* gains (without, in the ideal case, depreciating the value of the capital itself), in extra-economic areas such as the state educational system, the partnership market, or social media, intangible assets are valuable because, without being depleted, they can be "exchanged" for other *non-monetary* assets. Here, the "exchange goods" – that is, what one "receives" for one's singularity capital – are such things as talented and especially motivated students, desirable potential partners, or clicks, likes, and followers. The fact that this does not exclude monetary consequences is demonstrated by the market of cities. In that a city's singularity capital attracts interested people (residents, visitors, investors), it indirectly leads to monetary advantages in the form of higher tax income or a lively local economy, for example. Of course, non-monetary cultural capital shares similar features with monetary capital. Singularity capital, too, can be "capitalized," which means that it can be accumulated and repeatedly exchanged for other goods. Ideally, this can be done in such a way that the capital itself is not depleted.

To summarize, many of the features of cultural capitalism in the economy also apply to the cultural economization of the social as a whole, and affect all of society. The winner-take-all model of competition, which characteristically results in polarization between winners and losers, has spread into other spheres. There are now education markets (with their polarity between ambitious schools and "problem schools"), partnership markets (with their "successes" and "failures"), markets for cities (with their polarity between boomtowns and "left-behind" regions), and online attention markets (in which a few shining stars stand in contrast to legions of invisible participants). Moreover, the considerable emotional appeal that the goods of cultural capitalism hold for consumers can also be observed in all of these spheres, which are not related to the economy in the strict sense. In this way, cultural capitalism has gained enormous influence and significance throughout all of late-modern society and in the everyday lives of its individuals.

After the financial crisis of 2008, many commentators intoned that it would be wise for Western nations to refocus on the real economy.[72] Often, what they meant by the "real economy" was not only the economy outside of the financial sector. It was also insinuated that we should (or could) return to sturdy old industrial production – to the hard work, useful production, and transparent prices that had characterized the *trente glorieuses*. In light of the structural transformation that the economy has undergone over the last few decades, such an idea sounds absurd – or like pure nostalgia. The shift in employment away from industry toward the polarized services is just as much a reality as the rise of cognitive-cultural capitalism, with its intangible assets, knowledge work, its culturalization and singularization of goods, and its extreme market structures. The "real economy" – understood as a stalwart and rational economy removed from the interplay of prices, ascriptions of value, emotions, and future hopes – has always been a fiction.[73] This did not become apparent until the central role of the post-industrial, immaterial economy was fully recognized. Since then, the connections between knowledge and the economy, culture and the economy, and emotions and the economy have become abundantly clear. Cognitive-cultural capitalism is not a reversible deviation from the path of the "real," industrial economy. It is, rather, its successor: a more expansive and extreme form of capitalism. It shines on account of the emotionally seductive power of its world of goods, but it also leads to extreme asymmetries between the wealth that is produced by market winners and by market losers. These asymmetries pose a serious challenge, but instead of dreaming about restoring the idyll of national industrial economies, we should contend with the new situation as it is.

4

The Weariness of Self-Actualization: The Late-Modern Individual and the Paradoxes of Emotional Culture

A popular topic in today's cultural-critical debate is the fact that the late-modern individual and his or her lifestyle have fallen into a state of crisis. In this context, what Alain Ehrenberg called "the weariness of the self" is being lamented on all sides.[1] The risks of being overworked and overstressed seem to characterize the late-modern subject, and exhaustion-related illnesses (such as depression and burnout) and psychosomatic disorders have become the epoch's defining syndromes. The commentators diagnosing the present situation have developed a special interest in seeking causes for this crisis in large-scale social developments such as capitalism and digitalization.[2] Moreover, the fields of psychology and psychotherapy have also made contributions to this analysis and to the phenomenon of individual self-observation. To an unprecedented extent, late modernity is a thoroughly psychologized culture that encourages individual self-reflection and self-transformation.[3]

By now, however, it is easy to forget that the culture of the self, which emerged during the epochal shift of the 1970s, was associated with the hope that the subject might be liberated from the fetters of seemingly repressive industrial modernity and its "petit-bourgeois" everyday culture. It was expected that subjects would become more emancipated, hedonistic, sensitive, and vibrant, and that they would be more oriented toward their own needs and having "the good life" than toward the old norms of self-discipline. "Self-actualization" was and remains the guiding maxim of this advanced subject. At least since the 1990s, however, self-development has been the *new norm* of late-modern subjectivity, and its association with the normalization of the psychological complex, consumer capitalism, the demands of the post-industrial working world, and the structures of attention-obsessed digital culture has made it increasingly clear that this subject culture has produced intractable paradoxes. In an unprecedented way, late-modern culture promises individual self-fulfillment and suggests that subjects have a *right* to realize this goal, and yet it repeatedly makes it seem as though this very self-fulfillment is a phantasm that hardly anyone – except, perhaps, in certain exceptional moments – ever really achieves.

In this context, emotions and affects have taken on a central role. The late-modern culture of the subject is, in a certain sense, a *radically emotionalized culture*.[4] Fully in line with so-called "positive psychology," it extols the creation of *positive* emotions as a central aspect of life: satisfaction, pleasure, fulfillment, lived experience, enjoyment, desire, excitement, ease, social harmony, playfulness, "intensity," "resonance," and the development of the self in all of its (pleasant) facets and possibilities. This *positive culture of emotions* has meanwhile become such a matter of fact that it is easy to forget that both the bourgeois culture of the nineteenth century and the industrial culture of most of the twentieth century – not to mention earlier European ways of life, such as those propagated by Christianity or classical philosophy – maintained a far more skeptical attitude toward emotions. The traditional perception that it is hazardous to fall prey to one's feelings has almost entirely given way in late modernity to a culture of positive emotions. At least in its gratifying form, emotionality has become central to the late-modern way of life.

However, the paradox of this way of life, centered as it is on positive emotions, is that it unintentionally, systematically, and increasingly creates *negative* emotions: feelings of frustration and envy, rage, fear, despair, and meaninglessness.[5] In a sense, the underbelly of the positive culture of emotions is the reality of negative emotions, and while this culture refuses to acknowledge this dark side, the latter adheres to it all the more stubbornly. And yet there is no legitimate place for dealing with these negative emotions in late-modern culture, and there are no recognized methods for circumventing them in everyday life. It is no surprise, then, that these negative emotions therefore seek "illegitimate" forms of expression. These are either inwardly destructive (self-destructive) and manifest themselves in the psychosomatic illnesses mentioned above, or they are outwardly destructive, for instance in the form of aggressive hate speech on social media, or even in acts of hatred such as shooting sprees. In light of these social consequences, it seems warranted to concern ourselves with the causes behind the paradoxical production of negative emotions. Before doing so, however, it will first be necessary to understand the basic structures and social conditions of the late-modern, self-actualizing subject.

From Self-Discipline to Self-Actualization

The individual is not an autonomous entity, but rather a social product. It is only in society that *subjects* emerge from the basic physical and mental characteristics of human beings. Subjects are socially valuable beings who, in the ideal case, internalize the competencies, structures of desire, and mentalities that a given form of society requires. The mental structure of subjects is thus always a psycho-social structure. This is easy enough to see in the differences between the historical subject forms of different cultures: the society of ancient Rome produced different structures of the self – a different "habitus" (in Pierre Bourdieu's terms) – from those created by ancient Chinese society; the society of the heavily Christian European Middle Ages had different structures from those of early-modern aristocratic culture; and the structures of the self that predominated during the bourgeois era of the nineteenth century differed from those of twentieth-century industrial modernity. Regarding the epoch under consideration here, we have to ask to what extent it is possible to speak of late modernity's subject culture or social character. To what extent does "the human" today differ from that of 1960 (or even of 1900 or 1800)? A more precise answer to this question would require a more comprehensive historical and sociological analysis of modern culture.[6] For our purposes, however, it will be sufficient to compare the subject of late modernity, as it has been developing since the 1970s and 1980s, with its immediate precursor: the subject of industrial modernity.

The subject culture of industrial modernity is still familiar to many of our contemporaries – to those, that is, who experienced the old West Germany during the 1950s and 1960s.[7] However, this was a general phenomenon of Western societies. Three features were characteristic of this subject form: the guiding principle of social adjustment, "objectivity" (or a skeptical attitude toward emotions), and the ideals of self-discipline and the fulfillment of duties. Three important studies (each concerned with the United States, which played the leading cultural role in this era) have vividly elucidated these different features. In his classic book *The Lonely Crowd*, which was written shortly after the Second World War, the sociologist David Riesman characterized the subject of his time as an "other-directed character."[8] Unlike the "inner-directed character" of early, bourgeois modernity, this "new man" no longer found the criteria for his action in an internalized value compass (with guilt as the typical feeling that one experiences when deviating from this compass), but rather in the fluctuating social norms of his environment. In his or her behavior, the subject of industrial society was oriented first and foremost toward peer groups: young people of the same age, colleagues at work, or neighbors. This subject was oriented toward social adjustment, with the goal of demonstrating social normality. Here, deviation and individuality were causes for suspicion. Accordingly, the parenting practices during this era were also oriented toward ensuring that one's child would inconspicuously fit in with his or her social group. In general, the expansion of large corporations in the working world and the influence of television as a mass medium seem to have been important institutional parameters of the other-directed self.

In his book *American Cool*, the cultural historian Peter Stearns described the dominant lifestyle of industrial modernity (from the 1920s to the 1960s) as one defined by widespread skepticism toward the emotions.[9] The ideal was a "cool," sober subject who had negative emotions such as fear, sadness, or rage completely under control, but also did not excessively celebrate positive emotions such as pleasure or joy. The psychology of this time accordingly propagated the ideal of the distanced, socially adjusted self. Characteristically, the relationship between parents and children was also sober and matter-of-fact. Emotions were generally regarded as a weakness and as a sign of immaturity that always bordered on causing embarrassment. Not only relationships at work, but even one's personal and intimate relationships were ideally objective and unemotional. Finally, with a series of case studies in his book *The Road to Character*, the cultural critic David Brooks has outlined how the ideal subject during the first half of the twentieth century often lived according to the model of fulfilling his or her social duty, and how this necessarily entailed a great deal of personal sacrifice.[10] The guiding principle of this model is the idea that the subject has to exercise self-discipline in order to overcome negative or otherwise problematic inclinations, with the ultimate goal being to fulfill his or her social obligations and to find personal meaning in the "imposed" obligations themselves.

The three analyses outlined above may differ from one another in certain details, but they nevertheless piece together an image of subject culture that was typical in Western societies until the end of the 1960s, and whose three main features were: fitting into a social context, maintaining a skeptical attitude toward emotions, and practicing self-discipline in order to fulfill social obligations. As of the 1970s, this subject culture increasingly receded into the background and made way for a new one, which happens to follow the model of self-actualization.

The initial approaches of this new culture of the self took place in countercultural and subcultural circles – for instance, in the youth cultures of the 1960s and the alternative culture after 1968. However, the late-modern culture of the subject in its developed form at the beginning of the twenty-first century – today, its ideal-typical form can be found in the new, well-educated middle class in Western metropolitan regions – is not a mere copy of the late-1960s counterculture. Rather, it has a complex structure that combines two cultural models that were originally oppositional to one another: the model of a self whose primary goal is to actualize his or her desires and potential, *and* the model of a self who is oriented toward achieving high social status and the successful self-portrayal that comes with it. In cultural historical terms, the subject of late modernity has therefore synthesized two initially inimical ideals: the "Romantic" ideal of self-actualization, which originated around the year 1800 and has since been repeatedly adopted by countercultures and subcultures,[11] and the "bourgeois" ideal of a way of life that strives for social status via achievement and by means of investing in one's own status, which flourished in the nineteenth century and endures today in the middle class. Now, essentially, the subject of late modernity wants to have both: self-development *and* social success.

What are the causes of the profound transformation that the Western subject has undergone since the last third of the twentieth century? It is impossible to trace this transformation back to a single cause; rather, several cultural, social, economic, and techno-logical factors have had a compound effect.[12] The much-discussed "value shift" away from values of duty and acceptance toward those of self-development is closely related to the rise of a new middle class that benefited from the expansion of education and from the years of economic growth enjoyed during the *trente glorieuses*.[13] In the form of this new middle class, the values of self-actualization, which in the nineteenth century and early twentieth century were "lived" by just a few subcultures (above all in the field of art), have now found for the first time a broader social basis, from which they radiate into society as a whole. In the economic sphere, the shift of the Western economy from industrial to consumer capitalism – which is based on satisfying the unquenchable needs of mobile consumers for things, services, media formats, and events – has propelled this transformation of subject culture,[14] but so has the shift of the working world of highly qualified employees toward a postindustrial "new spirit of capitalism," according to which work is ideally no longer about earning a living but is, instead, something that provides meaning and creates satisfaction.[15] Since the turn of the millennium, moreover, digital culture has intensified consumer capitalism, and ubiquitous social media have provided subjects with a platform for self-representation that (at least in this form) is historically novel. Finally, two additional factors should be mentioned, both of which are supported by the engagement or private interests of the new middle class: first, the shift of the political climate toward "subject-sensitive" liberalization (i.e., the expansion of subjective rights); second, the triumph of so-called positive psychology.[16]

Successful Self-Actualization: An Ambitious Dual Structure

Positive psychology deserves special attention because many of the widely used concepts of today's new subject culture derive from it. Resting on the shoulders of Romantic philosophy, this psychology has done much to propagate the ideal of a good life based on self-development or "self-growth."[17] Thus, Abraham Maslow, a leading figure in this psychological approach and the inventor of the term "positive psychology," argued in 1954 that people can essentially follow one of two ways of life:[18] human lives are driven either by D-motivation (that is, deficiency motivation) or B-motivation (that is, being motivation). The aim of the first way of life is to correct material, social, and mental deficits in order to achieve prosperity, security, and acceptance. Here, accordingly, everyday activity is never an end in itself but, rather, always a means to an end. In the second way of life, which tends to become an option when one's basic needs have been met, everything revolves around "being" – that is, everything revolves around actualizing the self for its own sake. Subjects motivated in this way strive for unique lived experiences ("peak experiences," as Maslow called them) that are not means to an end but are rather enjoyed for their own sake, be it in the case of work or love, in play, nature, or art. From the perspective of positive psychology, it is only possible to lead a genuinely good life in the mode of B-motivation. This is closely connected to notions of emotional intensity, authenticity, and creativity.

Self-actualization thus represents an unusual philosophical and psychological ideal. Since the 1970s, however, it has nevertheless gone beyond particular subcultures and seeped into the social mainstream, where there now seems to be no alternative to it. Late-modern subjects want to develop themselves and are expected to do so – what other option is there? They consider themselves to be entitled and empowered to self-actualize. Ideally, entire segments of one's daily life should not (only) be a means to an end, but should involve activities that are done for their own sake and are thus emotionally fulfilling and subjectively meaningful. This is just as true of one's leisure time (with its trips, body cultures, political engagement, and events) as it is of one's work, which should not merely serve to make ends meet but should also be intrinsically motivating, meaningful, and satisfying. This is also true of one's personal relationships (partnerships, friendships, and family), which should involve fulfilling common activities. From the perspective of late-modern culture, many constellations that were entirely typical during industrial modernity seem deficient: working simply to earn money, getting (and staying) married simply to fit in with social conventions or to have financial security, participating in a leisure activity simply to relax and recover from work.

In the culture of late modernity, self-actualization is closely associated with an ideal of authenticity, the authentic life, and an authentic self.[19] Here, authenticity means "genuineness" in the sense that what one does, possibly without compromise, is oriented toward one's own "true" self (toward one's own desires, emotions, and values), with the aim being to act "individually" and thus not "like everyone else." Accordingly, it is ideal to strive to have a job in which one can rise to one's talents, a partnership in which both members feel as though they have found a perfect match, a family in which the parents and children create a little world of their own, a therapy or body culture that is tailor-made for one's own specific needs, or a political project with which one can fully identify.

In their pursuit of self-actualization, late-modern subjects engage in the ongoing process of valorizing and singularizing all possible elements of their lives. In the end, it is only possible for subjects to actualize themselves and feel authentic by cultivating a corresponding set of practices and activities that make them feel as though they have "developed." This is always a matter of introducing new elements into one's life: elements that seem valuable in themselves, are experienced as unique, and seem to be harmonious with one's own character. This process involves *valorization* because individuals look beyond mere instrumentality, utility, and efficiency and strive for what is valuable; they strive, that is, for that which has "value" and is therefore worth doing for its own sake – especially with respect to aesthetics (a yoga retreat, for instance) and ethics (a Montessori kindergarten, for example). This process involves *singularization* because subjects do not strive for what is uniform or standardized, but rather for what is individual, special, and non-interchangeable – from particular neighborhoods to tailor-made professional activities. The late-modern subject can only find development in the singular, in that which is *experienced* as singular. And only that which is experienced as singular (and not as something humdrum or standardized) seems authentic.

In a fundamental way, the late-modern subject culture of self-actualization is a culture of positive emotions. It cultivates the emotions – at least as long as they are positive – and these emotions and one's subjective lived experience are the standard by which the quality of one's life is measured. It is precisely this that distinguishes, in Maslow's work, D-motivation from B-motivation. When driven by the former motivation, one lives a largely unemotional daily life. Within the framework of the latter, on the contrary, the decisive factor is how one's life "feels" (or, to be more precise, how its individual moments "feel"). Here, the ideal seems to be "peak experiences," which are positive lived experiences of the greatest intensity. Of course, not every moment can meet this standard; essentially, however, one's everyday praxis is viewed in terms of how it is subjectively experienced and in light of how it emotionally "affects" the subject. If something repeatedly causes negative emotions – one's job, partnership, etc. – then this is regarded as fundamentally problematic. Yet even if something gives rise to just neutral emotions or to no emotions at all, this too seems unsatisfying. Ideally, *all* elements of one's life should elicit positive emotions; such is the model of the late-modern culture of self-development.

As mentioned above, the "Romantic" aspect of *inwardly* oriented self-actualization on the part of the subject is coupled with a second aspect that makes the late-modern way of life especially contradictory. In a sense, the late-modern subject is a Romantic and a member of the bourgeoisie at the same time, and this bourgeois orientation directs his or her gaze *outward* toward society, in which one hopes (and is expected) to achieve things and have social success. In order to achieve, maintain, or enhance a certain degree of social prestige, subjects actively invest in their status, and in doing so they rest on the shoulders of bourgeois culture.[20] It is necessary to attain achievements on a permanent basis in order to optimize one's own social position. To this end, subjects invest in various "forms of capital" (in Bourdieu's terms): in economic capital, for instance in the form of asset accumulation; in cultural capital, for instance in the form of education and competencies; in the social capital of useful social networks; and in psycho-physical capital, which consists in physical fitness and psychological balance. In the late-modern subject culture, the inwardly directed aspiration for self-development and the outwardly directed aspiration for social success are tightly intertwined; indeed, status work has turned out to be a *boundary condition* for successful self-actualization. Late-modern subjects are neither hippies nor anarchists; they are realists. They know that self-development cannot be achieved *against* or *outside of* society (nor is it expected to be); rather, this can only be achieved with the help of the forms of capital that are mediated *by* society. In the ideal case, these forms of capital furnish the subject with the resources that are necessary for realizing self-development: money, education, competencies, networks, good health, psychological balance. The ideal subject is thus not a world-averse Romantic, but rather a world-embracing creative person and self-promoting entrepreneur who skillfully mobilizes forms of capital in order to achieve satisfaction and wellbeing in the various segments of his or her life.[21]

Finally, there is still another, third side to the late-modern subject. In addition to pursuing authentic moments and striving for social status, which optimally blend together in the form of *successful self-actualization*, there is also the matter of performance. Late-modern subjects want (and are expected) to *present themselves* as people leading happy and authentic lives that are successful and rich in experiences.[22] This is the model of *performative self-actualization*. The paradigmatic late-modern subject makes his or her interesting life *visible* (on Instagram or other social media, for instance) and thereby transforms it, in whole or in part, into singularity capital within the framework of an attention economy.[23] In other words, subjects accumulate capital – *by means of* their interesting jobs, friendships, trips, political activity, etc. – and on this basis they themselves achieve the reputation of being singular and seemingly non-interchangeable. The late-modern subject is thus always engaged in a sort of "double-entry accounting," with both (inward) authentic self-development and (outward) presentation on the ledger: Do I feel as though I *myself* am authentic? Do *others* perceive me to be incomparable in a positive sense? Taking an extraordinary trip can ideally be entered twice on the credit side of the balance sheet: it can provide the subject with an interesting lived experience, and it can create a reputation in the eyes of others that this subject is leading a distinctive and *attractive* life.

In the late-modern subject culture, the ideal of authenticity is thus linked to that of *attractiveness*. Attractiveness means social recognition, which is fed by a subject's emotional appeal to others. Such appeal does not typically derive from the fact that the subject acts according to the general norms of expected behavior. Instead, it arises from his or her perceived *uniqueness*, which is what distinguishes this type of social recognition from that which was typical for the subjects of industrial modernity. In the latter case, it was sufficient to fulfill one's functional role: as a father or mother, at work, or in one's sports club. At that time, recognition was earned in a rather matter-of-fact and "unemotional" manner. Late-modern social recognition, which is earned via attractiveness, functions differently. It requires individuals to have a degree of "charisma," which stems from their extraordinariness: an extra-ordinary professional achievement (which causes someone to "rise to the top"), extraordinary leisure activities or interests, an extra-ordinary biography, etc. What is decisive is that recognition via attractiveness is acknowledged in the form of positive emotions, for instance in the form of *fascination* (such as the fascination that one has for a celebrity or loved one). The radiant victor in a sporting event, the famous YouTube star, the prominent entrepreneur, the charismatic actor, artists, activists, but also the "woman next door," who has conspicuously mastered her own unusual destiny, and so on and so forth – all of such people are, in their own way, the heroes of late-modern culture.

The Culture of Self-Actualization as a Generator of Negative Emotions

We have seen that the late-modern culture of successful and performative self-actualization is an extremely ambitious culture of the self. From this culture, subjects *desire* the utmost for themselves, and the utmost is *expected* from them at the same time. This coincidence of social expectations and subjective desires (which, for their part, were of course socialized by this very culture) is characteristic. Late-modern subjects *desire* the "authentic" development of their potential, from which they hope to gain subjective satisfaction, and at the same time they would like to be perceived and recognized by others as being especially attractive. In both cases, moreover, there are social expectations for a successful life, and individuals feel as though they have to fulfill these expectations: individuals, in other words, are *expected* to be authentic and attractive. Accordingly, late-modern society offers a number of formats for fulfilling these expectations: the urban creative type and the power wife, the satisfying family life and the media superstar, the "house on the sea" and the luxurious cruise, the political activist and the designer kitchen. Paradoxically, everywhere one looks there are cultural *formats* that promise subjects a life that is not average or "off the rack" but is literally *extraordinary* – that is, singular.

It has become increasingly clear, however, that the risk of failure is an inherent component of this ambitious late-modern subject culture. For some time, the dilemmas of contemporary subjectivity, its fault lines, and its precipices have been the object of various discourses, and such things have been explored with particular clarity in the field of art. To name just a few telling examples from recent years: in her original 2013 novel *The Interestings*, Meg Wolitzer follows a group of former classmates, who had forged a close bond during a summer camp, from the 1970s to the present. In an impressive manner, the author reveals the more or less subtle dissatisfaction and failures of each and every one of them over the course of their lives, while the characters themselves constantly observe and evaluate one another with an attitude of friendly jealousy. Far more drastically and aggressively (almost to the point of caricature), Virginie Despentes's three-part novel *Vernon Subutex* (2015–17) depicts an array of middle-aged people from the Parisian new middle class – with the character of Vernon, a former record store owner who has since become homeless, at the center of the plot – whose lifestyles have all led them to a personal dead end. Sonja Heiss's debut novel *Rimini* (2017) also takes place in the milieu of educated urbanites, and portrays middle-aged lawyers and psychoanalysts whose shattered hopes are apparent but nevertheless open up surprising new opportunities in their lives.[24] Whereas, in these examples, comparisons between people of the same age lend the stories their dynamic, the inter-generational comparisons made in recent films also provide revealing insights. In Maren Ade's film *Toni Erdmann* (2016), the restless life of a business consultant is juxtaposed with that of her concerned, 68er father. In Hans-Christian Schmid's *Home for the Weekend* (2012), a pair of grown siblings living in the city visit their parents in the country, and this reunion causes both generations to look back and reevaluate their lives. Finally, Richard Linklater's detailed coming-of-age drama *Boyhood* (2014) depicts, over the course of more than 10 years, the laborious efforts of two parents to achieve a "successful life" from the perspective of their growing son Mason.

From a sociological perspective, it can be shown more precisely how the risk of failure is to some extent built in to the late-modern subject culture. As mentioned above, the paradoxical structure of this subject culture manifests itself on the level of emotions. In the bright light of public attention, late-modern culture dances around the golden calf of "positive emotions" and yet, at the same time, furtively gives rise (not coincidentally, but systematically) to intense negative emotions. The latter are based on the *disappointment* that is induced by perceived discrepancies between expectations and reality. The experiences of disappointment generated by late-modern culture are intricately connected to strong negative feelings: to various shades of anxiety, sadness, or rage. In particular, the late-modern production of disappointment is caused by six socio-cultural mechanisms: the Romanticism–status paradox; the competitive structure of so many aspects of social life; the perpetuation of social techniques of comparison; the fragility of the standards for measuring "subjective lived experience"; the cultural ideal of exhausting all possibilities; and, finally, the lack of cultural resources for dealing with negative "uncontrollabilities" in general.

The Romanticism–status paradox is an especially powerful mechanism for producing disappointment. In that the neo-Romantic ideal of self-actualization and the neo-bourgeois ideal of social success are now joined at the hip, the late-modern subject has turned out to be inherently contradictory. Of course, if everything is going well, subjective fulfillment and social recognition coincide as desired. There is, however, a fundamental risk that this structure might translate into a double-bind situation, with the result that individuals can find themselves in the predicament of having oppositional expectations about their own lives. For example, if individuals lean too heavily toward self-actualization – in their job, family, education, etc. – they run the risk of losing social status. In contrast, those who place too much weight on investing diligently in their own status and security might at some point feel as though they have missed out on an opportunity to live up to their full potential. In modern cultural history, the Romanticism–status paradox can be traced back to the nineteenth century, when certain people had to face the question of whether they wanted to be an artist or a responsible member of the bourgeoisie.[25] Thus, many well-heeled members of the bourgeoisie yearned for the freedom of the artist's life, while many artists longed for the stable and secure life of the bourgeoisie. In late modernity, this dilemma, which affected just an exclusive circle of people during bourgeois modernity, has now become a paradox that is relevant throughout broad sectors of society.

A second mechanism that produces disappointment is the increasingly more intensive economization of the social, which has been observable since the 1980s.[26] Economization does not necessarily mean commercialization; on a more elementary level, it implies a gradual transition of social structures into the mode of competition, which itself takes place in non-commercial sectors. In this way, markets have emerged where they never (or hardly) were before. Contrary to the prophecies of market apologists, who giddily cheer the spread of win-win constellations in which everyone involved can "only win," the late-modern economization of the social has frequently given rise to win-lose constellations, which inevitably and simultaneously produce winners and losers. In especially drastic cases, this has resulted in winner-take-all or winner-take-the-most markets, in which the excessive gains (in recognition, satisfaction, etc.) made by a few people stand in contrast to the losses and frustration of the many. Here, market competition resembles a sporting event, at whose end the winner of the gold medal (and perhaps also the winners of the silver and the bronze) stand far above the legions of anonymous other competitors, who walk away with little to nothing.[27]

Such a marketization of the social can be observed in many areas of life. The late-modern working world, for instance, is not only characterized by the opposition between highly qualified employees in the knowledge economy and low-qualified workers in the simple services. Even *within* the sector of highly qualified labor – and therefore among the members of the new middle class, who live according to the model of "successful actualization" – there are often clear asymmetries between those who are successful and those who are not. Here, formerly predictable career paths have been replaced by win-lose constellations that pit against each other employees who work in the same industry and have the same formal qualifications. Such competition can be seen, for instance, in the fields of medicine, law, academia, journalism, architecture, computer science, and in the creative industry as a whole.

This sort of marketization, moreover, has spread into areas beyond the working world and has established constellations of winners and losers there as well. For instance, as Eva Illouz has discussed at length, increasingly extensive markets (enhanced by digital dating platforms) have formed within the sphere of intimate relationships.[28] Here, men and women literally take their attractiveness to market, so that success and failure are in turn never very far from one another: a few highly sought-after people stand in contrast to the many others who lose out or find themselves "stuck" in unsatisfying relationships.[29] Furthermore, a battle is now raging between various educational institutions over the status of excellence, so that a few distinguished schools and universities now stand head and shoulders above numerous "mid-level" institutions, which, unbeknown to many students enrolled, offer limited career opportunities. An additional sphere that has been affected by drastic tendencies toward marketization is that of real estate, especially in metropolitan regions. Here, on one side, there are attractive residential areas and the people who own property there (either through inheritance or shrewd investment), while on the other side there are bad neighborhoods and the unlucky victims of real-estate speculation.

In general, it can be said that the economization of the social distributes life opportunities and possibilities for satisfaction in a highly unequal manner without offering any legitimate explanations to those who have failed on the market. For the many who are disappointed, this inequality often violates their sense of justice, for they feel as though their achievements and efforts have been devalued. The legitimacy of the market, on which "every man is the architect of his own fortune," seems to be reduced to absurdity when (un)fortunate coincidences or unpredictable developments – on the labor market, the partnership market, the real-estate market, or the educational market – can be the deciding factor between success and failure.

This production of disappointment is fueled all the more by the ubiquitous technologies that facilitate comparison. Of course, human beings have always compared themselves to one another. Published in 1755, Jean-Jacques Rousseau's *Discourse on the Origin of Inequality* makes the case that one of the main problems of modern, civilized society is the fact that individuals, aware of their inequality, constantly compare their wealth and reputation to the wealth and reputation of others, and are thus perpetually discontent.[30] Late-modern society, however, has made it possible for people to compare themselves to others in an unprecedentedly systematic and intensive way; in doing so, it has turned comparison into a social compulsion. Digital technologies, in particular, have made it easy to view the lifestyles of others – in the form of images, above all – and this visibility simply invites comparisons: the vacation destinations and home furnishings of others are only just a few clicks away on Instagram, and the number of clicks and likes that an image receives is the method with which popularity is measured. As soon as people participate on social media and leave traces behind, they themselves are necessarily subjected to these mechanisms of quantified comparison. In addition, there are also more official ratings and rankings – of cities, universities, and brands, for instance – as well as widely discussed social statistics about such things as income and wealth distribution or the distribution of academic degrees, and all of this information helps to institutionalize a social logic of comparison.[31] This logic instructs people to keep a constant eye on where they stand in relation to others, whether in terms of formal parameters (such as income and education) or in terms of the "attractiveness" of their own lifestyle. Thus, even subtle social and cultural differences are made visible in a way that was not the case – and was not even possible – during industrial modernity. Then, comparisons were made within one's immediate local and social vicinity (residential area, neighbors, family), whereas the mass media at the time – aside from focusing on a few glamorous stars – offered little insight into the lives of others. It goes without saying that today's permanent mode of comparison can easily lead to disappointment. This disappointment can in turn transmute into sadness, or even rage. Envy, above all, is therefore an emotion that the culture of late modernity systematically cultivates.[32]

A fourth mechanism of disappointment is related to the enormous value that has been ascribed, in general, to subjective *lived experience* and, in particular, to the (positive, neutral, or negative) *feelings* that the late-modern individual has when evaluating aspects of his or her life.[33] Regarding one's happiness in life, the culture of self-actualization lends subjective lived experience and feelings a level of significance that they have never had before. The quality of older ways of life tended to be evaluated according to objective, "material" criteria or standards: social status in the sense of income or family reputation, the absence of need, the fulfillment of duties, conformity with religion or tradition, etc. In the industrial modernity of the 1950s or 1960s, the question of whether one was leading a successful life (that is, a life that corresponded to the standards of the time) was relatively easy to answer. Reliable indicators included a halfway decent job, an intact family with well-behaved children, a certain degree of comfort, and some free time for leisure activity. Ever since subjective lived experience, the feeling of authenticity, and the desire for self-actualization have gained significance, however, the way in which people evaluate the quality of their lives has become more demanding and complex, on the one hand, and more unpredictable and fragile on the other.

This is the case because positive lived experiences do not automatically occur even if the external framework for such experiences is put in place: having success at a highly interesting job can subjectively be perceived as tedious; a seemingly full family life can be experienced as alienating or draining; an adventurous vacation that seems enviable according to all standards can turn out to be a disaster, and so on. Furthermore, there is also the fact that subjective lived experience is often ambivalent and can change over time: jobs, partners, or places of residence that once seemed "perfect" can lose their appeal after a certain amount of time, and for obvious reasons it is not always easy to change such things. In fact, an absolutely positive lived experience is a rather rare phenomenon, and yet the late-modern culture of positive emotions has developed a poor understanding of *ambivalences*. The result is a generally low tolerance for ambiguity. Because of this, any feeling that cannot neatly be classified as positive or negative tends to be placed on the negative side of the ledger.[34]

Finally, the extreme sensitivity of late-modern subjects to their own inner worlds of lived experience and feelings also means, of course, that they are just as sensitive to their own *negative* reactions and emotions (and also to the "disturbing" or "hurtful" behavior of others) – and these are things that an emotionally less sensitive culture had not even perceived at all. If sensitivity implies an increased capacity for differentiation (thereby making ever more complex structures perceptible), then late-modern subjects have also become more sensitive to the elements that do not fit into their desired parameters: to the irritating characteristics of a partner, to the subtle annoyances at work or when interacting with colleagues, to the slight shifts in one's own body and mind between health and sickness. Because subjective lived experience has become one of the central aspects that determines whether one is living a good and successful life, the potential for moments of happiness has admittedly become greater, but so has the potential for disappointment and the sadness, anxiety, or rage that comes with it.

The fifth mechanism that produces disappointment concerns the typically late-modern idea that subjects have to experience everything to the fullest, and, if possible, savor every aspect of life. Here, the model of self-development is related to the ideal of an expansive and experimental self, which functions as a standard that subjects apply to themselves and others. In this case, self-actualization always entails striving for the *unlimited self*. Strictly speaking, of course, self-actualization does not have to be understood in this way: it could also mean that everyone is simply attempting to develop his or her "innate" self. As soon as this self has indeed been developed – that is, as soon as someone has discovered the appropriate forms and practices – this development then comes to a happy ending that "only" has to be reproduced. Late modern culture, however, is characterized by an apparently boundless dynamic of self-actualization. In the pursuit of the unlimited self, self-development thus follows the model of unlimited growth.[35] Ideally, subjects never rest content with the way of life that they have already developed; instead, they are always seeking the challenge of developing a new and better one.[36]

This goes hand in hand with a remarkable aversion to renouncing or missing out on things. In the eyes of late-modern subject culture, forgoing experiences is regarded as something negative, even pathological. The following principle seems to hold true: in one's own life, one must experience everything that can be experienced in human life as a whole. This is clear to see, for instance, in the norms that define the late-modern private sphere: personal relationships, partnerships, sexuality, family life, and so on. On the one hand, this sphere is more pluralistic and liberal than ever before; single mothers, same-sex couples, divorces, and sequential monogamy, for example, are all possible and respected. The late-modern flipside to this, however, is that subjects who do not intentionally try out multiple options in this sphere are increasingly looked upon with suspicion: people, for instance, who renounce sexuality for religious or personal reasons (asexuality); people who refuse to have a partner and prefer instead to live alone; women who, for whatever reason, make a conscious choice to forgo motherhood. They are all suspected of not taking advantage of their full range of possibilities and of failing to "live out" certain aspects of their personality, for the culture of self-development presumes the following: shouldn't everyone experience sexuality, have a partner, and experience the joys of parenthood? Is a life without these things a life lived in full? The ideal of the unlimited self puts pressure on subjects to experience as much as possible in their own lives, despite their natural limitations. It is not enough to know that *others* have experienced something.

A sixth important mechanism that produces disappointment goes back to the blatant deficiency in the way that late-modern culture deals with negative "uncontrollabilities" (to borrow Hartmut Rosa's term).[37] In broad terms, any event that evades subjective control can be designated as such, though events that remain uncontrollable in a negative and painful respect seem especially problematic. Of course, paradigmatic (because existential) uncontrollabilities include sickness and death, but accidents, (natural) catastrophes, and onerous family situations (into which one is born) also fall under the category of negative uncontrollabilities, as do unfortunate occurrences in one's social life, such as the contingencies of the job market. In general, modernity can be interpreted as a society whose goal is to eliminate negative uncontrollabilities: social progress is supposed to render them superfluous. Examples of this include the modern project of dominating nature and its dangers, as well as the modern project of medicine, which aims to eradicate all illnesses. Attempts to plan social processes and stave off life's risks (via social security programs, for instance) also represent mechanisms that modernity employs to make life predictable and reduce contingencies.

Despite all of these attempts to control and plan things, however, negative uncontrollabilities have obviously not been done away with altogether. Here, modernity repeatedly pushes up against its limits. Illnesses cannot be cured, deleterious family circumstances cannot be evaded, fluctuations in the market cannot be controlled, etc. Interestingly, however, modern culture offers little consolation in these situations. Beyond its attempts to manage such situations with various techniques of control and optimization ("the war against cancer," "lifelong learning," etc.), it lacks models, narratives, and attitudes for dealing with these uncontrollable aspects of life, which seem utterly meaningless (and not only from the perspective of the subjects affected by them).[38] In earlier times, religions could be relied on to provide instruments of contingency management. In today's broadly secular cultures, subjects can often do little more than despondently observe the failure of their life planning – or, in an effort to circumvent their own powerlessness, they can take the path of projection by identifying someone or something as being responsible for their own personal misery (this approach forms a breeding ground for conspiracy theories). In late modernity, which is based on an especially promising model of the self-determined and successful life, it is painfully clear that there are no cultural models whatsoever to help people make their peace with negative uncontrollabilities.

Ways Out of the Spiral of Disappointment?

Despite the inherent paradoxes of the late-modern lifestyle, there is no reason to resort to crude cultural-critical defeatism. Ultimately, every cultural way of life has its share of contradictions and dissatisfaction. However trivial this may seem, moreover, it should not be forgotten that in matters of health, nutrition, housing, working hours, job security, and education, Western societies have achieved a level without historical precedent, even though – by far – not all members of society have equally benefited from this.[39] That said, the risk of disappointment is considerable among those leading the highly ambitious late-modern way of life. It is true, of course, that disappointments do not have to be problematic per se. They can cause people to abandon certain expectations and change their goals, and they can also inspire people to work harder to achieve their desired goals in a different way. However, in the event that such expectations are firmly culturally embedded and repeated efforts to achieve them remain unsuccessful, the danger exists that disappointments will produce persistent negative emotions: either in the "inwardly" oriented form of sadness (about what has been lost or unrealized) and anxiety (on account of failure) or in the "outwardly" oriented form of rage (about one's lack of success and those allegedly responsible for it). Persistent disappointments can therefore turn into depressive lived experience or aggressive behavior. It is no surprise that late-modern society has both a depression problem and an aggression problem.[40]

What opportunities present themselves for transforming the late-modern way of life and its orientation toward self-actualization? Where would one have to begin in order to instigate such a transformation, and in what directions might it lead? Because a nostalgic return to classical (petit-)bourgeois culture is neither possible nor desirable, the question at hand is one of developing the late-modern way of life further and in a critical manner. From a sociological perspective, the first thing to do would be to examine the nuts and bolts of society that might easily be reconfigured. The economization of the social, for instance, could be subjected to revision. It would be possible for governments to add a higher degree of predictability to certain basic conditions of life – healthcare, housing, and education, for instance – and one could also imagine the implementation of certain measures to reduce the gaping divide of social inequality that has arisen from polarized labor markets.[41] Independent of government authorities, such a *de-economization of the social* could also be achieved by subjects themselves in their personal relationships. For instance, the unpredictability of partnership markets and family circumstances could be undermined by developing long-term solidary relationships in the form of friendship networks that minimize personal disappointments and are difficult to "break up with." That said, state institutions could also do more than they have done to consider the desires of individuals for self-actualization, for instance by implementing an educational policy that is more clearly tailored to the singularity of learners, by fostering a working world that respects the special qualities of individuals (such as their family situations), and by enacting a social policy that encourages them in their uniqueness.[42]

However, the fact that, in many respects, the cultural model of self-actualization eludes social or even government control should not be underestimated. Social parameters can admittedly be put in place to modify things slightly in one direction or another, but what about the psychological core of the culture of self-development? Is there anything beyond self-actualization? In this regard, two strategies come to mind that, in the future, might be able to push the culture of self-actualization beyond its limits, and both of these strategies are already present in the psychological discourse of self-help: on the one hand, a strategy that involves reflecting upon and tolerating contradictions; on the other hand, a strategy that involves distancing oneself to a greater extent from one's own (negative and positive) emotions. Both can be understood as alternatives to positive psychology.

A way of life that does not perceive contradictions and ambivalences as problems to be solved, but rather as a given to be accepted (and from which one can create reflexive distance) can benefit from certain versions of psychoanalysis. Unlike positive psychology, psychoanalysis proceeds from the basic assumption that life contains paradoxes which can neither be resolved nor turned into something positive. This situation is no different in modernity. A feeling of sadness in response to loss, for instance, is not regarded by psychoanalysts as something to overcome, but rather as something that can be constructively processed. The discrepancy between the pleasure principle and the reality principle is unavoidable (according to Freud), as is the imbalance between the id and the symbolic order (in Lacan's terms). From this perspective, it always comes down to how one deals with paradoxes. Here, psychoanalysis can be employed alongside socio-analysis, which examines the social contingency of many paradoxes and thus enables individuals to have a fuller understanding of their situation. In this way, subjects can be made aware of the Romanticism–status paradox, or the consequences that result from evaluating their lives according to the standard of subjective lived experience, and at the same time they can be made to understand that such difficulties cannot be fully resolved. What is needed is thus a way of life that *tolerates ambiguities* and recognizes that the modern belief in progress is not something that can simply be transferred and applied to everyone's individual biography.[43]

The second strategy consists in loosening the fixation that the late-modern model of self-actualization has on emotions. We have seen that the celebration of strong positive emotions invariably brings strong negative emotions into play, and that it can be difficult to deal with the latter. Why, in general, should such an extreme orientation toward feelings lie at the heart of an entire way of life? In light of the skepticism toward emotions that characterized bourgeois and (especially) industrial culture, it is understandable why late-modern culture emphasizes that feelings are a necessary aspect of a successful life. However, it has no answer for the inevitable presence of disappointments and negative emotions. One counterstrategy would be to acknowledge the presence of emotions but to avoid becoming dependent on them within the framework of one's life – and this applies to both negative and (what is more difficult) positive feelings alike.

To suggest that this would be a possible path forward for Western culture is to underscore the attractiveness of Buddhism (in its reaccentuated, Westernized form) and the psychological–philosophical techniques associated with it.[44] One cause of subjective suffering in late-modern Western society is the excessive extent to which individuals identify with their emotions – positive and negative – as well as with the ideal of an autonomous ego. Subjects are not forced, however, to surrender to their feelings; they can also take a step back and observe them as a volatile psychological process that neither constitutes nor defines their entire identity. From such a perspective, negative emotions thus lose their potency. The flipside of distancing oneself from negative emotions, however, is that positive emotions, on which the culture of self-actualization is so fixated, are relativized and "disempowered" as well. This is a matter of emancipating individuals from the vagaries of their emotions overall. Seen in this way, Western Buddhism offers an attitude that is reminiscent of classical stoicism, which the Danish psychologist Svend Brinkmann, for instance, has advocated in his work.[45] From this standpoint, what is needed is a more sober view on the uncontrollabilities of life.

Clearly, it would be an imposing challenge to step away from the late-modern culture of emotions and adopt a form of emotional control that hinges on emotional distancing. The same can be said of withdrawing from the culture of self-optimization in favor of "tolerating" contradictions. This would be a challenge because, in these cases, what is at stake is no less than the idea of progress and of the quest for happiness as a personal project, both of which are deeply embedded in the cultural code of modernity. The late-modern model of successful self-development can be understood as an especially ambitious version of this *pursuit of happiness* because, now, subjects themselves are expected to experience the same progress as society at large. This model of growth, however, has meanwhile reached its ecological limits, and not only on the level of society as a whole. Regarding subjects, too, one could say that they have reached the "limits to growth." In this sense, a way of life that is less prone to disappointment would also be a more ecological way of life – ecological, that is, in relation to the finite mental (and physical) resources of the subject.

5

The Crisis of Liberalism and the Search for the New Political Paradigm: From Apertistic to Regulatory Liberalism

Since 2010, there have been increasing indications that the societies of Europe and North America have entered a fundamental political crisis. In short, this can be interpreted as a crisis of Western liberalism, various versions of which have been defining the political agenda since the 1980s. Its most important symptom is what could be summarized as an international *populist revolt*: a multifaceted movement against liberal elites and their economic and cultural hegemony, in the name of an imagined "people."

Overwhelmingly, this has been a populist revolt from the right, but it has also come in part from the left or from a faction whose worldview is difficult to classify. Its particular national manifestations are well known: the election of Donald Trump as the President of the United States and the Brexit referendum in Great Britain represent the two most spectacular and internationally successful examples. Similar tendencies, however, have shown up in other places as well. In France, the 2017 presidential election culminated in a run-off vote between the liberal candidate Emmanuel Macron and Marine Le Pen, the leader of the National Front; in 2018 and 2019, the country was shaken by the protests of the *gilets jaunes*. In Italy, a government was formed in 2018 by the right-wing populist Northern League in conjunction with the broadly left-wing populist Five Star Movement. Among mid-sized and smaller European countries, the right-wing populist governments of Hungary and Poland, which were elected in 2010 and 2015 respectively, stand out in particular. Although Germany has yet to be affected as strongly by this populist revolt, the rise and infighting of the Alternative for Germany, which gained 94 seats in the 2017 parliamentary election, are being closely monitored. Everywhere, anti-establishment movements and parties are gaining traction, and this has put pressure on the entire spectrum of the established party system, from the social democrats to the conservatives. It seems as though we have reached a point in Western democracies where the future developments of the political agenda are up in the air.

In order to understand the current developments, we have to situate them within a broader context of the political history of Western societies after 1945. We are accustomed to interpreting political processes of change in terms of the schema of "left" and "right," which has been in place since the French Revolution. According to this schema, the political landscape represents a locus of apparently endless conflict between social-democratic (or progressive) and conservative parties in the broadest sense. Accordingly, the story of political history is commonly told as a sequence of regime changes from the right side to the left, and vice versa. We are all familiar with this from the way that history is often represented. A political shift took place from the CDU governments of Konrad Adenauer and Ludwig Erhard (with the intermezzo of the grand coalition) to the SPD governments of Willy Brandt and Helmut Schmidt, from the Democrat Jimmy Carter to the Republican Ronald Reagan, from the Conservatives Margaret Thatcher and John Major to the Labour government of Tony Blair, from the conservative Nicolas Sarkozy to the socialist François Hollande, and so on. With the populist revolt over the last 10 years, however, it has become clear that this common left–right schema alone is no longer sufficient for understanding political developments. No attentive observer has failed to notice that the populism that has arisen over these years has something "right-wing" about it, but it also has something "left-wing," and that the establishment affected by this revolt is – in its own way and at the same time – a liberal, left-wing, and conservative establishment. In broad terms, it ranges from the neoliberal bankers and managers in London or New York to the progressive bourgeois-bohemians ("bobos") in Paris or Berlin.

At issue, however, is more than just the political classification of today's populism. The left–right schema lost its explanatory power some time ago; in fact, this schema is inadequate for fully grasping the overall structural change that has taken place in Western politics since 1945. My thesis is that, over the last 70 years, the development of politics in Western nations can only be properly understood if we recognize that a sequence of abstract *political paradigms* has been at work "beneath" this left–right distinction. What this means is that an overarching political paradigm defines the political discourse and government activity for a few decades; after it has exhausted its ability to solve problems, it is replaced by another overarching political paradigm. Each of the political paradigms that have historically succeeded one another offers a fundamentally different answer to the question of how and to what extent politics intends to configure *social order*. What is important is that, during its time of dominance, a paradigm typically encompasses nearly the *entire* political spectrum from the center-left to the center-right. In other words, there are both left-leaning and right-leaning *versions* of each paradigm in question; they exist as patent variations of an overarching political manner of thinking and governing whose abstract foundation is often overlooked by those who are living at the time. Each political paradigm experiences a history of ascendancy, dominance, and decline that are all closely related to corresponding phases of social development. During the phase of its dominance, a given paradigm seems to be the "only way" and it determines, by regulating what can be thought and said (in Foucault's terms), how society and its form are politically conceived and governed. During the phase of a paradigm shift, this hegemony crumbles and fundamental debates are held about which new paradigm should follow. We now find ourselves in just such a transitional phase.

This may sound abstract, but it is easy to demonstrate in concrete terms. Since the end of the Second World War, and in nearly every Western nation, it is possible to identify two of these grand political paradigms, which are based on contrary ideas of social order. The first to arise and dominate was a *social-corporatist paradigm*, which spanned from Franklin D. Roosevelt's New Deal and the Scandinavian welfare state to the conservatism of Konrad Adenauer and Charles de Gaulle. It experienced a fundamental crisis over the course of the 1970s and was gradually replaced after 1980 by the paradigm of *apertistic* ("opening") *liberalism*, which ranged from neoliberal "Reaganomics" and New Labour to the red–green alliance in Germany. Broadly speaking, whereas the social-corporatist paradigm is economically and culturally oriented toward social regulation and the creation of order, apertistic liberalism strives to open up and dynamize cultural and economic social development. Since 2010, the paradigm of apertistic liberalism has, for its part, clearly fallen into a state of fundamental crisis, a symptom of which is the ongoing populist revolt. The question is: Which paradigm will come next? And to this I would answer: A good case can be made that it will (and should) be the paradigm of *regulatory liberalism*, which aims to regulate and establish order both socio-economically and culturally, though in a way and from a social background that differ from those of the old paradigm of social corporatism.

Political Paradigms and Political Paradoxes

Let us first take a closer look at the concept of the political paradigm, which I consider a key to understanding the political development of postwar societies. By talking of political "paradigms," I am transferring an influential concept, which the historian of science Thomas

S. Kuhn had devised to analyze large-scale trends in the (natural) sciences, to the political sphere and its development.[1] According to Kuhn, paradigms are vocabularies for problem-solving. They assert themselves when they turn out to provide answers to problems – in Kuhn's case, the problems of scientific explanation – and they encounter critique or enter a state of crisis when the number of "anomalies" that they fail to explain surpasses a significant threshold. After a crisis-ridden period of transition, a paradigm shift therefore takes place and a new language game is established that successfully solves newly discovered scientific problems for some time – until this new paradigm is likewise exhausted and replaced by the next, which is better able to explain newfound challenges. Kuhn believed that, within a given period of time, there is always just *one* leading paradigm, which provides a framework that is shared by more or less all scientists. Every paradigm shift thus entails a new beginning and *relative* progress. Seen in this way, the history of paradigms is a process of progress (with visible fractures) that casts aside previous paradigms but never fully devalues them. These old paradigms had "their time," but within the new context at hand they simply no longer seem sufficient.

As I understand them here, *political* paradigms share certain features with Thomas Kuhn's paradigms, but the analogy should not be taken too far. I intend to relate the concept to a precise social context: to the liberal-democratic, pluralistic systems of the so-called West (which, at the same time, are capitalist systems). The political paradigms that have characterized Western political history since 1945 can likewise be understood as complexes for problem-solving, and particularly as discourses and government techniques for dealing with *social* problems. In fact, the political sphere monitors society as something which poses problems that call for a political solution – economic crises, inequality, social disintegration, alienation, violence. Political paradigms therefore always emerge in a particular context of historical crisis, and they develop their own techniques of government as "problem-solving formulas" (the welfare state, marketization, diversity, etc.), for which they mobilize support and which they put into political practice. When a political paradigm has been implemented, when it works effectively from the perspective of its proponents, and when it succeeds in dominating the discourse with its way of thinking (including the discourse of its original opponents), then it seems to lack alternatives and to represent "the one and only accepted view of things." It becomes, in other words, hegemonic.

Times change, however, and new problems emerge that the formerly dominant political paradigm cannot solve, or at least not sufficiently. Ultimately, in fact, this paradigm is deemed to have failed. Of course, that which becomes a "problem" is not an

objective matter; rather, it is defined as such by social authorities
– the public sphere, political movements, experts, voters, etc. – so
that conflicts invariably arise about how things should be defined.
Like the implementation of a political paradigm, efforts to define
problems are a struggle for power; it is a question of who holds
sway over the discourse, and how resources are distributed between
various groups of actors and collective interests. Unlike the scientific
paradigms that Kuhn had in mind, however, political paradigms are
not only cognitive programs for solving problems; rather, they are
normative through and through: they involve decisions about value,
antagonisms over value, and utopian visions of desirable values.
Every individual version of a political paradigm therefore possesses
an enormous amount of potential for people to identify with it.
Unlike Kuhn's paradigms, which seem relatively self-contained, a
political paradigm is essentially more heterogeneous. Every political
paradigm exists in various versions – left-leaning and right-leaning
varieties, for instance – which can be "opposed" to one another, even
though they share certain common perceptions of problems and
common ideas about how to solve them.

A *political paradigm shift* is therefore fundamentally more
dramatic and profound than a mere change of government from
left to right or right to left (even if some of these transitions did
indeed usher in or give voice to a political paradigm shift, which is
typically only apparent in retrospect). Unlike the case of a "simple"
change of government between parties, which "only" entails the
replacement of one version of the paradigm by another, a political
paradigm shift means that an entire political manner of thinking
and governing is ousted by a new one, which will then impose itself
over the entire programmatic spectrum for many years to come. This
transition, however, does not at all take place smoothly, and this is
because of a complication that affects political paradigms and scientific paradigms in different ways. Governed by its own set of laws,
nature, which scientific theories attempt to understand, does not
change; society, however, which is the focus of politics, *changes*, and
it often does so *by means of* the intervention of politics (and often
in unexpected ways).

This therefore brings the concept of the *political paradox* into
play. By this, I mean the process in which a political paradigm, by
solving an existing social problem at a point in time t and thereby
justifying the long-term implementation of its policies, *creates* a new
social problem at a point in time $t + 1$ that it is no longer able to
solve. For modern societies, of course, social change is the normal
situation in any case, so that a successful political paradigm will
inevitably be usurped at some point if it remains unchanged. In
the case of the political paradox, however, it is the politics *itself*
for which, having allowed a new set of problems to emerge as an

unintended consequence of its own activity, the prevailing political paradigm can no longer offer a solution.

To cite a few examples: as an answer to the social question, the expansion of the welfare state has created the problem of a "culture of dependency"; as an answer to government overregulation, neoliberalism has resulted in the neglect of infrastructure and in drastic social inequalities; as an answer to migration processes, the politics of multiculturalism has contributed to the formation of parallel societies; as an answer to an underqualified society, the expansion of education has indirectly created both a social stratum that has missed out on this opportunity entirely and another stratum of highly ambitious people for whom life in a Fordist bureaucracy would no longer be thinkable. Broadly speaking, an initially "suitable" political approach is eventually made obsolete by the results of its own actions. In a sense, we are dealing here with a dialectical process: an initially "up-to-date" form of political action rises to the summit, and from this tipping point it then rapidly loses its persuasiveness and is replaced by a contrary form of political action that seems fit to tackle the problems at hand – though, again, only for a limited time.

As related specifically to the two aforementioned political paradigms of postwar history, this means that, after 30 years of dominance, the social-corporatist paradigm, which proved to be an extremely successful answer to the social and cultural problems of industrial modernity after 1945, entered a state of crisis on account of the fact that (among other things) it became a victim of its own political paradoxes. For its part, the paradigm of apertistic liberalism, which at first succeeded in making the stalled society more dynamic, seems to have become increasingly paradoxical since 2010, which indicates that it will soon be replaced. This background should be kept in mind, but before we can examine political developments more closely and address the question of how the next political paradigm might look, it will first be necessary to introduce a few more useful distinctions: the distinction between different sorts of social problems, the distinction between the paradigm of regulation and that of dynamization, and the distinction between the left-leaning and right-leaning versions of one and the same paradigm.

Problems and Solutions: Between the Paradigms of Regulation and Dynamization

As mentioned above, a political paradigm can be understood as an answer to a particular set of social problems. In principle, the relevant actors and discourses can regard any number of circumstances as a "social problem" in need of political solution. In the development of political paradigms since 1945, however, at least three complexes of problems have been present: *socio-economic problems, socio-cultural problems*, and *democratic-functional problems*. Though interrelated, they cannot be reduced to one another. What is important is this: in every phase of crisis – before the beginning of the social-corporatist paradigm (in the early 1930s, at least in the United States), during the 1970s (when the latter paradigm burned out), and in the current phase since 2010, as apertistic liberalism is coming to its end – problematic situations are apparent *on all three levels*.

Socio-economic problems include, for instance, economic crises (which go beyond mere boom-and-bust fluctuations), long-term economic stagnation, financial crises, high rates of long-term unemployment, glaring social inequality, high levels of government debt, or low levels of innovation. Socio-cultural problems include, among other things, social experiences of alienation, forms of cultural disintegration, as well as crises of legitimacy and motivation. Finally, democratic-functional problems are those that affect the legitimacy and functionality of the political system itself and raise questions about the validity of participating in the liberal-democratic system and about the efficiency of the political order. In acute crisis situations, it is typically the case that only some of these problems are at first perceived by various political camps. In actuality, however, when a dominant political paradigm finds itself in a state of crisis, this crisis usually pertains more or less to *all three areas simultaneously*. Conversely, it can also be said that if a new political paradigm wants to persuade people, win votes, and influence government policy, it has to offer a solution and a recon-figuration on all three levels.

Because the sequence of previous political paradigms does not really fit within the framework of the left–right schema, this poses the question of how we can systematize them in a different way. Such a systematization is also necessary and informative because it will enable us to have a better understanding of the process of forming a new paradigm – a process that is presently under way. My assumption is that a systematization of this sort is in fact possible, but it has to proceed from a point of reference that is more abstract than that offered by the historically traditional distinction between the left and the right. In their deep structure, the previous political paradigms distinguish themselves in the way that they respond to the fundamental social problem of *forming and dissolving orders*, and thus also in the way that they deal with the question of stabi-lizing or destabilizing social boundaries.

From this perspective, it becomes clear that, in previous developments, *paradigms of regulation* and *paradigms of dynamiz-ation* alternated with one another. In a paradigm of regulation, socio-economic and socio-cultural (as well as democratic-functional) problems are interpreted as problems that have resulted from a *lack of social order* and social regulation. To this extent, this paradigm relies on discourses and government techniques that revolve around the establishment of order, and it does so in an effort to create uniform conditions. This also (and especially) involves the establishment of firm boundaries. The social-corporatist paradigm, which was dominant into the 1970s (from Franklin D. Roosevelt's New Deal to Ludwig Erhard's "well-ordered society") is just such a paradigm of regulation. In a paradigm of dynamization, on the contrary, socio-economic and socio-cultural (as well as democratic-functional) problems are interpreted as problems that have arisen from an *excess of collective regulation* and a *lack of dynamism*. To this extent, this paradigm is based on opening up and deregulating orders in the broadest sense – in favor of individual freedoms, groups, markets, etc. It is based on tearing down rigid structures in the name of difference and variety. It aims to facilitate social movement and mobility and to welcome contingency. This also includes opening up various sorts of boundaries. The paradigm of apertistic liberalism –in both its neoliberal and its progressive-liberal manifestation, both of which decidedly endorse globalization – is just such a paradigm of dynamization. It can be presumed that this paradigm will be followed by a new paradigm of regulation. In light of the fundamental social changes that have since taken place, however, this new paradigm of regulation will certainly not have the same form as the old social corporatism.

The distinction between the paradigms of regulation and dynamization also sheds new and informative light on the traditional distinction between the left and the right (see Table 5.1). Let me stress: the left–right distinction is by no means irrelevant, neither historically nor for present and future developments. However, its significance is more limited than it is typically thought to be. If, in its form as a paradigm of regulation or dynamization, the prevailing political paradigm represents an abstract deep structure of political thought and action, then this structure is filled out in different specific ways by the left and the right. Conversely, it is also true that both the political left and the political right have an affinity for *both* paradigms. Throughout the entire timeframe in question (and, in fact, since the nineteenth century), the political left has had

Table 5.1 The left–right distinction and political paradigms

	The paradigm of regulation	**The paradigm of dynamization**
Left	Statist social democracy	Progressive liberalism
Right	Conservatism	Economic liberalism

both a "regulatory" side (in the form of statist social democracy) and a "dynamic" and "opening" side (in the form of various liberal emancipation movements). On the political right (in the broadest sense!), both versions are represented as well: classical conservatism is based on regulation and order, while economic and market liberalism are based on dynamization.

From this perspective, it is possible to decipher the tensions that exist *within* the left and *within* the right. Conversely, it also becomes clear that, in their specific historical manifestations, the paradigms of regulation and dynamization have been oriented both toward the left *and* the right, which in practice means that only *certain* traditions of the left and the right can be attended to at a given time, while others recede into the background. The social effects of a left-leaning or right-leaning instantiation of a paradigm's deep structure are undoubtedly relevant. It is possible to identify such effects on two levels. Whether the paradigm is being interpreted by the left or the right will decide whether government policies tend to promote equality or inequality, traditional or post-traditional ways of life. Within the same paradigm, the left and the right thus approach the interests and values of various social groups in a different way. There are historical differences, for instance, between the "Adenauer version" of social corporatism and the "Brandt version," just as there are between the "Blair version" of apertistic liberalism and the "Thatcher version." Furthermore, it is only within the medium of the left–right distinction that the paradigm is fully grasped by the political discourse, which can then associate it with specific social ideals and thus turn it into something that people can identify with. In a sense, the paradigm remains an imperceptible "code" as long as it never appears on the user interface in the conflict between the left and the right. As its underlying code, however, the paradigm fully determines how this interface functions.

In what follows, I would like to outline the sequence of previous political paradigms in light of this interpretive framework (see Table 5.2). The central question is why the corporatist paradigm of regulation and the liberal paradigm of dynamization fell into a state of crisis and what this means for current developments.

The Rise of the Social-Corporatist Paradigm

Up into the 1970s in Western Europe and North America, as mentioned above, political activity from the left to the right was dominated by a way of thinking that can be called the social-corporatist paradigm. In Western Europe, this was closely related to the reconstruction of nations that had been destabilized by the Second World War. It was supported by the political rise of Social

Democracy, on the one hand, and by that of Christian Democracy on the other. The historical context is somewhat different in the United States. Here it was the experience of the economic crisis after the stock market crash in 1929, to which Franklin D. Roosevelt responded in 1933 by instituting his "New Deal," that would lead to the most effective national version of the social-corporatist paradigm. In Western Europe, this paradigm was implemented by social democrats in the form of the Scandinavian welfare state and its cultural model of the "people's home" (*folkhemmet*) – to cite one example from the left – and it was implemented by Christian Democrats in the form of the social market economy and the "well-ordered society" of West Germany – to cite one example from the right.[2]

The structural background of the social-corporatist paradigm consisted of a fully developed industrial society, as well as a functional nation state as a controlling authority. Additional preconditions included urbanization, which had a transformative effect on all of society, and a relatively high level of cultural homogeneity within the populations of the countries in question (even despite the intensive migration movements that had taken place at the beginning of the twentieth century). Within this framework, the social-corporatist paradigm can be understood as a response to the massive crises that industrial societies had experienced during the 1930s and 1940s, which were socio-economic, socio-cultural, and

Table 5.2 *Political paradigms and social problems since 1945*

	Response to socio-economic problems	Response to socio-cultural problems
1945 The social-corporatist paradigm / the paradigm of regulation	Keynesianism / welfare state	"*Folkhemmet*" / the "well-ordered society"
1970 The crisis of overregulation		
1980 Apertistic liberalism / the paradigm of dynamization	Neoliberalism	Progressive liberalism
2010 The crisis of over-dynamization		
2020 Regulatory liberalism?	New economic regulation?	A new establishment of cultural orders?

democratic-functional crises all at once. This is clearest to see on the socio-economic level: the global economic crisis at the beginning of the 1930s gave rise to a drastic increase in unemployment and rampant poverty across broad sectors of the population. The renewed virulence of the "social question" at the time was indicative of the ineffectiveness of an economically and politically weak state. At the same time, the cultural and democratic crisis was ubiquitous, and this was interpreted by contemporaries as a "moral crisis" as well: the transition from an agrarian to an industrial society was associated with a normative "evacuation" of the social, which thinkers such as Émile Durkheim could describe as a condition of anomie. One aspect of this anomie manifested itself in (partially violent) political polarization, which characterized much of Europe in the 1930s. In Germany, this culminated in the collapse of the political system and the rise of totalitarian National Socialism. The cultural crisis was thus closely intertwined with a democratic-functional crisis: liberal democracies, whose structural roots go back to the nineteenth century, were put on the defensive throughout the continent and were challenged by the alternative systems of communism and fascism.

Against this crisis-ridden postwar backdrop, the social-corporatist paradigm asserted itself on a broad front as a form of government that promised to – and did – *regulate* the social, cultural, and political conditions by bringing them into *order* and subjecting them to this order. As mentioned above, this was at its heart a paradigm of regulation.[3] After 1945, the government policies of both the Social Democrats and the Christian Democrats represented comprehensive systems for creating social order, and at the center of these systems was an active state. Such order was achieved most prominently in the areas of economic and social policy. The (nation) state under the social-corporatist paradigm perceived itself as the central authority of economic control whose task was to restrain the capitalist system and its immanent crises and, at the same time, to distribute its production of wealth throughout the population. Anti-cyclical and demand-oriented economic policies – "Keynesianism" – served as an important instrument for planning economic processes and offsetting market failures. Moreover, the paradigm gave rise to a redistributive welfare state that provided a safety net against risks (health insurance, pensions), regulated the labor and housing markets, and guaranteed the availability of general education and infrastructure. The leitmotif of this model – a "society of equals," as Pierre Rosanvallon called it – was its effort to achieve comparable living conditions for one and all.

It should not be overlooked, however, that the social-corporatist paradigm was not just a response to economic crises; it also set in motion a comprehensive program of societal configuration that was based on a strong concept of the *social*. According to this understanding, the individual had a reciprocal relationship with society. He or she received support and protection from it, but was also expected to do something for society in return. In a sense, the individual was thought to be "indebted" to society. Within the framework of this paradigm, there was also (besides the state) a diverse set of *corporations* that were responsible for imbedding individuals into society at large: political parties, labor unions, churches, professional associations, community organizations, schools, companies with permanent workforces, etc. In the social-corporatist paradigm, an aspect of community was supposed to be integrated into society, and this was just as clearly pronounced in the Scandinavian "people's home" as it was in the West German "well-ordered society." The result was an actively and politically promoted leveled middle-class society in which cultural differences, individuality, "deviant behavior," and violations of patriarchal gender norms and its model of the nuclear family were typically viewed with suspicion. In democratic-functional terms, the social-corporatist paradigm was based on a model that synthesized pluralism, the guarantee of equal rights, and skepticism toward the "will of the people," and thus it enforced the structural outline of representative democracy with a mass base in strong people's parties and organizations. On the one hand, the democratic model of the postwar era was influenced by the experience of fascism, with its readily violent masses; on the other hand, it was influenced by its confrontation with the anti-pluralistic state socialism in Eastern Europe.[4]

The Crisis of Overregulation

As a system, the social-corporatist paradigm survived multiple decades without ever being challenged by an alternative. In the 1970s, however, it fell into a fundamental crisis that ultimately led to its undoing. During these years, the social conditions transformed – not least because of politics itself, though partially independent of it as well – so radically that, by the end, the paradigm seemed to create more problems than it could ever solve. In a striking manner, two moments of crisis converged at this time – an economic and a cultural crisis – and both of them can be interpreted as symptoms of social *overregulation*. The occurrence of severe economic crises, with the oil crisis of 1973 as the turning point, shook society's faith in the plannability of the economy. After 30 years with high growth rates and steadily increasing affluence, the economy entered a stage of stagnation, high unemployment, high inflation, and high government debt. One began to hear diagnoses of government failure and of a "crisis of crisis management" (as Claus Offe put it). At the same time, and apparently independently (or so it seemed at first), there also occurred a cultural crisis of legitimacy. The anti-authoritarian student protests of 1968 and the related non-conformist "alternative" movement indicated that well-educated young adults – the functional elite of tomorrow – were increasingly dissatisfied with the regulated "system" in place, which led not only to social equality but also to uniformity and conformism.

If one digs deeper, it becomes clear that these publicly visible crises were caused by fundamental processes of social change, which, structurally, more or less "pulled the rug out from under the feet" of the social-corporatist paradigm. On the economic side, the model of national industrial societies reached its limits in the 1970s.[5] After the end of the postwar era, industrial production found itself in a saturation crisis; the tendencies of deindustrialization and post-industrialization were on the rise. With the advent of post-industrialization – that is, with the gradual rise of the knowledge economy on the one hand, and of simple services on the other – the social base of industrial society also began to erode, particularly the industrial workforce. As engines of growth, the Fordist system of large corporations with specialized mass production had reached its zenith, while more flexible post-Fordist forms of organization were increasingly making their presence felt in the economy. Production, moreover, was becoming increasingly globalized, and this process gained even more intensity after 1980. National economic policies thus lost a great deal of their effectiveness as instruments of control. On top of that, the end of the era of high economic growth pushed the expansion of the welfare state to a limit that governments could only exceed by accumulating more and more debt.

Alongside this socio-economic shift, there was also a socio-cultural transformation that likewise undermined the foundations of the social-corporatist paradigm. What took place in Western societies was a profound shift in values and a push toward cultural liberalization, which promoted a culture of individualism and singularism and gradually replaced the culture of reciprocal social obligations that had characterized the "society of equals." The traditional values of duty and acceptance were ousted by the values of individual self-actualization, from which perspective the institutions of classical industrial society seemed to limit individual opportunities. Here, "1968" and the counterculture were merely the spearhead of a more fundamental cultural transition. In short, the "people's home" no longer represented the great promise of one's homeland, but instead an authoritarian entity that one would rather leave behind. Accordingly, many corporations (people's parties, labor unions) lost their power to identify with people. The most important impetus behind this shift in cultural weight was the new middle class of highly qualified individuals who had benefited from the expansion of education. This shift in values went hand in hand with the institutionalization of the norms and desires of consumer society. The tendency of the consumption-obsessed middle class (and upper class) to appreciate public handouts has thus been declining since the 1970s – and so has the legitimacy of the redistributive welfare state. Furthermore, the 1970s also experienced moments of democratic-functional crisis. Over the course of the international student movement, the model of representative democracy supported by strong corporations with a mass base saw itself being challenged, and especially by the critical intelligentsia. What emerged were the "new social movements" – the women's movement, the environmental movement, citizens' initiatives, for example – which articulated new and previously neglected political themes "from below," and thus demanded a greater share of political participation.

The social-corporatist paradigm was not immediately responsible for the post-industrialization of the economy and the cultural shift in values. Rather, the latter followed a dynamic of their own that confronted politics with new structures, and the ability to manage these new structures came at the cost of a political paradigm shift. At the same time, however, the political paradox of this paradigm became clear. Without intending to do so, the social-corporatist project laid the foundation for the very structural change that would later make it seem obsolete. This is true of both the economic and cultural side of things. The postwar political project of increasing prosperity for everyone within the framework of national industrial societies led to the exhaustion of all production possibilities in national industrial economies. Therefore (and on account of capitalism's inherent logic of growth), it became necessary to develop a post-industrial and increasingly globalized economic structure in order to ensure continued growth on the production side, and to satisfy consumers with new and advanced goods. In conjunction with the politically driven expansion of education, this development led to the formation of an increasingly ambitious new middle class that has been oriented toward self-actualization, interested in private consumption, politically critical of traditional social and Christian democracy, and uninterested in participating in the cultural model of the self-effacing "well-ordered society." Overall, the picture that emerged was that of a crisis of overregulation. The postwar paradigm of regulation wore out its welcome in the middle of the 1970s; the initially legitimate and necessary concern for creating social order turned into an excess of regulation that inhibited economic change and restricted the cultural opportunities for individual self-development.[6]

The Rise of the Paradigm of Apertistic Liberalism

The political paradigm shift that began to take place in Western countries in the 1980s is often described in terms of the rise of neoliberalism, which is thought to have superseded the era of classical social democracy and thus to have instigated a changing of the guard from the left to the right. This interpretation, however, only touches on part of the truth, which is more complicated. For one thing (and this should be clear by now), the paradigm of regulation from the 1950s to 1970s was more than just social-democratically oriented; rather, the social-corporatist practice of government dominated from the center-left to the center-right. It contained not only the socio-economic model of the Keynesian welfare state but also a cultural model based on the community and the collective, which could also be interpreted conservatively. Since the 1980s, accordingly, the social-corporatist paradigm has not simply been replaced by neoliberalism but, in the medium term, by a synthesis between two sides of a new form of liberalism, one of which can be classified as on the right and the other as on the left. Here, in addition to neoliberalism, there is also progressive liberalism (or social liberalism), which emerged from the civil rights movements of the 1960s and 1970s, among other causes. By reducing this *New Liberalism*, which has dominated the last 30 years, to neoliberalism alone, one underestimates its effectiveness, which derives from *both* of its sides (even though the actors involved on either side often view each other with mutual distrust).[7]

Structurally, the rise of apertistic liberalism has been supported by the transition from industrial society to post-industrial society, by the process of (economic but also socio-cultural) globalization, and by the cultural shift in values toward social liberalization. At the same time, the new political paradigm has impelled these very processes of transformation. Over the course of recent decades, it has become clear that New Liberalism has a well-defined (in socio-structural terms) and central group of proponents: the new middle class of highly qualified individuals, which is concentrated in metropolitan regions and is distinguished by its high degree of geographical mobility.[8] Some of its factions are neoliberally oriented, while others lean toward progressive liberalism; in part, the new middle class is also both at the same time.

The overarching characteristic of New Liberalism is its general tendency to deregulate, dynamize, and open up previously rigid social structures. Historically, of course, there have been many variants of liberalism; in this case, we are dealing with what can be called *apertistic* liberalism ("apertistic," that is, in the sense that it opens things up). What is clear is that the paradigm of regulation has been replaced by a *paradigm of dynamization*. Whereas neoliberalism is based on opening up the markets and reducing government regulations in the economy and society, progressive liberalism is based on opening up identities and empowering individuals and cultural groups. Under the social-corporatist paradigm, the function of the state was to control affairs and create order – and, if necessary, it would even exercise this function *against* the market and *against* the unique characteristics of individuals. Both wings of apertistic liberalism, in contrast, assign the state no more than an instrumental function: the function of making room for markets to operate, and the function of securing the subjective rights of individuals and particular, as well as local, collectives.

In abstract terms: whereas the social-corporatist way of thinking – informed as it was by the experiences of the interwar period – was based on stabilizing boundaries in order to maintain social order, and was thus closely associated with the nation state, apertistic liberalism – informed as it is by the experiences of the 1970s – pursues the ideal of transgressing and dissolving boundaries. It is no surprise that the process of globalization, which has been ongoing since the 1980s, has been enforced by this New Liberalism, in particular as a globalization of markets *and* as a globalization of culture and its identities. Structurally, neoliberalism and progressive liberalism – a pair of often hostile "brothers" – turn out to be two sides of enforced globalization, anti-statism, and resolute individualism. Moreover, they also represent two sides of the politics of difference, which has replaced the old politics of equality: on the one hand, the mobilization of differences between competitors on various markets; on the other hand, the mobilization of differences between individuals and collectives in the cultural sphere. The overriding structure is brought to light by the fact that both sides share a common enemy: the seemingly rigid, inhibitive, and collectivistic paradigm of social corporatism.

As is well known, the politics of *neoliberalism* was first put into practice by the Thatcher government in Great Britain and the Reagan government in the United States, after its intellectual groundwork had been laid by a neoliberal school of economic policy (Friedrich von Hayek, Milton Friedman, Gary Becker et al.). Afterwards, it quickly spread in a variety of forms, including versions endorsed by social-democratic parties. Its features have meanwhile become familiar, and they boil down to what Bob Jessop fittingly referred to as the replacement of the "Keynesian national welfare state" by the model of the "Schumpeterian competition state,"[9] whose point of departure is global capitalism (the "world market"), which places individual nations, individual cities, individual companies, and individual employees in a permanent state of competition with one another. This therefore makes the economic sector fundamentally and inherently dynamic, and the goal of government policy must be to ensure, and even promote, *competitiveness*. According to Schumpeter's theories, innovation and entrepreneurship are the central factors that repeatedly create new advantages in a competitive economy. To be oriented toward innovation is, not least, to promote the post-industrial economy. However, neoliberal politics is not content with increasing competitiveness in existing markets; rather, it actively endeavors to implement market structures in areas that had previously evaded the logic of competition – areas such as infrastructure, housing, education, and culture. At the heart of this approach to government is the general idea that the "invisible hand" of the market, with its internal dynamics, is the optimal instrument for increasing efficiency, innovation, and prosperity. Even the global financial sector has now been deregulated, and taxes on income and capital have systematically been reduced. Finally, neoliberalism also aims to restructure the labor market and the welfare state, a transformation that can be described as a paradigm shift from "welfare" to "workfare." The social-democratic versions of neoliberalism in particular – as represented by the governments of Clinton, Blair, and Schröder, for instance – have done much to limit social support in order to encourage people to reenter the labor market.

Although *progressive liberalism*, which has been expanding since the 1980s, has different historical roots from those of neoliberalism, it has proved to be the second effective wing of the paradigm of apertistic liberalism. One example of the rise of progressive liberalism is the transformation of the Democratic Party in the United States. Here, following the civil rights movement, the political concerns of groups that had been disadvantaged on account of their "identity" were avidly pushed to the forefront of the party's program. Its politics are now guided by the image of a society that is neither egalitarian nor homogeneous, but is instead (and ought to be) diverse and multicultural.[10] The identity politics of disadvantaged groups, which have been creating new self-awareness in this context, may in many respects be a distinctly American phenomenon, but Western progressive liberalism goes beyond this. Just as neoliberalism has radicalized the old tradition of economic and market liberalism, progressive liberalism has likewise radicalized an old idea – namely, the liberal principle that every individual possesses subjective rights that must be acknowledged by other individuals and by the state. However, because these subjective rights seem to have been inadequately realized, progressive liberalism has endorsed a program for systematically actualizing and expanding such rights and for "empowering" individuals.[11]

Regarding the individual as a legal subject, this has made it necessary to think in terms of two opposing categories at the same time: the categories of generality and of particularity. In light of the triumph of the concept of human rights since the 1970s, all individuals are thought to possess the same general rights; at the same time, progressive liberalism has developed – within the framework of a society of singularities – a special sensitivity for the uniqueness of the individual, which also deserves to be protected. Rather than focusing on the rights of workers, which were so central to the social-corporatist paradigm, progressive liberalism concentrates instead on the constellations in which individuals are denied recognition on account of their socio-cultural identity. The equal rights of men and women may be its primary political concern, but progressive liberalism also fights for the rights of sexual minorities, ethnic groups, and disabled people (inclusion). It also firmly stands for the rights of local groups (so that their voices are heard in government planning, for instance) and for the indirect rights that have been ascribed to nature within the framework of the environmental movement.

The social model of progressive liberalism is thus based on the two fundamental goals of expanding the subjective rights of individuals and achieving cultural diversity within society. In general, the actualization of subjective rights, which also then include the rights of cultural groups, is meant to bring about a society that is as free as it is diverse. Against the backdrop of this positive evaluation of diversity, progressive liberals also regard migration movements and the creation of multicultural constellations within national societies, which break up the homogeneity of national cultures, in an essentially positive light.

The apertistic liberalism from the years 1980 to 2010 corresponded to a specific praxis of democracy.[12] Formally, this praxis did not differ from that of the previous paradigm, though now there was not any "system competition" from the people's democracies of Eastern Europe, which imploded around 1990. Beyond its formal structures, however, the political system was thoroughly transformed. Its basis in national corporations and people's parties eroded, while international institutions gained significance: international organizations and their economic expertise (the WTO, the World Bank, and the European Commission, for example) became important decision makers, and globally active NGOs influenced the political agenda (as regards, for instance, environmental and climate policy). Domestic policy was driven more and more by the increasingly close relations between politics and economics, on the one hand, and between politics and law on the other. Political–economic hybrid organizations – in the form of public–private partnerships, for instance – gained relevance, as did the political influence of the judicial system, which, by making fundamental legal rulings, became an instrument for establishing the law instead of applying it. The democracy of apertistic liberalism therefore uncoupled itself from the national "demos" in favor of a network of supranational and sub-political actors.

The Threefold Crisis of Apertistic Liberalism

The evidence has been growing: for some time – and clearly since around 2010 – the political paradigm of apertistic liberalism has for its part been in a state of crisis, and it is possible to observe a development that structurally resembles that which had brought about the downfall of social corporatism. A formerly effective, socially attractive, and promising praxis of government now seems to create more problems than it solves. The (right-wing) populist revolt has made this paradigm crisis patently obvious and politically controversial, but the revolt is only one of its symptoms, and it is neither the cause of the crisis nor its long-term solution. On the one hand, it can be said that the unintended and problematic consequences of the politics of apertistic liberalism have become increasingly clear. On the other hand, the overall structural transformation from industrial to post-industrial modernity (which, at the same time, is a society of singularities) has given rise to features that have also turned out to be problematic. Here, the problems that have emerged may not be the direct fault of politics, but, regardless, the paradigm of apertistic liberalism is no longer able to deal with them productively.

However, if we interpret the crisis of apertistic liberalism through the lens of paradigms and paradigm shifts, two things become apparent. First, the crisis is not a catastrophe; in fact, it is absolutely *normal*. In light of the nature of social change, any overriding political paradigm necessarily has just a limited amount of time in which it can act in a way that is sensitive to the problems at hand. At a certain point, it will be taken down by a socio-structural transformation that causes new problems and requires new solutions. Such was the case with the social-corporatist paradigm in the 1970s, and now this situation is repeating itself. Furthermore, the crisis of a political paradigm is not a systemic crisis. That said, such a crisis pertains to a system's ability to define and solve problems, and thus it catapults the political public sphere into a state of contingency that causes uncertainty and can be characterized by fierce political conflicts. This is what distinguishes the phase of a dominant political paradigm from that of a paradigm shift: whereas, in the former, the basic framework of thought seems to be fixed, in the latter situation it is a matter of debate. Although many commentators seem to have forgotten this, the political conflicts during the transitional phase of the 1970s were intense, and they even led to left-wing extremist terrorism in West Germany and Italy, and to heated battles between labor unions and the government in Great

Britain. We now find ourselves yet again in the phase of a "normal" but conflict-laden paradigm shift. During this transitional phase, it has been characteristic of political debate to subject the politics of the recently dominant paradigm to an extensive critique that makes it seem fundamentally flawed. The level of historical awareness in these debates, however, is extremely low. Within the acrimonious situation of a paradigm shift, during which a struggle is waged for the future of politics, few people tend to consider the political paradox that a particular form of politics in a previous situation *n* may have been *suitable*, but it is *no longer suitable* in the situation *n* + 1 (and this ultimately does nothing to discredit the politics of the past). Typically, this paradox only becomes clear after the fact from a long-term historical and sociological perspective.

A second aspect has also become apparent: we can only understand the crisis of apertistic liberalism if we recognize that we are dealing with a socio-economic crisis *and* a socio-cultural crisis at the same time, and that these two crises have also given rise to a democratic-functional crisis. Such a combination of crises characterized the phase before the establishment of the social-corporatist paradigm, and it was characteristic of its downfall as well. It does not seem easy, however, to see all three moments of crisis together, as is clear from the current discourses about the present crises. Here, the left–right schema clearly gets in the way. Since the financial crash of 2008, for instance, the left has worked out every detail of the weaknesses and problems of neoliberalism and all the features of the socio-economic crisis, while almost entirely ignoring the cultural crisis that has been taking place. Conservatives, for their part, have focused on the weaknesses and problems of progressive liberalism and have identified every feature of the socio-cultural crisis while systematically downplaying the socio-economic crisis that is under way. It is essential, however, to recognize the combination of socio-economic, socio-cultural, and democratic-functional crises in order to formulate an appropriate response and devise a suitable new political paradigm.

Let us take a closer look, then, at this crisis and examine it in its full complexity. First of all, it undoubtedly has a socio-economic dimension. Neoliberalism, the globalization of markets, and the rise of the knowledge economy bestowed a new dynamic to economic development, but the underbelly of this dynamism was made drastically clear by the financial crisis in 2008. Deregulation and the dismantling of government control mechanisms pushed financial markets to the brink of collapse and, in many cases, led to a radical increase in government debt. It was telling to see how unpredictably the markets behaved without any government intervention. Moreover, neoliberal tax policies, which essentially reduced taxes in favor of private consumers, fostered the creation of a small group of super-rich individuals whose income and assets have surpassed every former measure, thereby lending a new dimension to social inequality.[13] In many places, neoliberal politics has also resulted in the neglect of general public services and basic social infrastructure, from transportation and education to healthcare and housing. Often, the marketization of the social did not lead to more efficient services, but rather to the insufficient maintenance of public goods. In metropolitan regions, in particular, one can see how the market-ization of housing has intensified social-geographical inequality. Overall, it can be said that neoliberalism is caught in a crisis of deregulation – a crisis of excess dynamization – and that this crisis resulted from a lack of social and government oversight in economic markets.

Beyond these *immediate* consequences of neoliberal politics, the fundamental dark sides of the structural transformation from indus-trial to post-industrial society have also become clear, as has the fact that neoliberalism obviously lacks the sensitivity and instruments to deal with them. Central in this regard is the replacement of the old leveled middle-class society with an (economically, culturally, and geographically) polarized social structure.[14] In the course of the post-industrialization of the economy, various lifeworlds in Western societies have increasingly grown apart; the new middle class of highly qualified individuals stands at the opposite end to a new precarious class. Stuck between these two classes is a numeri-cally reduced old middle class that oscillates between maintaining status, losing status, and being culturally devalued. Whereas, as a supporter of apertistic liberalism, the new middle class adheres to the ideal of social progress via globalization, singularization, and post-industrialization, the precarious class and parts of the old middle class are confronted with experiences of loss. The polari-zation between high-skilled and low-skilled jobs, between academic and vocational education, and between progress-oriented and regression-oriented perceptions of society corresponds to the new geographical disparity that exists between thriving metropolitan regions and rural areas that have been "left behind." It would be shortsighted to hold neoliberalism responsible for all of these social developments. Although neoliberalism has certainly made indirect contributions to them – by forcing deindustrialization and creating urban knowledge clusters, for instance – we are essentially dealing with an unplanned economic, cultural, and socio-structural process with its own dynamics and with a high level of complexity. What is decisive, however, is that the ideas of neoliberalism have proven unable or unwilling to regulate this process.

Yet the crisis of apertistic liberalism has a second, cultural dimension, which mostly has to do with the repercussions of progressive liberalism. Like the economic aspect of this crisis, this

cultural dimension has also been the subject of much debate. In
the strict sense, the issue at hand is that of identity politics and the
politics of multiculturalism; in a broader and more fundamental
sense, the cultural element of this crisis is related to the dissolution
of reciprocal connections within a "thoroughly liberalized" society.
The critique has often been expressed – even by self-reflective
voices from the social-liberal camp itself – that the convergence of
increased migration into Western nations since the 1990s with the
liberal politics of multiculturalism has fueled a process of cultural
disintegration in the immigration countries. Liberal identity politics,
which gives discriminated social groups the chance to develop
collective self-consciousness and which rightly promotes social
participation and respect for cultural traditions, also contains the
risk of encouraging cultural communities to self-isolate according
to criteria such as ethnicity and religion – a development that, in
many places, has meanwhile given rise to a new, "white" form of
identity politics. Since 2010, the widespread discussion of the need
for *cultural* integration has essentially been a critique of the liberal
desire for multiculturalism.[15]

However, the fundamental problem of the "liberalism of rights"
runs even deeper, and this brings us to the second of the two topics
mentioned above, which was discussed as early as the 1980s within
the framework of an extensive philosophical debate about liberalism. In this debate, the proponents of so-called communitarianism
and republicanism argued against the proponents of (progressive)
liberalism that the latter position, by relying on ostensibly neutral
mechanisms of social coordination such as the law and by leaving
it up to individuals (and groups) to implement their desires and
subjective rights, requires social and cultural structures in society
that it is not only unable to create itself but also, in the worst case,
even *weakens*.[16]

Actual social developments have since overtaken this philosophical argumentation. In the society of singularities, individuals
have internalized the liberal program of expanding subjective rights
and have transformed into "entitled subjects" with apparently
natural claims to various rights: as citizens, consumers, employees,
employers, students, spouses, etc. Now, in the culture of late
modernity, what began as the welcome emancipatory empowerment
of responsible citizens is ultimately threatening to turn into the
egoism of individuals against institutions. The risk has meanwhile
become obvious: the web of norms that define our reciprocal obligations, which these institutions support, will only become thinner
if individuals insist on their (idiosyncratic) desires and rights and
perceive norms and duties as nothing more than limitations on
their opportunities for individual growth. In the end, late-modern
culture is therefore threatened by a more fundamental cultural

disintegration that goes far beyond the special issue of integrating migrants into broader society.

The coarsening of communication on social media, which has been observable since 2010 and is widely lamented, can be regarded as a prominent example of the erosion of cultural consensus regarding the general norms for coexistence. Of course, the liberal politics of subjective rights is not fully responsible for this process. The development of mentalities and media technologies follows a dynamic of its own. However, the liberal politics of subjective rights has proven to be helpless when it comes to countering this process of disintegration, just as neoliberal politics has had no answer to the socio-economic crisis at hand. In this case, too, the crisis of apertistic liberalism has turned out to be a crisis of deregulation – namely, a crisis that has emerged from a *shortage of cultural regulation*.

Finally, the socio-economic and the socio-cultural crises are closely related to a third crisis: the crisis of late-modern democracy.[17] This comes as something of a surprise to the liberal members of the new middle class, but the signs have been clear to see for a long time: not only in the form of populism but also in waning voter participation, which indicates that growing portions of the population have been losing faith in the institutions of liberal democracy. The political system is quite obviously struggling with a problem of legitimacy.[18] To be sure, one reason for this is the fact that, for several years, the dominant paradigm of apertistic liberalism has proven to be less than suitable for solving the social and cultural problems that have become so apparent. It is also true, however, that the institutional reconfiguration of the political system since the 1990s has also contributed to this loss of faith. The growing power of international organizations and judiciary systems, both of which exist outside of immediate democratic control, and the imposition of economic austerity measures formulated by experts – tendencies such as these have done much to "de-democratize" democracy; that is, they have taken important political decisions out of the hands of elected representatives. The few opportunities that have arisen for direct democracy – the Brexit referendum, for instance – have turned out to be desperate attempts on the part of the public to "win back control."

There are two other noteworthy factors that are indicative of the general malaise of liberal democracy. First, since around the year 2010, digital media have developed into a venue that enables public opinion to form in an accelerated, combative, and highly emotional way. This online discourse, which has its own rhythm and structure, is poorly synchronized with the classical institutions of liberal democracy. With its decisions and discussions, in fact, traditional politics always seems to lag behind the digital public debate. Second, members of parliament are not representative of the populations

that they serve. Whereas the era of social corporatism took the
views of labor unions into account (for instance) and thus sought
to ensure that various political milieus were represented politically, today's parliaments are increasingly dominated by politicians
with university degrees.[19] Regardless of their political affiliation,
the overwhelming majority of parliamentarians come from the
educated middle class, so that there is a discrepancy between the
lifeworlds of elected representatives and those of large portions of
the population.

Populism as a Symptom

The (right-wing) populist movement, with which the political system
has been confronted more and more since 2010, perceives itself
as a solution and response to the crisis of apertistic liberalism.
Of course, it will not be fully possible to evaluate the significance
of this movement until it has become a matter of history. In my
interpretation, however, populism is not the new and overarching
paradigm of government that will replace apertistic liberalism for
the long term; rather, it is a *symptom* of the crisis of this liberalism
and an important collective force during a conflict-laden transitional phase in which an old paradigm is losing legitimacy and a new
paradigm must emerge. What does it mean, however, that populism
can be understood as a symptom of the present crisis facing the
paradigm of dynamization? As a concept, populism is controversial,
polysemous, and it has polemical undertones, which is why many
commentators have chosen to avoid it entirely. I have nevertheless
decided to use it because it encapsulates so well many of the novel
political tendencies over the past few years. When discussing the
features of populism, it is important to consider three different
levels at the same time: its political form, its political content, and
its socio-cultural base.

The specific nature of populist parties and movements can be
identified first of all on the level of its political form. Populism
proceeds from an "alternative" model of democracy, and this model
is not that of liberal democracy but, rather, one of antiliberal
democracy.[20] From the dominant political perspective that has
characterized Western societies since 1945, democracy and liberalism are linked to one another. The basic political consensus – from
the social democrats on the left to the conservatives on the right
– has presumed that *democracy*, as a means of governing people,
must go hand in hand with *liberal* principles such as the rule of
law and the existence of checks and balances between institutions.
Here, the basic assumption is that modern society is undeniably
pluralistic and that the different facets of this pluralism have to find

a voice within the political system. The populists' view is completely different. They fundamentally endorse the model of an antiliberal democracy in which the will of the people should immediately be translated into politics. Populists therefore claim to be the sole representatives of what "the people" want. In their eyes, pluralism, moderation between different interests, and compromise, which are typical of liberal democracy, now seem superfluous and like attempts to weaken the "will of the people" (thus their highly skeptical and suspicious attitude toward the established media). Populism is thus characterized by a sort of "us-versus-them" antagonism, with the "us" being the voice of the people and the "them" designating the elites, cosmopolitans, and migrants who are allegedly different from "the people." Populism has to regard the people as a homogeneous social community. This homogeneity can be defined in cultural or social terms: culturally by means of national identities and certain moral principles (such as those represented by "real" Americans, Germans, etc.), socially by being an "average" person who is part of the "working population" and "supports the country," etc. The democratic-functional crisis of apertistic liberalism has led populists to conclude that liberal, pluralistic democracy in its known form generally needs to be overturned or modified – for instance, by dismantling the authoritative bodies that protect pluralism and the rule of law. Populist rhetoric, which is often offensive and antagonistic, is thus not merely meant to mobilize voters; rather, it is based on a different model of democracy that is used to reconstruct institutions in cases where populists have long-term political ambitions.

Besides this fundamental political form, populism is also characterized by its particular political content. In this respect, the individual parties – the National Rally in France or the Freedom Party in Austria, for example – differ from one another, and their positions are constantly changing. Essentially, however, one can conclude that populism represents a type of politics that concentrates on mechanisms of *national regulation*, to the point of implementing policies of *national isolationism*. It is important to recognize that this regulation concerns both the socio-economic and the socio-cultural spheres. In both respects, populists reject the politics of apertistic liberalism out of hand. Whereas the latter aims to open up society economically and socially, the fundamental position of populists is to regulate both, and generally to close things off on the national level. It is therefore no surprise that the focal points of populist politics happen to be economic and social policy, on the one hand, and migration and cultural policy on the other. The aim of populist economic policy is to strengthen the national economy (with protectionist instruments, if necessary), while populism's intensified social policy is meant to operate in favor of the national population. With respect to cultural and migration policies – whose goals intersect with those of so-called identitarian movements and with those of the white supremacy movement in the United States – the aim is to reduce immigration and to install a politics of national identity. In both economic and cultural terms, populism is therefore firmly against globalization.

Third, and finally, it is necessary to consider populism's socio-cultural base.[21] In principle, this base can be found in all milieus, classes, and regions, but certain population groups are overrepresented here, while others are underrepresented. A characteristic feature of this base is that its members generally tend to share a sense of social devaluation, a sense of imminent social and cultural loss, and the feeling that they have been "cheated" by social developments, which means that they feel as though they have been overtaken or marginalized by other social groups. Since the 1990s, according to political scientists, a new line of conflict has emerged between "cosmopolitans," who welcome globalization and the new liberal dynamization of culture and the economy, and "communitarians," who favor the security of the nation state and compliance with social rules.[22] In this light, the supporters of populism can be found among those who hold communitarian values, feel resentment toward elites and globalists, and fear that they are losing out. In socio-structural terms, these supporters come predominantly from portions of the traditional middle class and the precarious class, whereas they are distinctively underrepresented among the educated new middle class. Accordingly, support for populism tends to be higher among residents of small towns and rural areas, and lower among those living in metropolitan regions.[23]

If populism is examined on all three of these levels, it becomes clear why it has become such a vibrant topic in public discourse. On the left, too, there are now some supporters of (left-wing) populism, who agree with the general critique of liberalism and want "common people" to redress the injustices committed by the elite.[24] If my diagnosis is true – that the recently dominant paradigm of apertistic liberalism is now embroiled in socio-economic, socio-cultural, and democratic-functional crises – then it is plain to see why populism is currently enjoying so much success: it has recognized these crises and offered a radical counter-agenda. In the present political landscape, if there is an absolute opponent to apertistic liberalism, this opponent is (right-wing) populism. What is remarkable about this is that populism (unlike most of the left-leaning or right-leaning establishment) has in fact perceived the full context of all three crises and has formulated responses to each of them: the socio-economic crisis of neoliberalism should be countered by regulating economies on the national level; the socio-cultural crisis of progressive liberalism should be countered by strengthening national identities and opposing cosmopolitanism and immigration;

and the democratic-functional crisis of "post-democracy" should be countered by promoting an illiberal form of democracy that equates politics with the will of the people. Against the backdrop of late modernity's polarizing class structure – in which the new middle class, the old middle class, and the precarious class are all in opposition to one another – populism therefore resonates with those in the traditional (small-town and rural) middle class and the (native) precarious class who harbor resentment toward liberal elites and fear that they are losing status and cultural value in society at large. Abstractly, populism is opposed by apertistic liberalism and liberal (post-)democracy; concretely, it is opposed by the cosmopolitan and urban new middle class that espouses apertistic liberalism.

Populism is thus a product of the crisis of apertistic liberalism. There are good reasons to doubt, however, that it will form the next lastingly effective and overarching political paradigm. Above all, there are two main reasons to be skeptical. First, previous leading paradigms served a long-term integrative function in society (a function that only began to erode when these paradigms were coming to an end). The paradigms in question therefore accommodated different progressive and conservative versions, which spanned the entire political spectrum; in a sense, they were inherently pluralistic and thus spoke to a wide range of social groups. This is just as true of social corporatism's paradigm of regulation as it is of apertistic liberalism's paradigm of dynamization. It was only for such reasons that these paradigms ultimately managed to dominate the discourse and to seem like the one and only alternative, at least for a certain amount of time. The political form of populism, however, is firmly opposed to such an integrative function. Populism is based on elementary antagonism; inwardly, it requires homogeneity, while outwardly it portrays large portions of late-modern society as its enemy: the liberal new middle class, large sectors of the post-industrial economy, the local governments of metropolitan regions, migrant members of the population, the established media, and educational institutions – all of these things are regarded by populism as essential opponents. It remains unlikely, however, that a new integrative and lastingly effective political paradigm could take hold while opposing half of society, along with its most prosperous regions and economic sectors.

Second, there is also good reason to doubt whether populist politics can demonstrate the same ability to solve problems that characterized previous dominant paradigms, and thus whether it will ever be sufficiently convincing to rise to dominance itself. It has to be kept in mind that the paradigms of regulation and dynamization always *accepted* the foundations of the respective social structures at hand in order to reconfigure them subsequently. Populism, in contrast, seems to be at war with three fundamental structures of late-modern society, and not even politics seems capable of undoing them: the globalization of the economy, in which national economies now depend on global production chains, financial streams, and the migration of workers; the post-industrialization of the economy, in which the former centrality of industry has been replaced by the duality of high-skilled knowledge work and simple services; and, finally, the cultural heterogeneity of society, which has resulted from the pluralization of milieus, the differentiation of classes, and the effects of global migration processes.

From a sympathetic perspective, one could say that populism hopes to respond to apertistic liberalism's crisis of over-dynamization by imposing social and cultural regulations. It quickly becomes clear, however, that the tempering forms of regulation endorsed by populists will ultimately culminate in *nationalistic isolationism*. In the end, their aim is not to institute new structures and *reconfigure* the consequences of globalization, post-industrialization, and cultural heterogeneity; rather, their goal is to *fight against* globalization, post-industrialization, and cultural heterogeneity. Essentially, populism endorses a nostalgic form of politics that yearns to restore a bygone condition – a condition of sovereign nation states, regulated industrial societies, and cultural homogeneity.

To the extent that it is possible to draw conclusions about the present and future on the basis of the past, the new paradigm shift that we are currently experiencing will not be dictated by the populist margins but by the broad center of the political landscape. Just as fundamental political principles, which were held by the whole political spectrum from the center-left to the center-right, shifted during the 1940s and again during the 1970s, it seems as though a similar development is currently in progress. In fact, such a development *should* be in progress if we do not want the system to remain mired in an endless feedback loop of ongoing conflict between today's new form of liberalism (which already seems "old" by now) and the new form of populism that has arisen. A real danger of right-wing populism is that it might potentially inhibit the necessary learning process of social democrats, progressives, and conservatives in the political mainstream. One hardly needs to be a populist, however, to recognize and criticize the weaknesses of apertistic liberalism and to promote the involvement of politics in culture and the economy!

"Regulatory Liberalism" as the Paradigm of the Future?

In the political development of Western countries, a new overarching paradigm will emerge to replace apertistic liberalism's paradigm of dynamization and provide a new framework for the entire political spectrum, but how will it look? My basic assumption is that the new political paradigm will (and should) adopt the contours of *regulatory liberalism*, for which three elements are essential. First, at its core, it will be a paradigm of regulation, though it will not be identical with social corporatism. Thus, its principal concern will not be to liberate social forces but, rather, to establish social order. Second, the new paradigm will respond by regulating a new socio-cultural issue: in late modernity, there is a "crisis of the general," and the new paradigm will attempt to revitalize generality, both socially and culturally.[25] Third, the new paradigm will maintain a liberal foundation in two respects – first, by preserving the institutional framework of liberal democracy and its pluralism; and second by perpetuating certain insights of apertistic liberalism regarding the late-modern dynamics of culture and the economy. Here, the dynamic nature of identities, markets, and globalization will not be eliminated, but will rather be *embedded* within newly established parameters.[26] In both regards, this new form of liberalism will differ fundamentally from populism.

As I have already mentioned, apertistic liberalism suffers quite clearly from a *shortage* of social regulation; it shuns establishing order in favor of creating a maximum amount of freedom for markets, multinational actors, individual rights, and cultural identities. Its crisis is not one of overregulation but rather of *over-dynamization*. This is not to say that there is a sort of endless cycle in which every paradigm of dynamization is necessarily followed by a paradigm of regulation. Moreover, we cannot know what future developments and challenges lie in store. Nevertheless, it is *presently* the case that a paradigm of dynamization has come to an end and that the response to its downfall will likely involve new forms of regulation.

In fact, a new political paradigm's ability to solve problems is also revealed in the way that it deals with the previous paradigm. There are two general possibilities here: either a radical break from the old paradigm, or a constructive form of integration. Both possibilities presented themselves when apertistic liberalism replaced social corporatism. In Great Britain, for instance, Thatcherism's departure from the welfare state was far more radical than was the case in Germany, where many of the achievements from the social-corporatist era were maintained (in retrospect, this turned out to be advantageous in some respects). In the present political conflict, it is populism that endorses a complete break from apertistic liberalism. My strong assumption, however, is that the rise of a new paradigm will depend on how and whether it perpetuates the proven successes of apertistic liberalism while *simultaneously* situating them within a different framework, and my guess is that this new framework will be one of social and cultural "embeddedness."

The liberalism from the 1980s to the 2000s has meanwhile received a great deal of bad press from commentators on both the left and the right. Neoliberalism has become a target of the left, which often views it only in terms of unfettered capitalism in favor of the super-rich, while progressive liberalism has become a target of conservatives, who can associate it in a single breath with the counterculture of 1968 and with the rise of political correctness. In light of this escalating critique – which now suspiciously overlaps with the populist critique of liberalism – it seems necessary to keep in mind that both branches of liberalism contain certain insights that might be helpful during the present paradigm shift. Which insights are these?

Because it systematically promotes the rights of people who have been disadvantaged and discriminated against legally, socially, and culturally, progressive liberalism essentially belongs to the history of emancipation movements, which goes back to the eighteenth century. Progressive liberalism thus endorses the comprehensive legal empowerment of all individuals, regardless of their gender, ethnic background, religion (etc.), and every failure to achieve this empowerment can be regarded only as regression. Achieving the equal rights of women is certainly one of its most important accomplishments. In societies with an increasingly multi-ethnic character, moreover, progressive liberalism has also rightly encouraged people to respect the ethnic and religious differences between individuals and groups. Here, progressive liberalism proceeds from the fundamental idea that populations are heterogeneous and that it is necessary for society to deal with this heterogeneity. This basic assumption seems truer today than ever before, and it will likely remain true in the future.

Whereas the significance of progressive liberalism in the West lies in its contributions to the political development of a system of norms, the achievements of neoliberalism have to be viewed more pragmatically in terms of the ongoing problem of calibrating an appropriate relationship between the market and the state. Though many people now regard neoliberalism as the root of all evil, there are reasons to reconsider this presumption. Even Colin Crouch, one of the most prominent critics of neoliberalism, emphasized some of its positive aspects in his latest book.[27] In fact, one of the problems identified by neoliberalism remains valid today: we no longer exist in national economies but, rather, in a global economy – in a global form of capitalism in which individual countries and regions have to compete for capital and labor. This applies especially to the relationship between the economies of the global North and those of the global South, many of which are fighting to increase their share in global prosperity. Accordingly, it has become an ongoing challenge for Western national economies to create new branches and to leave the old behind. After all, this is the only way that they will be able to maintain their economic power, which is also necessary for their state and welfare budgets. Obviously, some of the components of Schumpeter's competition state will remain indispensable to ensuring the future production of wealth.

Despite its accomplishments, the paradigm of apertistic liberalism has exhausted itself in large part because of its naïve belief that legal rights and market forces would necessarily bring about social progress without there being both winners and losers. Its shortcomings – and the signs of crisis that I have already mentioned – indicate that this is not the case. To solve this problem, the new regulatory liberalism will have to begin with the insight that it is necessary to implement social, cultural, and (to some extent) government-run systems to regulate markets and subjective rights. Apertistic liberalism failed to build new regulatory systems to suit the changing conditions. Instead, it allowed both the law and the market to serve an independent and quasi-political function, and to do so it paid the price of not having a robust concept of society, culture, and the state. The political challenge of the coming decade (and thus also the task of regulatory liberalism) will thus be to address the *social* issues of increasing inequality and decreasing social provisions as well as the *cultural* issues of cultural disintegration and the erosion of reciprocity. By responding to these new social issues, regulatory liberalism would be a new form of *social liberalism*; by responding to these new cultural issues, it would also represent a new form of *cultural liberalism*. None of this will be possible, however, without new *government* (and civic) regulations.[28] Under the paradigm of regulatory liberalism, the state will once again have an active role, but this role will clearly differ (and must differ) from that which the state played during the era of social corporatism.

In order to work, it is important for regulatory liberalism to avoid two things: it should set aside any visions of forming a "new community," which is often evoked by populists; and it should shelve any fantasies of planning and controlling a "new society," which might be tempting to establish by means of government regulations. Late-modern society is not a community; it is not a homogeneous collective, and it never will be. Its lifestyles are varied; its classes are stratified and multi-ethnic. The challenge will lie in creating a general component of society that can be claimed by everyone, despite social differences and cultural heterogeneity. Unlike a "community," late-modern "society" does not have a binding and universally shared way of life, and the individuals who constitute it are each irreducibly singular. Despite – or because of – this, late-modern society is dependent on rules and their implementation, and it requires forms of recognition that individuals will acknowledge both *in* and *despite* their diversity.

Just as there will be no new community, there will also be no completely new society. Such a vision would be based on the idea that social structures can be planned, determined, and controlled by the state, but this idea fails to take into account the willfulness and inherent dynamics of social, cultural, and economic processes. The end of the postwar era's social-corporatist paradigm was brought about by (among other factors) its euphoria for social planning, which at best was briefly successful under the exceptional labor conditions of the *trente glorieuses* (autonomous nation states, global growth, cultural homogeneity). In order to emphasize its difference from this one-dimensional model of social regulation, I will insist on calling the paradigm that will succeed that of apertistic liberalism a form of *liberalism*. As already mentioned, regulatory liberalism will support the structures of liberal democracy and will further perpetuate certain insights of apertistic liberalism. Yet it will also be an instantiation of liberalism in a more basic sense. What sense do I have in mind? Political philosophy and intellectual history have provided numerous definitions of what constitutes liberalism. The idea of freedom plays a role in these definitions, of course, but so do ideas of plurality, the critique of authority, subjective rights, equal rights, progress, individualism, and the priority of markets and achievement.[29] Here, however, I would like to adopt the abstract but fitting understanding of the term proposed by Michel Foucault, who defined liberalism as a particular form of *governmentality*.[30]

In short, liberalism is a form of government that acknowledges the inherent dynamics and indeterminable nature of society. Liberalism does not proceed from the idea that it is possible to sit at the drawing board to plan, regulate, and enforce the structure of society. For it recognizes that social processes – that is, the economic processes of markets and the socio-cultural processes of individuals and groups, with their various interests and values – can only be nudged in one direction or another. Moreover, technological, media, and ecological processes are unpredictable and self-regulating in such a way that they are impervious to any rigid and external government planning. Society's primacy over the state is therefore not just a normative matter; in reality, it also functions in ways that are always more complex than the state could ever predict. In Foucault's words, "reality develops, goes its own way, and follows its course according to the laws, principles, and mechanisms of reality itself."[31] It is possible to acknowledge this, however, without endorsing a simple laissez-faire approach to government. The dynamics of society require certain restrictions, and "freedom" cannot be regarded as unlimited. From the perspective of liberal government, however, the regulation of social processes can only take place *indirectly* by means of incentives and disincentives, and such regulation has to be prepared to deal with the unintended consequences that it might cause. In Foucault's estimation, "a power thought of as regulation can only be carried out through and by reliance on the freedom of each."[32] With respect to this indirect sort of control, regulatory liberalism will have to be more active than apertistic liberalism ever was, but it cannot revert to believing in the effectiveness of universal (national) social planning.

In the final section of this chapter, I would like to discuss five problem areas in which the new paradigm of regulatory liberalism will have to act in order to overcome the present crisis.

Challenges Facing Regulatory Liberalism

Beyond meritocracy Critics have often – and rightly – pointed out that late-modern societies are suffering from increasing social inequality. This has more than just a material dimension, for there is also inequality with respect to social recognition, and this creates feelings of contempt and devaluation among large segments of the population. Regulatory liberalism will have to provide an answer to this, but before doing so it will have to examine the causes of this growing disparity more closely. The most important cause of today's social inequality should be sought in the fundamental transformation from the industrial to the post-industrial economy. In the structure of employment, this transformation has given rise to a new dualism between the knowledge economy (with its highly qualified workers) and the simple services (with its so-called low-skilled workers). It has therefore created a new *status hierarchy*, which is a paradoxical consequence of the well-intended, and also beneficial, expansion of education.[33] The problem is that the social status of those on the lower rungs of this hierarchy – that is, most of the members of the new service class – is far lower than that of the labor force during the bygone era of industrial society, and that such workers accordingly receive less social recognition, pay, and security. Late modernity is thus suffering from the full effects of a *meritocracy problem*, which Michael Young clairvoyantly predicted as early as 1958 in his book *The Rise of Meritocracy*.[34] The creation of the knowledge economy, upon which politics has placed such great hopes, has invariably produced losers as well. To those who have lost out during this development, however, it is now implied that they are responsible for their own falling status because they failed to achieve "upward mobility" through the educational system. Conversely, according to Young, people with high qualifications are quick to refer to their own education and achievements with the self-assurance of those who feel as though they have "earned" their respective positions in society.

The meritocratic notion of education overlooks a central fact: the ability of society to function is just as dependent on the work of so-called low-skilled employees as it is on the work of highly qualified employees, and society as a whole will probably break apart if the "uneducated" workers performing routine and physically demanding jobs continue to be denied the social recognition that they deserve (not to mention basic job security and health insurance). What is decisive here is that the solution to the problem cannot lie in simply calling for more education, because this will only reproduce the present situation of winners and losers, especially if all the reserves of talent happen to be exhausted. What is needed is, instead, a new social contract, which, following the classical idea of the division of labor, fundamentally recognizes the equal necessity of *all* types of work and thus moderates the social differences between them. Such a contract is not just a matter of government policies (minimum wage, tax laws, social benefits); it also pertains to the symbolic dimension of a society that has grown accustomed to distinguishing between those who have "made it" and the rest. To borrow a term from Robert Fuller, the problem that has to be dealt with is that of a culture of "rankism," in which differences in social status (especially as such status relates to employment) translate into considerable and ultimately unjustifiable discrepancies in the extent to which individuals are valued.[35]

The urban–rural divide In late modernity, the dynamics of market processes have also created substantial social inequalities in terms of social geography and the living conditions associated with it. The widening discrepancies between prosperous metropolitan regions and stagnating rural and small-town areas will be a central challenge for regulatory liberalism. This is especially true of the conditions in the United States, Great Britain, and France. In Western Germany, such geographical discrepancies are perceptible but more subtle, while in Eastern Germany they are prominent. In this case, too, the problem has to be properly diagnosed before any therapy can be applied; yet again, the driving force behind this inequality happens to be the dynamics of post-industrialization. It is this factor that has caused the knowledge economy and the educated middle class (but also a large portion of the service class) to cluster in metropolitan regions, which has in turn caused ambitious people to leave rural areas and smaller cities, thereby draining their populations. Two vicious cycles are under way: already successful metropolitan regions attract more and more capital and residents (partially from abroad) and, in the absence of regulation, this leads to overheating effects in the form of shortages of space, inadequate transportation systems, and rising housing costs. Rural areas, in contrast, are suffering from an exodus of qualified young people, which only causes such areas to seem more unattractive, thereby inciting even more people to leave and enticing even fewer people to move there. In a sense, the result of all this has been the development of two (geography-based) parallel societies,[36] and it will be essential for future politics to address the problems of metropolitan and rural regions independently, and to make efforts to regulate the "natural" market processes that are taking place in both cases. The overheating problem in large cities can be tempered, for instance, by regulating the real-estate market and constructing affordable housing; in rural areas and small cities, the problem of depopulation can be addressed through the targeted promotion of regional development (increasing educational opportunities, opening regional branches of businesses, and so on).

The provision of infrastructure The neoliberal economization of the social privatized many of the institutions that provide elementary resources to the population – transportation, healthcare, energy, affordable housing, education, public security, and the like – and therefore subjected these institutions to market mechanisms. At issue here, ultimately, is the privatization of social infrastructure in the broad sense. Often, however, this marketization of infra-structure did not strengthen it (as planned) but, rather, weakened it, also with respect to its equal accessibility to everyone. During the era of apertistic liberalism, the portions of infrastructure that did remain in the hands of government were often neglected. For regulatory liberalism, however, the maintenance and improvement of this public infrastructure will have to be of central importance. Here, as members of the Foundational Economy Collective have underscored, we are dealing with the fundamental elements of the economy, and the ability of these elements to function repre-sents the basis of everyone's quality of life.[37] They provide citizens with security and predictability in basic matters. Over the last few decades, governments have seemingly deemed it more important to promote personal consumption – from lowering income taxes to increasing childcare benefits for families – than to provide less spectacular but essential infrastructural goods and services. In this area, however, things need to be reconsidered. Private consumption cannot replace the necessity of public infrastructure, for, whenever such provisions are inadequate, the wealthy and educated can compensate with private means (private security services, private schools, private health insurance), while everyone else has to rely all the more on insufficient infrastructure that is publicly available.

The challenges posed by meritocracy, the urban–rural divide, and the neglect of public infrastructure are all challenges of a socio-economic sort, and thus regulatory liberalism will have to emerge here as a socio-economic regulative authority that exercises control over the markets and counteracts the comprehensive economization of the social. However, a timely and effective political paradigm is also able to recognize the need for regulation that exists in the socio-cultural sphere. For, as I have already discussed above, late-modern society's deregulation problem has not one but *two* sides to it, and there is an intimate relationship between these two aspects that is often overlooked. Above all, it is not especially helpful to view the socio-economic problem as a traditional issue on the left, and to view the socio-cultural problem as a traditional issue among conservatives and communitarians. Both sets of problems are only superficially related to the old left–right schema; both, in fact, have arisen from the conflict between regimes of regulation and regimes of dynamization. To this extent, and for a paradigm concerned with reconstituting generality, they thus turn out to be two sides of the same coin.

The search for basic rules The cultural pluralization of ways of life is a *fait accompli* in late-modern societies. The post-industrialization of the economy and the cultural shift in value have given rise to a number of different milieus, which, on a more abstract level, have taken on the form of cultural classes. In many places, meanwhile, this cultural heterogeneity has resulted in a constellation of polarization and antagonism, especially between the new and the old middle class.[38] At the same time, migration movements have created not only multi-ethnic but also multicultural conditions whose consequences – beyond the inevitable existence of different background stories and the influences of diverse cultural traditions – can even include the establishment of "parallel societies" of individual ethnic groups. In light of this situation, regulatory liberalism will not simply be able to perpetuate, without further ado, the progressive liberal model of multiculturalism. Rather, a central political challenge for the development of late-modern society will be to work toward developing basic rules and values that everyone will accept. Formulated in the sociological tradition of Émile Durkheim, the task at hand is that of *cultural integration*, and this applies equally to immigrants and to non-immigrants from various milieus and classes. Cultural integration, in other words, applies to the "redneck" in Alabama just as much as it applies to the "hipster" in California. This is to stress that the question of cultural integration goes far beyond the issue of migration.

The work needed to establish, convey, and implement basic cultural values and universally shared cultural practices can no longer be neglected in the manner of laissez-faire liberalism, for which "culture" is merely a matter for the private or economic sphere. Following Niklas Luhmann, one could, of course, ask whether modern society might be able to function even without such a consensus of cultural values.[39] However, the answer to this question seems to be no. Social practices in all areas of life – in the public sphere, in the working world, and certainly in the case of political debate – require a particular, and often unspoken, set of generally recognized cultural values in order to take place success- fully and peacefully. Often, these requirements are not noticed until they are gone. What counts as valuable and what does not is a matter of ongoing negotiation within society as a whole. Public educational systems can play a central role in the conveyance of common values, but also recently created spheres such as online social media have turned out to be spaces in which the establishment of basic rules seems especially urgent (in the case of social media, such rules would pertain to communication).

In working to establish a set of generally binding basic rules, a future regulatory liberalism will have to navigate within two fields of tension: between collective acceptance and heterogeneity, on the one hand, and between universalism and national cultures on the other. In contrast to the cultural politics of right-wing populism, the aim of cultural liberalism cannot be to negate the irreducible heterogeneity of late-modern ways of life; rather, it will have to work toward creating a common framework *within* this respected hetero- geneity of ethnicities and lifestyles.[40] The basic rules in question do not exist *a priori*, and they are not fixed – also, they are not a matter of abstract principles. Rather, they will have to be worked out in an ongoing fashion and in relation to the specific cultural practices to which they apply. This also means, for instance, that constitutional law – with its matrix of fundamental values (to which the theory of constitutional patriotism is quick to refer) – will not be sufficient. Legal norms require specific everyday cultural practices – practices of cooperation, civil conflict, exchange, solidarity, friendly indif- ference, ritual, play, etc. – in order to become socially effective. At least from the perspective of Western societies, many of these basic rules have a universalistic character and are thus relatively indifferent to individual national cultures. At the same time, however, nation states remain the central political entities that organize education and the public sphere. The culture that cultural liberalism regards as valuable is therefore always a culture of the general contained within a culture of the particular – the culture of a nation as well as that of a diverse set of lifestyles.

A culture of reciprocity Within the framework of the general question of the basic cultural rules of social coexistence, the question of the culture of reciprocity turns out to be an important subtopic. In fact, one could argue that one of the greatest short- comings of apertistic liberalism is that it weakens a culture of reciprocity and unilaterally enforces a culture of subjective interests and subjective rights. Here, interestingly, the effects of both sides of the paradigm are similar: neoliberals proceeded from the model of a utility-maximizing individual who participates in markets and represents his or her interests there, while progressive liberals proceeded from the model of an individual who claims his or her subjective rights vis-à-vis others. The one side turns citizens into self-centered consumers, while the other side turns them into demonstrators for their own individual causes. But where does that leave the role of the citizen as a political entity with feelings of responsibility for society as a whole? In this model, there no longer seems to be any room for society as a space of reciprocity – that is, as a space for mutual social benefits, with laws and obligations that seek a balance between one's own individual interests and those of others.

It is no surprise that there has recently been growing support for reviving a culture of reciprocity, in which individuals have a sense of obligation for others and for society at large.[41] Certainly, there is something unpopular about such a form of politics, given that voters have grown accustomed to articulating their own rights and interests (and, in the populist mode, social obligation is almost exclusively demanded of "others" – preferably of migrants and wealthy cosmopolitans). This view of politics would insist that society could expect something in return from those who have received social benefits, and it would prompt discussions about the following questions (among others): Do those who have benefited from public education not also have an obligation to society to use their talents and abilities for the welfare of everyone (and not simply for their own monetary gain)? Do families who have received government support not also have an obligation to raise their children to become responsible members of society (and not just rational egoists)? Do people who have accumulated vast wealth via (legally protected) capital gains not also have a duty to repay portions of these gains to society? These complexes of problems can in part be regulated by legal means, but they extend beyond the law because they pertain to the general conception of what constitutes the body politic.[42]

It is an open question, of course, how a new political paradigm of regulatory liberalism might form its ideas and translate them into practical politics. If this paradigm does come about, then it goes without saying that there will be more progressive and more conservative versions of it, as was already the case with the two preceding paradigms. The progressive versions (which I myself would support) will clearly emphasize the importance of social infrastructure for all and will be more strongly oriented toward cultural universalism, while the conservative versions will be more nationally oriented and will be more tolerant of social inequality. In general, the social base of regulatory liberalism will differ from that of apertistic liberalism: whereas, during the late phase of its development, the latter was supported primarily by the new middle class of highly qualified people in metropolitan areas, there is a chance that regulatory liberalism might attract support not only from the enlightened and self-critical portion of this new middle class but also from portions of the old middle class and the precarious class, some members of which presently endorse populism. If the difference in values between the new middle class and the old middle class can be described as a contrast between pro-globalization cosmopolitans and pro-regulation communitarians, then regulatory liberalism could perhaps lead to a "historical compromise" between the two.

In one respect, however, regulatory liberalism will differ in an essential way from the two previous paradigms: it will have to be more skeptical of its own ability to bring about progress. As already mentioned, the social-corporatist paradigm was highly optimistic about the ability of the state to control things. Yet apertistic liberalism cultivated an understanding of progress that was no less optimistic, though now it was directed toward the inherent dynamics of socio-economic development. Today, both of these optimistic attitudes toward progress seem naïve, and – despite all its hopes for reconfiguring the politics of the future – regulatory liberalism will have to think twice before reverting to such optimism.

In general, we have to acknowledge the fact that society's development in the twenty-first century will come with (and already has come with) *experiences of loss* that cannot be cured by being ignored. These losses have to be identified and processed in order for society to avoid falling into a permanent populist spiral of outrage and grievance. They have three systematic causes. First, the transformation from industrial to post-industrial society, which has further been fueled by digitalization, has brought about the loss of the secure industrial world of routine physical and administrative jobs, which was able to provide the model of a "society of equals" with a basis in everyday reality. Second, globalization has led to the economic and political rise of the global South – especially in Eastern and Southern Asia – so that "the West" is in the process of irretrievably losing its hegemony, its privileged ability to accumulate wealth, and its political dominance. Third, increasingly dire ecological problems, which have been caused by the industrial and post-industrial way of life and which are culminating in climate change, will entail the irrecoverable loss of a model of social development which assumed that it would be possible to increase material wealth indefinitely. The traditional concept of progress, which has served as a measure of political and social development since the Enlightenment, will itself need to be revised in the twenty-first century.

Notes

Introduction

1 On the rise of Donald Trump, see Steven Levitsky and Daniel Ziblatt, *How Democracies Die* (London: Penguin, 2019).
2 Francis Fukuyama, *The End of History and the Last Man* (New York: The Free Press, 1992).
3 Reinhart Koselleck, *Futures Past: On the Semantics of Historical Time*, trans. Keith Tribe (New York: Columbia University Press, 2004).
4 Oswald Spengler, *The Decline of the West*, trans. Charles F. Atkinson (New York: Oxford University Press, 1991); José Ortega y Gasset, *The Revolt of the Masses*, trans. Anthony Kerrigan (Notre Dame University Press, 1985).
5 Interesting in other ways are recent fictional dystopias, such as those depicted in film. Examples include *Blade Runner 2049*, directed by Denis Villeneuve (Burbank, CA: Warner Bros. Pictures, 2017); and *War for the Planet of the Apes*, directed by Matt Reeves (Los Angeles: 20th Century Fox, 2017).
6 For a critique of the disappearance of society's ability to tolerate ambiguity, see Thomas Bauer, *Die Vereindeutigung der Welt: Über den Verlust an Mehrdeutigkeit und Vielfalt* (Stuttgart: Reclam, 2018).
7 Andreas Reckwitz, *The Society of Singularities*, trans. Valentine A. Pakis (Cambridge: Polity, 2020).
8 Pierre Rosanvallon, *The Society of Equals*, trans. Arthur Goldhammer (Cambridge, MA: Harvard University Press, 2013).
9 See Reckwitz, *The Society of Singularities*.
10 The term "individualism" is usually used to denote a culture that favors the self-responsibility of the individual over social solidarity, and "individualizing" is typically used to denote the process of "freeing" the individual from such collective bonds. See Ulrich Beck, *Risk Society: Towards a New Modernity*, trans. Mark Ritter (London: SAGE, 1992).
11 On the topic of singularization, see also Igor Kopytoff, "The Cultural Biography of Things," in *The Social Life of Things: Commodities in Cultural Perspective*, ed. Arjun Appadurai (Cambridge University Press, 1986), pp. 64–91.
12 The work was first published online as "Zwischen Hyperkultur und Kulturessenzialismus," *Soziopolis* (October 24, 2016), https://soziopolis.de/beobachten/kultur/artikel/zwischen-hyperkultur-und-kulturessenzialismus. On April 30, 2017, a revised version of the text – now titled "Hyperkultur und Kulturessenzialismus: Der Kampf um das Kulturverständnis" – was broadcast as part of Deutschlandfunk's radio series *Essay und Diskurs*.

1 Cultural Conflicts as a Struggle over Culture

1 Samuel P. Huntington, *The Clash of Civilizations and the Remaking of World Order* (New York: Simon & Schuster, 1996).
2 Raymond Williams, *Culture and Society, 1780–1950* (New York: Columbia University Press, 1958).
3 On these various concepts of culture, see Andreas Reckwitz, *Die Transformation der Kulturtheorien: Zur Entwicklung eines Theorieprogramms* (Weilerwist: Velbrück Wissenschaft, 2000), pp. 64–90.
4 Ernst Cassirer, *The Philosophy of Symbolic Forms*, trans. Ralph Manheim, 3 vols. (New Haven, CT: Yale University Press, 1955–7).
5 See Reckwitz, *The Society of Singularities*, pp. 19–80.
6 Émile Durkheim, *The Elementary Forms of Religious Life*, trans. Joseph Ward Swain (London: G. Allen & Unwin, 1915).
7 Max Weber, *The Protestant Ethic and the Spirit of Capitalism*, trans. Talcott Parsons (New York: Charles Scribner's Sons, 1930).
8 On the relevance of "culture" in postmodernity, see Fredric Jameson, *Postmodernism, or, the Cultural Logic of Late Capitalism* (London: Verso, 1991); and Scott Lash, *Sociology of Postmodernism* (London: Routledge, 1990).
9 For a model of culture as a "resource," see also George Yúdice, *The Expediency of Culture: Uses of Culture in the Global Era* (Durham, NC: Duke University Press, 2003).
10 On the particular structure of markets for cultural goods, see also Pierre-Michel Menger, *The Economics of Creativity: Art and Achievement under Uncertainty* (Cambridge, MA: Harvard University Press, 2014).
11 For further discussion of cultural capitalism, see Scott Lash and Celia Lury, *Global Culture Industry: The Mediation of Things* (Cambridge: Polity, 2007); and Chapter 3 below.
12 Richard Florida, *Cities and the Creative Class* (New York: Routledge, 2005).
13 Georg Simmel, *Sociology: Inquiries into the Construction of Social Forms*, trans. Anthony J. Blasi et al. (Leiden: Brill, 2009).
14 On the new middle class, see Chapter 2 in this book.
15 This tendency is the impetus behind the postcolonial critique of the cultural appropriation of the powerless by the powerful.
16 On the concept of diversity, see Steven Vertovec, "'Diversity' and the Social Imaginary," *European Journal of Sociology*, 53:3 (2012), pp. 287–312.
17 On the concept of hybridity, see Jan Nederveen Pieterse, "Globalization as Hybridization," in *Global Modernities*, ed. Mike Featherstone et al. (London: SAGE, 2002), pp. 45–68.
18 See Bernhard Giesen, *Kollektive Identität: Die Intellektuellen und die Nation 2* (Frankfurt am Main: Suhrkamp, 1999); and Manuel Castells, *The Power of Identity* (Cambridge, MA: Blackwell, 1997).
19 See Benedict Anderson, *Imagined Communities: Reflections on the Origin and Spread of Nationalism*, 2nd edn. (London: Verso, 1991).
20 For further discussion of this phenomenon, see Reckwitz, *The Society of Singularities*, pp. 286–309.
21 Of course, identity conflicts can also, in part, assume the form of cultural class struggles.
22 See Martin Riesebrodt, *Rückkehr der Religionen? Zwischen Fundamentalismus und der "Kampf der Kulturen"* (Munich: Beck, 2000), pp. 59–60; and Ronald F. Inglehart and Pippa Norris, "Trump, Brexit, and the Rise of Populism: Economic Have-Nots and Cultural Backlash," Harvard Kennedy School Working Paper, no. RWP16-026 (2016). For further discussion, see also Chapter 2 below.
23 See Pankaj Mishra, *Age of Anger: A History of the Present* (New York: Farrar, Straus & Giroux, 2017); and Sebastian Conrad, *What Is Global History?* (Princeton University Press, 2016).
24 Beyond this strict dichotomy, there are also interesting hybridizations between the two regimes of culturalization. Muslim teenagers, for instance, can be

portrayed by the media as having an "attractive style" within the framework of Western youth culture, and thus as functioning within the logic of Culturalization I. In this regard, they are participants in hyperculture's markets of attention and valorization. However, if they are recruited to join an Islamist cause – to fight for ISIS, for instance – it is immediately thought that they have abandoned this logic and have firmly switched over to the logic of Culturalization II.

25 See Will Kymlicka, *Multicultural Odysseys: Navigating the New International Politics of Diversity* (Oxford University Press, 2007).

26 Karl Popper, *The Open Society and Its Enemies: New One-Volume Edition* (Princeton University Press, 2013), originally published in 1945.

27 For such a critique of hyperculture, see for instance Guillaume Paoli, *Die lange Nacht der Metamorphose: Über die Gentrifizierung der Kultur* (Berlin: Matthes & Seitz, 2017).

28 The result of incorporating individual goods into a global system of markets and appropriation is that, by claiming to be incomparable, the individual goods of hyperculture are in fact all the more likely to be compared with one another. This is the reason why, from a cultural-critical perspective, the elements of hyperculture happen to seem so similar that one often hears complaints about the absence of things that are radically "other" or different. On this topic, see Byung-Chul Han, *Hyperkulturalität: Kultur und Globalisierung* (Berlin: Merve, 2005).

29 See Terry Eagleton, *The Idea of Culture* (Oxford: Blackwell, 2000); and François Jullien, *There Is No Such Thing as Cultural Identity*, trans. Pedro Rodriguez (Cambridge: Polity, 2021).

30 On the culture of Romanticism, see Isaiah Berlin, *The Roots of Romanticism*, ed. Henry Hardy (Princeton University Press, 2014).

31 See Friedrich Schiller, *On the Aesthetic Education of Man in a Series of Letters*, trans. Elizabeth M. Wilkinson and L. A. Willoughby (Oxford: Clarendon Press, 1983).

32 On the distinction between community and society, see Helmuth Plessner, *The Limits of Community: A Critique of Social Radicalism*, trans. Andrew Wallace (New York: Humanity Books, 1999).

33 The leading ideas of global culture, global museums, and global cultural heritage all point in such a direction. In this regard, see Christoph Antweiler, *Inclusive Humanism: Anthropological Basics for a Realistic Cosmopolitanism*, trans. Diane Kerns (Göttingen: Vandenhoeck & Ruprecht, 2012).

34 See, for instance, John Dewey's foundational book *Democracy and Education: An Introduction to the Philosophy of Education* (New York: Macmillan, 1916).

2 From the Leveled Middle-Class Society to the Three-Class Society

1 Ulrich Beck, "Jenseits von Stand und Klasse? Soziale Ungleichheiten, gesellschaftliche Individualisierungsprozesse und die Entstehung neuer sozialer Formationen und Identitäten," in *Soziale Ungleichheiten*, ed. Reinhard Kreckel (Göttingen: Schwartz, 1983), pp. 35–74.

2 Branko Milanović, *Global Inequality: A New Approach for the Age of Globalization* (Cambridge, MA: Harvard University Press, 2016).

3 Robert D. Putnam, *Our Kids: The American Dream in Crisis* (New York: Simon & Schuster, 2015).

4 Arlie Russell Hochschild, *Strangers in Their Own Land: Anger and Mourning on the American Right* (New York: The New Press, 2016).

5 David Goodhart, *The Road to Somewhere: The Populist Revolt and the Future of Politics* (London: Penguin Books, 2017).

6 Christoph Guilluy, *La France périphérique: Comment on a sacrifié les classes populaires* (Paris: Flammarion, 2015).

7 Didier Eribon, *Returning to Reims*, trans. Michael Lucey (Cambridge, MA: MIT Press, 2013).

8 Thomas Piketty, *Capital in the Twenty-First Century*, trans. Arthur Goldhammer (Cambridge, MA: Harvard University Press, 2014).

9 Gerhard Schulze, *Die Erlebnisgesellschaft: Kultursoziologie der Gegenwart* (Frankfurt am Main: Suhrkamp, 1992). The publications of the SINUS Institute can be accessed at www.sinus-institut.de/en/publications/downloads.

10 My concept of class thus has a different emphasis from that of Marx; instead, it has certain parallels to that of Pierre Bourdieu.

11 Pierre Bourdieu, "The Forms of Capital," in *Handbook of Theory and Research for the Sociology of Education*, ed. John G. Richardson (Westport, CT: Greenwood Press, 1986), pp. 241–58.

12 For a more detailed analysis of what I will discuss below (and for an abundance of empirical data), see Milanović, *Global Inequality*, pp. 10–45. For further discussion of this topic, see also Heinz Bude and Philipp Staab, eds., *Kapitalismus und Ungleichheit: Die neuen Verwerfungen* (Frankfurt am Main: Campus, 2016).

13 Milanović, *Global Inequality*, pp. 10–18.

14 There is, in addition, the *upper class*, which I treat as a special case on account of its limited scope. To be more precise, one would have to speak of a 3-plus-1 class model.

15 Oliver Nachtwey, *Germany's Hidden Crisis: Social Decline in the Heart of Europe*, trans. David Fernbach and Loren Balhorn (London: Verso, 2018).

16 Jean Fourastié, *Les Trente glorieuses, ou la revolution invisible de 1946 à 1975* (Paris: Fayard, 1979).

17 Helmut Schelsky, "Die Bedeutung des Schichtungsbegriff für die Analyse der gegenwärtigen deutschen Gesellschaft," in *Auf der Suche nach Wirklichkeit: Gesammelte Aufsätze* (Düsseldorf: E. Diederichs, 1965), pp. 331–6. Regarding the political structures of industrial modernity, see Rosanvallon, *The Society of Equals*.

18 See Karl Martin Bolte et al., eds., *Deutsche Gesellschaft im Wandel* (Opladen: Leske, 1967); and Beck, *Risk Society*.

19 From the 1950s to the 1970s, the Gini coefficient (a measure of social inequality) was relatively low. It was considerably higher during the first half of the twentieth century and it began to rise again after 1980, especially in the Anglo-Saxon countries. See Milanović, *Global Inequality*, pp. 46–117.

20 In the United States, only 40 percent of the population in the 1950s had a high school diploma (see Figure 2.2).

21 Ralf Dahrendorf's "house model." Originally published in Dahrendorf, *Gesellschaft und Demokratie* (Munich: R. Piper & Co., 1965), p. 516.

22 On the concept of working to improve one's status, see Uwe Schimank et al., *Statusarbeit unter Druck? Zur Lebensführung der Mittelschichten* (Weinheim: Beltz Verlagsgruppe, 2014).

23 William H. Whyte, *The Organization Man* (New York: Simon & Schuster, 1956).

24 Ibid., p. 363.

25 I discuss this phenomenon at greater length in Chapter 3.

26 On this topic, see Allen J. Scott, *A World in Emergence: Cities and Regions in the 21st Century* (London: Edward Elgar, 2012); and Daniel Bell's classic work *The Coming of Post-Industrial Society: A Venture in Social Forecasting* (New York: Basic Books, 1973).

27 See Stephen J. Rose, "Manufacturing Employment: Fact and Fiction," Urban Institute (April 13, 2018), www.urban.org/sites/default/files/publication/97776/manufacturing_employment_fact_and_fiction_2.pdf; and the data provided by the Federal Statistical Office of Germany at https://de.statista.com/statistik/daten/studie/275637/umfrage/anteil-der-wirtschaftsbereiche-an-der-gesamtbeschaeftigung-in-deutschland.

28 On deindustrialization, see Lutz Raphael, *Jenseits von Kohle und Stahl: Eine Gesellschaftsgeschichte Europas nach dem Boom* (Berlin: Suhrkamp, 2019).

29 See the sources cited above in note 27.

30 Maarten Goos and Alan Manning, "Lousy and Lovely Jobs: The Rising

Polarization of Work in Britain," *Review of Economics and Statistics*, 89 (2007), pp. 118–33.

31 On this topic, see Tanjev Schultz and Klaus Hurrelmann, eds., *Die Akademiker-Gesellschaft: Müssen in Zukunft alle studieren?* (Weinheim: Juventa, 2013).

32 See the information posted by the Federal Statistical Office of Germany at www.destatis.de/DE/Publikationen/Thematisch/BildungForschungKultur/BildungsstandBevoelkerung.html; Otto Hüther and Georg Krücken, *Hochschulen: Fragestellungen, Ergebnisse und Perspektiven der sozialwissenschaftlichen Hochschulforschung* (Wiesbaden: Springer, 2016), p. 78.

33 The source of this graph is the United States Census Bureau; see www.census.gov/content/dam/Census/library/publications/2016/demo/p20-578.pdf (p. 4).

34 It should be added that the increased availability of academic degrees has also led to hierarchization within the system of higher education.

35 See Ronald Inglehart, *Modernization and Postmodernization: Cultural, Economic, and Political Change in 43 Societies* (Princeton University Press, 1997).

36 See the data collected by the Federal Statistical Office of Germany: www.destatis.de/GPStatistik/servlets/MCRFileNodeServlet/DEHeft_derivate_00021684/Datenreport2016.pdf;jsessionid=E5C94A0A9F27899774E66A2BE50E59FF (p. 420).

37 See Abraham H. Maslow, *Motivation and Personality* (New York: Harper & Row, 1954).

38 This graph is of my own design. The distinction between different types of capital is borrowed from Bourdieu's essay "The Forms of Capital."

39 In 2014 in Germany, the average lifetime income of those with a vocational degree was estimated at 1.3 million euros, whereas the average lifetime income of university graduates was estimated to be 2.3 million euros. On these figures, see https://de.statista.com/statistik/daten/studie/288922/umfrage/durchschnittliche-lebensverdienste-in-deutschland-nach-bildungsabschluss. In 2009 in the United States, the median yearly earnings of people with just a high school diploma were $33,000, whereas people with an advanced degree earned, on average, $74,000. See www.census.gov/newsroom/cspan/educ/educ_attain_slides.pdf.

40 For a more detailed analysis of the new middle class, see Reckwitz, *The Society of Singularities*, pp. 199–251.

41 For early and trenchant analyses of the new middle class during its gradual rise, see, for instance, Paul Leinberger and Bruce Tucker, *The New Individualists: The Generation after the Organization Man* (New York: Harper Collins, 1991); Mike Featherstone, *Consumer Culture and Postmodernism* (London: SAGE, 1990); and David Brooks, *Bobos in Paradise: The New Upper Class and How They Got There* (New York: Simon & Schuster, 2000).

42 On the concept of hyperculture, see Chapter 1.

43 Annette Lareau, *Unequal Childhoods: Class, Race, and Family Life* (Berkeley: University of California Press, 2011).

44 See Wolfgang Merkel, *The Struggle over Borders: Cosmopolitanism and Communitarianism* (Cambridge University Press, 2019).

45 For further discussion of this topic, see Chapter 5 below.

46 This, in particular, is the topic of Chapter 4 below.

47 For insights into understanding the transformation of the traditional middle class, see Goodhart, *The Road to Somewhere*; Joan C. Williams, *White Working Class: Overcoming Class Cluelessness in America* (Boston: Harvard Business Review Press, 2017); and Hochschild, *Strangers in Their Own Land*.

48 Hochschild, *Strangers in Their Own Land*, p. 166.

49 On this concept, see Walter G. Runciman's classic study *Relative Deprivation and Social Justice: A Study of Attitudes to Social Inequality in Twentieth-Century Britain* (London: Routledge & Kegan Paul, 1966).

50 Since 2009 in Germany, the number of university students has exceeded that of people pursuing vocational training. In 2012, there were 2.5 million of the former, and 2 million of the latter. See https://de.statista.com/infografik/1887/zahl-der-studierenden-und-auszubildenden.

51 One of the first researchers to make this observation was Gøsta Esping-Andersen in his book *Changing Classes: Stratification and Mobility in Post-Industrial Societies* (London: SAGE, 1993).

52 See Heinz Bude, *Die Ausgeslossenen: Das Ende vom Traum einer gerechten Gesellschaft* (Munich: Hanser, 2008); Friederike Bahl, *Lebensmodelle in der Dienstleisungsgesellschaft* (Hamburger Edition, 2014); and Putman, *Our Kids*.

53 Regarding East Germany, an impressive document of this dying work culture is Andreas Dresen's film *Gundermann* (2018).

54 Piketty, *Capital in the Twenty-First Century*. On the upper class in general, see also Olaf Groh-Samberg, "Sorgenfreier Reichtum: Jenseits von Konjunktur und Krise," *Wochenbericht DIW Berlin*, 35 (2009), pp. 590–612.

55 Ralf Dahrendorf, "Die globale Klasse und die neue Ungleichheit," *Merkur*, 11 (2000), pp. 1057–68.

56 Of course, this is not meant to dismiss the fact that migrants deal with comparable experiences across class differences (discrimination, for instance) or that, across class divides, women in general (or men in general) face similar challenges.

57 In Germany, the number of women graduating from university has been greater than the number of men since 2006. See the data collected by the Federal Statistical Office of Germany: www-genesis.destatis.de/genesis/online/link/tabelleErgebnis/21321-0001.

58 This is also related to the new middle class's openness to homosexual and bisexual orientations and to transgender identities.

59 On these differences in partnership models, see Cornelia Koppetsch and Günter Burkart, *Die Illusion der Emanzipation: Zur Wirksamkeit latenter Geschlechtsnormen im Milieuvergleich* (Konstanz: UVK, 1999).

60 This is also the sector of society that has given rise to the anti-genderism movement.

61 An additional aspect is that, in the precarious class, involuntary single life (even in the middle-aged cohort) is a more relevant phenomenon than it is in the other classes. On the one side, there are many women who are single parents; on the other side, there are many men who have few personal assets to offer and thus fail to find a long-term partner. In these cases, the feeling of being left behind also has a private and personal side to it.

62 For these figures, see the *Malteser Migrationsbericht* (2017), which contains data prepared by the Federal Statistical Office of Germany: www.malteser.de/fileadmin/Files_sites/malteser_de_Relaunch/Angebote_und_Leistungen/Migrationsbericht/Malteser_Migrationsbericht_2017_es.pdf (pp. 11–12).

63 See Berthold B. Flaig, "Migrantische Lebenswelten in Deutschland," in *Praxis der SINUS-Milieus: Gegenwart und Zukunft eines modernen Gesellschafts- und Zielgruppenmodells*, ed. Bertram Barth et al. (Wiesbaden: Springer, 2018), pp. 113–24. The differentiation of milieus in this article can be translated into a class model.

64 In 2018 in Germany, 18 percent of employed people with a university degree had an immigrant background. See the statistics provided by the Federal Employment Agency in the following report from April of 2019: https://statistik.arbeitsagentur.de/Statischer-Content/Arbeitsmarktberichte/Berufe/generische-Publikationen/Broschuere-Akademiker.pdf (p. 18).

65 Boris Nieswand, *Theorizing Transnational Migration: The Status Paradox of Migration* (London: Routledge, 2011).

66 Guilluy, *La France périphérique*; Scott, *A World in Emergence*. The *gilets jaunes* protest during 2018 and 2019 in France had a clearly geographical dimension insofar as it was a protest by the old, small-town middle class against the new, metropolitan middle class and the government supported by it.

67 This is a point that Guilluy emphasizes in his book *La France périphérique*.

68 On socio-spatial segregation within cities in Germany, see Marcel Helbig and Stefanie Jähnen, "Wie brüchig ist die soziale Architektur unserer Städte? Trends und Analysen der Segregation in 74 deutschen Städten," WZB Discussion Paper

(2018), http://dennymoeller.de/wp-content/uploads/2018/10/WZB-Segregation. pdf.

69 SINUS is a German research institute situated in Heidelberg. Its analyses of contemporary milieus refer not only to Germany but to many other countries. The results concerning Western European and North American societies are relatively similar.

70 See https://www.sinus-institut.de/en/sinus-solutions/sinus-milieus.

71 Some of the SINUS milieus do not fit neatly into one class or another. This is true of the "established" milieu (which is split between the old and the new middle class), the "traditional" milieu (which is divided between the old middle class and the precarious class), and the "hedonist" milieu (which includes parts of the precarious class and the new middle class). Whereas, in the latter two cases, it is probably possible to draw a clear line between the different segments, the "established" milieu poses the fundamental problem that it is also home to a group of educated people who do not belong to the new middle class but, rather, to the old. Here one could speak of a new inconsistency with respect to status, which has political consequences as well.

72 Because the SINUS studies have been conducted since 1980, it is possible to track the changes in milieus over multiple decades. In 1985, the milieus of the new middle class – to the extent that it existed then at all – constituted 13 percent of the West German population (in this regard, see also Andreas Rödder, *21.0: Eine kurze Geschichte der Gegenwart* [Munich: C. H. Beck, 2015], p. 148), whereas in 2018 it made up 31 percent of the population (see Figure 2.4). This is an increase of almost 20 percent! For additional evidence of this contrast, see Figure 2.1.

73 See Wolfgang Merkel, "Kosmopolitismus versus Kommunitarismus: Ein neuer Konflikt in der Demokratie," in *Parties, Governments, and Elites: The Comparative Study of Democracy*, ed. Philipp Harfst et al. (Wiesbaden: Springer, 2017), pp. 9–23. Currently, the political landscape of the United States is certainly influenced by this new structure. From the outside, the two-party structure may seem stable, but the internal structure of both parties has changed considerably. Since the 1990s, the Democrats have increasingly become the party of the new middle class and its liberal cosmopolitanism, while the Republicans – with the Tea Party Movement and, ultimately, with Donald Trump – have trended toward right-wing populism and have catered to the "angry" faction of the white old middle class. Regarding the recent developments in the Democratic Party, see Thomas Frank, *Listen, Liberal: Or, Whatever Happened to the Party of the People?* (New York: Picador, 2016).

74 On recent political developments in France, see Bruno Amable and Stefano Palombarini, *L'Illusion du bloc bourgeois: Alliances sociales et avenir du modèle français* (Paris: Raisons d'agir éditions, 2018).

75 For further discussion of this topic, see Chapter 5.

3 Beyond Industrial Society

1 Adam Smith, *An Inquiry into the Nature and Causes of the Wealth of Nations*, ed. W. B. Todd et al. (Oxford University Press, 1976).

2 Karl Marx, *Capital: Volume One*, trans. Ben Fowkes (New York: Vintage Books, 1977).

3 Fourastié, *Les Trente glorieuses*.

4 Raphael, *Jenseits von Kohle und Stahl*.

5 See Amin Ash, ed., *Post-Fordism: A Reader* (Oxford: Blackwell, 1994); Bell, *The Coming of Post-Industrial Society*; Peter Drucker, *Post-Capitalist Society* (New York: Harper Collins, 1993); Hartmut Häußermann, *Dienstleistungsgesellschaften* (Frankfurt am Main: Suhrkamp, 1995); and Joseph B. Pine and James Gilmore, *The Experience Economy: Work Is Theatre & Every Business a Stage* (Boston: Harvard Business Review Press, 1999).

6 See Yann Moulier-Boutang, *Cognitive Capitalism* (Cambridge: Polity, 2011); Isabell Lorey and Klaus Neundlinger, eds., *Kognitiver Kapitalismus* (Vienna: Turia + Kant, 2012); and, with a somewhat different emphasis, Paul Mason, *Postcapitalism: A Guide to Our Future* (New York: Farrar, Straus & Giroux, 2015).

7 See Nigel Thrift, *Knowing Capitalism* (London: SAGE, 2005); and Luc Boltanski and Arnaud Esquerre, *Enrichment: A Critique of Commodities*, trans. Catherine Porter (Cambridge: Polity, 2020).

8 See Wolfgang Streeck, *How Will Capitalism End? Essays on a Failing System* (London: Verso, 2016); and Nick Srnicek, *Platform Capitalism* (Cambridge: Polity, 2016).

9 Jean Fourastié, *Le Grand Espoir du XXe siècle: Progrès technique, progrès économique, progrès social* (Paris: Presses universitaires de France, 1949).

10 On this concept, see also Olivier Bomsel, *L'économie immatérielle: Industries et marchés d'expériences* (Paris: Gallimard, 2010).

11 Hans-Werner Niemann, *Europäische Wirtschaftsgeschichte: Vom Mittelalter bis heute* (Darmstadt: Wissenschaftliche Buchgesellschaft, 2009).

12 See Nikolai Kondratieff, *The Long Wave Cycle*, trans. Guy Daniels (New York: Richardson & Snyder, 1984); and Joseph A. Schumpeter, *The Theory of Economic Development: An Inquiry into Profits, Capital, Credit, Interest, and the Business Cycle*, trans. Redvers Opie (Cambridge, MA: Harvard University Press, 1934).

13 See Scott Lash and John Urry, *The End of Organized Capitalism* (Cambridge: Polity, 1987).

14 On this transitional phase, see Anselm Doering-Manteuffel and Lutz Raphael, *Nach dem Boom: Perspektiven auf die Zeitgeschichte seit 1970* (Göttingen: Vandenhoeck & Ruprecht, 2008).

15 See the data provided by the Federal Statistical Office of Germany: https://de.statista.com/statistik/daten/studie/275637/umfrage/anteil-der-wirtschaftsbereiche-an-der-gesamtbeschaeftigung-in-deutschland; and Rose, "Manufacturing Employment: Fact and Fiction," p. 3.

16 See Berthold Herrendorf et al., "Growth and Structural Transformation," in *Handbook of Economic Growth*, vol. II, ed. Philippe Aghion and Steven Durlauf (Amsterdam: Elsevier, 2014), pp. 855–941.

17 This graph is of my own design, and it is based on data collected by the Federal Statistical Office of Germany.

18 Fourastié, *Le Grand Espoir du XXe siècle*; Bell, *The Coming of Post-Industrial Society*. For a good critical discussion of the three-sector theory, see Uwe Staroske, *Die Drei-Sektoren-Hypothese: Darstellung und kritische Würdigung aus heutiger Sicht* (Regensburg: Roderer, 1995).

19 On the transformation of consumption, see Featherstone, *Consumer Culture and Postmodernism*; and Manfred Prisching, *Die zweidimensionale Gesellschaft: Ein Essay zur neokonsumistischen Geisteshaltung* (Wiesbaden: Verlag für Sozialwissenschaften, 2006).

20 On this shift in values and the new middle class, see Chapter 2 above.

21 See Thrift, *Knowing Capitalism*.

22 Carlota Perez, "Technological Revolutions, Paradigm Shifts and Socio-Institutional Change," in *Globalization, Economic Development and Inequality*, ed. Erik Reinert (Cheltenham: Edwin Elgar, 2004), pp. 217–42.

23 On this new global division of labor, see Scott, *A World in Emergence*.

24 Michael J. Piore and Charles F. Sabel, *The Second Industrial Divide: Possibilities for Prosperity* (New York: Basic Books, 1984).

25 Maurizio Lazzarato, "Immaterial Labor," in *Radical Thought in Italy: A Potential Politics*, ed. Paolo Virno and Michael Hardt (Minneapolis: University of Minnesota Press, 1996), pp. 133–48.

26 On knowledge work, see Nico Stehr, *Wissen und Wirtschaften: Die gesellschaftlichen Grundlagen der modernen Ökonomie* (Frankfurt am Main: Suhrkamp, 2009). On the new forms of organization that such work has brought about, see

Luc Boltanski and Ève Chiapello, *The New Spirit of Capitalism*, trans. Gregory Elliott (London: Verso, 2005).

27 See Esping-Andersen, *Changing Classes*; and Bahl, *Lebensmodelle in der Dienstleisungsgesellschaft*.

28 The source of this graph is Goos and Manning, "Lousy Jobs and Lovely Jobs," p. 126. Examining the situation in the United States, Allen J. Scott reached similar conclusions in his book *A World in Emergence*. The data collected by Goos and Manning concern not only the tertiary sector but, rather, all employment sectors.

29 See Chapter 2 above.

30 See Manfred Moldaschl and Günter G. Voß, eds, *Subjektivierung von Arbeit* (Munich: Hampp, 2003).

31 See Stephan Voswinkel, *Welche Kundenorientierung? Anerkennung in der Dienstleistungsarbeit* (Berlin: Edition Sigma, 2005).

32 On the social structures and political implications of the new working world, see Chapters 2 and 5 in this book.

33 The digitalization of many branches of the economy (including the specialized segment known as the "digital economy"), which has been intensifying since 2010, has enhanced the polarizing tendencies of the workforce. On the one hand, it creates new jobs for highly qualified workers, for instance in the IT sector itself; on the other hand, digital technologies simplify even further what the simple services have to offer (transportation or delivery services, for instance). Moreover, digitalization has also reduced the number of Fordist jobs performed by people with mid-level qualifications. On this topic, see Srnicek, *Platform Capitalism*.

34 See Paul James, ed., *Globalization and Economy* (London: SAGE, 2007).

35 Bob Jessop, *The Future of the Capitalist State* (Cambridge: Polity, 2002). Regarding neoliberalism, see also Chapter 5 above.

36 See the articles collected in Paul Windolf, ed., *Finanzmarkt-Kapitalismus: Analysen zum Wandel von Produktionsregimen* (Wiesbaden: Verlag für Sozialwissenschaften, 2005); and Gerald F. Davis, *Managed by the Markets: How Finance Re-Shaped America* (New York: Oxford University Press, 2009).

37 This is Carlota Perez's argument in her book *Technological Revolutions and Financial Capital: The Dynamics of Bubbles and Golden Ages* (Cheltenham: Edward Elgar, 2002).

38 See Wolfgang Streeck, *Buying Time: The Delayed Crisis of Economic Capitalism*, trans. Patrick Camiller and David Fernbach (London: Verso, 2014).

39 Bell, *The Coming of Post-Industrial Society*.

40 Drucker, *Post-Capitalist Society*.

41 Moulier-Boutang, *Cognitive Capitalism*.

42 Boltanski and Esquerre, *Enrichment: A Critique of Commodities*.

43 In 2018 in Germany, for instance, public services accounted for 18 percent of gross value added. See www.deutschlandinzahlen.de/tab/deutschland/ volkswirtschaft/entstehung/bruttowertschoepfung-nach-wirtschaftsbereichen.

44 In 2018 in Germany, business-related services alone accounted for 11 percent of gross value added.

45 See the report on Germany by the World Travel & Tourism Council: www.wttc. org/-/media/files/reports/benchmark-reports/country-reports-2017/germany.pdf.

46 Jonathan Haskel and Stian Westlake, *Capitalism Without Capital: The Rise of the Intangible Economy* (Princeton University Press, 2018).

47 For a long time, economic statistics accordingly considered no more than the physical assets of companies. This has since changed.

48 This graph is from Haskel and Westlake, *Capitalism Without Capital*, p. 26.

49 See John Howkins, *The Creative Economy: How People Make Money from Ideas* (London: Penguin, 2001).

50 See Moulier-Boutang, *Cognitive Capitalism*.

51 Mason, *Postcapitalism*, p. 156.

52 See Daniel Cohen, *Three Lectures on Post-Industrial Society* (Cambridge, MA: MIT Press, 2009).

53 See Frank Trentmann, *Empire of Things: How We Became a World of Consumers, from the Fifteenth Century to the Twenty-First* (London: Allen Lane, 2016).
54 This topic is discussed in greater detail in Reckwitz, *The Society of Singularities*, pp. 81–130. The features of cultural capitalism are also systematically analyzed in Boltanski and Esquerre's book *Enrichment: A Critique of Commodities*. A much earlier study of this subject is Scott Lash and John Urry, *Economies of Signs and Space* (London: SAGE, 1994). On the significance of unique services in the late-modern economy, see Lucien Karpik, *Valuing the Unique: The Economics of Singularities*, trans. Nora Scott (Princeton University Press, 2010).
55 A paradigmatic example of the process of singularization is the revaluation of typical old apartments built around the year 1900. Whereas, during industrial modernity (with its focus on functionality), they were frowned upon as being less comfortable and "unmodern," they have gradually entered the register of "culture" in late modernity. What one now sees in them is the splendor of bygone epochs, the authenticity of parquet flooring, their stucco ornaments and double doors, their location in "urban" neighborhoods with a mixture of residences, small stores, restaurants, and so on. The narrative framework surrounding old apartments has thus changed; their functional quirks notwithstanding, they are now perceived and experienced as being culturally valuable, "full of character," and unique. The demand for them on the real-estate market has accordingly increased, and thus so has the price that one is willing to pay for them.
56 In the terminology used by Boltanski and Esquerre, the fate of fashion-oriented goods is determined by a society's "trend form," while reputation-oriented goods depend on its "collection form." See the seventh and ninth chapters of their book *Enrichment: A Critique of Commodities*.
57 Jens Christensen, *Global Experience Industries: The Business of the Experience Economy* (Aarhus University Press, 2009).
58 Because the "culturality" of cultural goods cannot be identified from any *external* features (as is the case with cognitive goods in general), the current statistics available on different branches of the economy are too crude or insufficient. This is because they are based on categories inherited from industrial modernity. A *qualitative* shift has taken place, and industry statistics have not kept up with this change.
59 This is an issue that economic sociologists have been studying for some time. See, for instance, Jens Beckert and Patrik Aspers, eds., *The Worth of Goods: Valuation and Pricing in the Economy* (Oxford University Press, 2011).
60 See Moulier-Boutang, *Cognitive Capitalism*, pp. 31–2. On the "transformation" of functional goods into cultural goods, see also the examples mentioned in Lash and Lury, *Global Culture Industry*.
61 This is no place to dive into the fundamental debate over what "value" means in the economy. This question has recently been discussed by Mariana Mazzucato in her book *The Value of Everything: Making and Taking in the Global Economy* (London: Allen Lane, 2018). My starting point is that the economic value of goods is generally the result of socio-cultural ascriptions of value, and of the constellations of power in markets and in social discourses. I do not presuppose that the value of a commodity can be determined "objectively," as was assumed to be the case by the political economists of the eighteenth century. It is itself a political and discursive strategy to assert that such an objective (labor) value exists.
62 See Haskel and Westlake, *Capital Without Capitalism*, pp. 65–6. The basic idea of scalability was developed by Paul Romer in the 1980s. Unlike Paul Mason, I do not see how this sort of scalability might lead to the collapse of capitalism. On the contrary, cognitive goods – and, even more so, cultural goods – have obviously revitalized capitalism by offering new possibilities for expansion, which industrial-Fordist capitalism failed to do. See Mason's book *Postcapitalism*.
63 See Menger, *The Economics of Creativity*.

64 Robert Frank and Philip Cook, *The Winner-Take-All Society: Why the Few on the Top Get so Much More Than the Rest of Us* (London: Virgin Books, 2010).
65 Boltanski and Esquerre, *Enrichment: A Critique of Commodities*, pp. 274–300.
66 See Georg Franck, *Ökonomie der Aufmerksamkeit: Ein Entwurf* (Munich: Hanser, 1998).
67 See, for instance, Uwe Schimank and Ute Volkmann, *Das Regime der Konkurrenz: Gesellschaftliche Ökonomisierungsdynamiken heute* (Weinheim: Juventa, 2017).
68 On this topic, see Dietmar J. Wetzel, *Soziologie des Wettbewerbs: Eine kultur- und wirtschaftssoziologische Analyse der Marktgesellschafte* (Wiesbaden: Springer, 2013).
69 On the new middle class, see Chapter 2 above.
70 See Richard Florida, *Who's Your City? How the Creative Economy Is Making Where You Live the Most Important Decision of Your Life* (New York: Basic Books, 2008).
71 See Eva Illouz, *Why Love Hurts: A Sociological Explanation* (Cambridge: Polity, 2013).
72 See, for instance, Saskia Sassen, "Vive l'économie réelle!" *Le Monde* (February 21, 2009), www.lemonde.fr/idees/article/2009/02/21/vive-l-economie-reelle-par-saskia-sassen_1158611_3232.html.
73 For different perspectives on this, see Christian Marazzi, *Capital and Affects: The Politics of the Language Economy*, trans. Giuseppina Mecchia (Cambridge, MA: MIT Press, 2011); and Jens Beckert, *Imagined Futures: Fictional Expectations and Capitalist Dynamics* (Cambridge, MA: Harvard University Press, 2016).

4 The Weariness of Self-Actualization

1 See Alain Ehrenberg, *The Weariness of the Self: Diagnosing the History of Depression in the Modern Age*, trans. David Homel et al. (Montreal: McGill-Queen's University Press, 2010).
2 See, for instance, Byung-Chul Han, *The Burnout Society*, trans. Erik Butler (Stanford University Press, 2015); and Sven Hillenkamp, *Negative Moderne: Strukturen der Freiheit und der Sturz ins Nichts* (Stuttgart: Klett-Cotta, 2016).
3 See Thomas Fuchs and Lukas Iwer, eds., *Das überforderte Subjekt: Zeitdiagnose einer beschleunigten Gesellschaft* (Berlin: Suhrkamp, 2018).
4 In recent years, the number of publications devoted to the topic of emotion in the social sciences and humanities has swollen considerably. Here, it is enough to recommend Monica Greco and Paul Stenner, eds., *Emotions: A Social Science Reader* (London: Routledge, 2008); and Jan Plamper, *The History of Emotions: An Introduction*, trans. Keith Tribe (Oxford University Press, 2012). In late modernity, however, the issue of emotions has been revived in a particular way. In this respect, see Deborah Lupton, *The Emotional Self: A Sociocultural Exploration* (London: SAGE, 1998).
5 Regarding some of these negative emotions, see Sianne Ngai, *Ugly Feelings* (Cambridge, MA: Harvard University Press, 2007). For a different interpretation of the connection between positive and negative emotions in late modernity, see Lauren Berlant, *Cruel Optimism* (Durham, NC: Duke University Press, 2011). Eva Illouz has also discussed the relevance of negative emotions as they relate to late-modern romantic partnerships – see her book *The End of Love: A Sociology of Negative Emotions* (Oxford University Press, 2019).
6 See Andreas Reckwitz, *Das hybride Subjekt: Eine Theorie der Subjektkulturen von der bürgerlichen Moderne zur Postmoderne*, new edn. (Berlin: Suhrkamp, 2020).
7 See, for example, Heinz Bude, *Deutsche Karrieren: Lebenskonstruktionen sozialer Aufsteiger aus der Flakhelfer-Generation* (Frankfurt am Main: Suhrkamp, 1987).
8 David Riesman, *The Lonely Crowd: A Study of the Changing American Character* (New Haven, CT: Yale University Press, 1950).

9 Peter N. Stearns, *American Cool: Constructing a Twentieth-Century Emotional Style* (New York University Press, 1994).
10 David Brooks, *The Road to Character* (New York: Random House, 2015).
11 See Charles Taylor, *Sources of the Self: The Making of Modern Identity* (Cambridge, MA: Harvard University Press, 1989).
12 For a more detailed discussion of this transformation, see Reckwitz, *The Society of Singularities*.
13 See Ronald Inglehart, *The Silent Revolution: Changing Values and Political Styles Among Western Publics* (Princeton University Press, 1977). For further discussion of the new middle class, see Chapter 2 above.
14 For more detail on the shift from industrial to consumer capitalism, see Chapter 3 above.
15 See Boltanski and Chiapello, *The New Spirit of Capitalism*.
16 On the role of psychology as a cultural force, see Eva Illouz, *Saving the Modern Soul: Therapy, Emotions, and the Culture of Self-Help* (Los Angeles: University of California Press, 2017).
17 See Duane Schultz, *Growth Psychology: Models of the Healthy Personality* (New York: Van Nostrand Reinhold, 1977).
18 Maslow, *Motivation and Personality*.
19 See Phillip Vannini and Patrick J. Williams, eds., *Authenticity in Culture, Self, and Society* (London: Routledge, 2016).
20 See Schimank et al., *Statusarbeit under Druck?*
21 On these subject figures, see also Ulrich Bröckling, *The Entrepreneurial Self: Fabricating a New Type of Subject*, trans. Steven Black (London: SAGE, 2016); and Andreas Reckwitz, *The Invention of Creativity: Modern Society and the Culture of the New*, trans. Steven Black (Cambridge: Polity, 2017).
22 On this point, see also Martin Altmeyer, *Auf der Suche nach Resonanz: Wie sich das Seelenleben in der digitalen Moderne verändert* (Göttingen: Vandenhoeck & Ruprecht, 2016).
23 See Franck, *Ökonomie der Aufmerksamkeit*.
24 Meg Wolitzer, *The Interestings* (New York: Riverhead Books, 2013); Virginie Despentes, *Vernon Subutex*, trans. Frank Wynne, 3 vols. (London: MacLehose Press, 2017–20); and Sonja Heiss, *Rimini* (Cologne: Kiepenheuer & Witsch, 2017).
25 See Peter Gay, *Pleasure Wars: The Bourgeois Experience, Victoria to Freud* (New York: W. W. Norton, 1988).
26 For a more detailed discussion of this topic, see Chapter 3 above.
27 On the logic of winner-take-all markets, see Frank and Cook, *The Winner-Take-All Society*. Regarding competitive sports as a model for late modernity, see Alain Ehrenberg, *Le Culte de la performance* (Paris: Calmann-Lévy, 1991).
28 See Illouz, *Why Love Hurts*.
29 In this regard, consider the phenomenon of INCELs, the movement of aggressively misogynistic and dissatisfied heterosexual men, one of whom was responsible for the terrorist attack on April 23, 2018, in Toronto.
30 Jean-Jacques Rousseau, *Discourse on the Origin of Inequality*, trans. Donald A. Cress (Indianapolis: Hackett, 1992).
31 See Steffen Mau, *The Metric Society: On the Quantification of the Social*, trans. Sharon Howe (Cambridge: Polity, 2019).
32 Pankaj Mishra has rightly emphasized that the comparison of lifestyles on digital media, which takes place on a global level, can be a cause of aggression for those who feel as though they have "fallen short" in comparison to others. See his book *Age of Anger: A History of the Present*.
33 I am inclined to interpret Hartmut Rosa's theory of resonance as an expression of neo-Romantic culture that understands lived experience – or, to be more precise, the extent to which one is subjectively affected by others (coded as "resonance") – as a central criterion for living a good life. See Hartmut Rosa, *Resonance: A Sociology of Our Relationship to the World*, trans. James Wagner (Cambridge: Polity, 2019).
34 See Bauer, *Die Vereindeutigung der Welt*.

35 On this mechanism of growth, see Gerhard Schulze, *Die beste aller Welten: Wohin bewegt sich die Gesellschaft im 21. Jahrhundert?* (Munich: Hanser, 2001).
36 In this respect, think of guidebooks such as Patricia Schultz's *1000 Places to See Before You Die* (New York: Workman, 2003).
37 See Hartmut Rosa, *The Uncontrollability of the World*, trans. James Wagner (Cambridge: Polity, 2020).
38 For a discussion of this topic from the perspective of a therapist, see Rainer Funk, *Der entgrenzte Mensch: Warum ein Leben ohne Grenzen nicht frei, sondern abhängig macht* (Gütersloher Verlagshaus, 2011).
39 See Michel Serres, *C'était mieux avant!* (Paris: Le Pommier, 2017).
40 Regarding depression, see Ehrenberg, *The Weariness of the Self*. Regarding aggression (and for a historical perspective), see Uffa Jensen, *Zornpolitik* (Berlin: Suhrkamp, 2017).
41 On the connection between social security and the reduction of stress, see Richard Wilkinson and Kate Pickett, *The Inner Level: How More Equal Societies Reduce Stress, Restore Sanity, and Improve Everyone's Well-Being* (New York: Penguin, 2018).
42 See, for instance, Remo H. Largo, *The Right Life: Human Individuality and Its Role in Our Development, Health, and Happiness*, trans. Ruth Martin (London: Allen Lane, 2019).
43 For an argument along these lines, see Adam Phillips, *Missing Out: In Praise of the Unlived Life* (London: Hamish Hamilton, 2012).
44 See, for instance, Matthias Ennenbach, *Buddhistische Psychotherapie: Ein Leitfaden für heilsame Veränderungen* (Oberstdorf: Windpferd, 2010); and Charles S. Prebish and Martin Baumann, eds., *Westward Dharma: Buddhism Beyond Asia* (Berkeley: University of California Press, 2002).
45 See Svend Brinkmann, *Stand Firm: Resisting the Self-Improvement Craze*, trans. Tam McTurk (Cambridge: Polity, 2017).

5 The Crisis of Liberalism and the Search for the New Political Paradigm

1 Thomas S. Kuhn, *The Structure of Scientific Revolution*, 4th edn. (University of Chicago Press, 2015). Kuhn's book was originally published in 1962.
2 On the special significance of Christian democracy in this regard, see Jan-Werner Müller, *Contesting Democracies: Political Ideas in Twentieth-Century Europe* (New Haven, CT: Yale University Press, 2011).
3 My discussion above is informed by Peter Wagner, *A Sociology of Modernity: Liberty and Discipline* (London: Routledge, 1994); Rosanvallon, *The Society of Equals*; and Jessop, *The Future of the Capitalist State*.
4 In general, the effect of "system competition" during this phase should not be underestimated. Throughout this period, there was a close affinity between the Western redistributive welfare state and the planned socialism of the East, for, after the crisis of the old bourgeois order, both sides were based on the comprehensive implementation of socio-economic, cultural, and political regulation. Western societies attempted to show that it was possible to bring liberal democracy, capitalism, and social regulation into a delicate balance.
5 For a more detailed discussion of this phenomenon, see Chapter 3 above.
6 In light of the schema suggested here, it turns out that the social-democratic governments of the early 1970s played a special role in political history. This is especially true of the social-liberal coalition of the Brandt government in West Germany. Socio-economically, the latter stuck firmly to the social-corporatist paradigm (before the oil crisis of 1973 initiated the collapse of this paradigm). However, this government had also been influenced by the protest movement of 1968, so that it began to implement the politics of the New Liberalism to come ("Let's dare to build a more democratic society," judicial reform, etc.). It was this unusual synthesis that enabled the social-liberal government to become so attractive in Germany.

7 Nancy Fraser has introduced the concept of "progressive neoliberalism" to describe this constellation. I have avoided this term, however, because it suggests that progressive liberalism is merely an appendage of neoliberalism. See Nancy Fraser, "From Progressive Neoliberalism to Trump – and Beyond," *American Affairs* (Winter 2017), https://americanaffairsjournal.org/2017/11/progressive-neoliberalism-trump-beyond.

8 For a detailed discussion of the new middle class, see Chapter 2 above.

9 Jessop, *The Future of the Capitalist State*. See also the articles collected in Thomas Biebricher, ed., *Der Staat des Neoliberalismus* (Baden-Baden: Nomos, 2016).

10 Regarding diversity, see Vertovec, "'Diversity' and the Social Imaginary." On the Democratic Party in the United States, see Frank, *Listen, Liberal*.

11 For a critical assessment of this development, see Christoph Menke, *Critique of Rights*, trans. Christopher Turner (Cambridge: Polity, 2020). For a positive view of it, see Judith N. Shklar, *Der Liberalismus der Rechte* (Berlin: Matthes & Seitz, 2017).

12 Colin Crouch has referred to this praxis critically as "post-democracy." See his book *Post-Democracy* (Cambridge: Polity, 2004).

13 Neoliberalism has been critiqued from several fronts. For representative contributions to this broad debate, see Wendy Brown, *Undoing the Demos: Neoliberalism's Stealth Revolution* (New York: Zone Books, 2015); Heiner Flassbeck and Paul Steinhardt, *Gescheiterte Globalisierung: Ungleichheit, Geld und die Renaissance des Staates* (Berlin: Suhrkamp, 2018); and Christoph Butterwegge et al., *Kritik des Neoliberalismus* (Wiesbaden: Verlag für Sozialwissenschaften, 2007).

14 For further discussion of this polarization, see Chapter 2 above.

15 For a critique of multiculturalism from the liberal camp, see Kenan Malik, *Multiculturalism and Its Discontents: Rethinking Diversity after 9/11* (University of Chicago Press, 2013).

16 On this debate, see the contributions in Axel Honneth, ed., *Kommunitarismus: Eine Debatte über die moralischen Grundlagen moderner Gesellschaften* (Frankfurt am Main: Campus, 1995).

17 On this topic, see Yascha Mounk, *The People vs. Democracy: Why Our Freedom Is in Danger and How to Save It* (Cambridge, MA: Harvard University Press, 2018).

18 In the United States, 71 percent of people born in the 1930s claim that it is highly important for them to live in a democracy. The situation is clearly different among those born in the 1980s – that is, among today's young adults. Within this group, only 29 percent say that it is highly important for them to live in a democracy, and 24 percent of them claim that they would be content to live under a strongman leader. See ibid., pp. 105–9.

19 In the 19th German Bundestag, 558 of the 709 parliamentarians (i.e., 78 percent) have a university degree, while this is true of just 16 percent of the total population.

20 See Jan-Werner Müller, *What Is Populism?* (Philadelphia: University of Pennsylvania Press, 2016).

21 This issue has recently been analyzed in detail. See Philip Manow, *Die politische Ökonomie des Populismus* (Berlin: Suhrkamp, 2018); Wilhelm Heitmeyer, *Autoritäre Versuchungen* (Berlin: Suhrkamp, 2018); and Pippa Norris and Ronald Inglehart, *Cultural Backlash: Trump, Brexit and Authoritarian Populism* (Cambridge University Press, 2019).

22 See Merkel, "Kosmopolitismus versus Kommunitarismus."

23 This is clear to see from the official statistics concerning the voter profiles of those who supported Marine Le Pen's candidacy during the first round of the French presidential election in 2017, and of those who supported the Alternative for Germany in the Bundestag election during the same year.

24 See Bernd Stegemann, *Das Gespenst des Populismus: Ein Essay zur politischen Dramaturgie* (Berlin: Theater der Zeit, 2017).

25 See my book *The Society of Singularities* (pp. 310–19), where I go into greater detail about the dual structure of liberalism and the counter-movements of cultural essentialism.

26 Regarding the economy, the concept of "embeddedness" stems from Karl Polanyi's book *The Great Transformation: The Political and Economic Origins of Our Time* (New York: Farrar & Rinehart, 1944).
27 Colin Crouch, *Can Neoliberalism Be Saved from Itself?* (London: Social Europe, 2017).
28 Regarding the idea of transforming liberalism in this way, see Lisa Herzog, *Freiheit gehört nicht nur den Reichen: Plädoyer für einen zeitgemäßen Liberalismus* (Munich: C. H. Beck, 2013).
29 See Edmund Fawcett, *Liberalism: The Life of an Idea* (Princeton University Press, 2014).
30 See Michel Foucault, *Security, Territory, Population: Lectures at the Collège de France, 1977–1978*, trans. Graham Burchell (New York: Palgrave Macmillan, 2007); and Michel Foucault, *The Birth of Biopolitics: Lectures at the Collège de France, 1978–1979*, trans. Graham Burchell (New York: Palgrave Macmillan, 2011). Foucault's concept of liberal governmentality is fully in accord with the concept of regulation proposed by systems theory, according to which "second-order control" is more significant and always more complex than "first-order control."
31 Foucault, *Security, Territory, Population*, p. 48.
32 Ibid., p. 49.
33 Regarding the effects of the expansion of education, see Chapters 2 and 3 above.
34 Michael Young, *The Rise of Meritocracy, 1870–2033: The New Elite of Our Social Revolution* (London: Random House, 1958). See also Frank, *Listen, Liberal*.
35 Robert W. Fuller, *All Rise: Somebodies, Nobodies, and the Politics of Dignity* (San Francisco: Berrett-Koehler, 2006).
36 Regarding the example of France, for instance, see Guilluy, *La France périphérique*.
37 Davide Arcidiacono et al., *Foundational Economy: The Infrastructure of Everyday Life* (Manchester University Press, 2018).
38 For a more detailed discussion of this antagonism, see Chapter 2 above.
39 Niklas Luhmann, *Observations on Modernity*, trans. William Whobrey (Stanford University Press, 1998).
40 On this set of problems, see Isolde Charim, *Ich und die Anderen: Wie Pluralismus uns alle verändert* (Vienna: Paul Zsolnay Verlag, 2018). See also Chapter 1 above.
41 In this regard, see Paul Collier, *The Future of Capitalism: Facing the New Anxieties* (New York: HarperCollins, 2018). Collier, however, tends to be too nostalgic for the social democracy of the 1950s and 1960s, and this is not a constructive approach. He fails to consider today's overall liberal orientation, which generally approves of globalization and heterogeneity. The idea of social cooperation is also at the heart of the "convivialist movement." See Frank Adloff et al., *Convivialist Manifesto: A Declaration of Interdependence*, trans. Margaret Clark (Duisburg: Käte Hamburg Kolleg / Centre for Cooperation Research, 2014).
42 Here I have neglected to address the difficult question of how a new paradigm will confront not only today's social and cultural crises but also the democratic-functional crisis into which the "expertocracy" of apertistic liberalism has fallen. In terms of intellectual history, one might here call to mind the republicanism that took a critical stance toward liberalism and that regarded individuals not primarily as private persons, but rather as citizens with common concerns within a body politic. Hannah Arendt made prominent attempts to revitalize this tradition. One could view the power of Emmanuel Macron's En Marche movement to mobilize people before the presidential election of 2017, or the popularity of the Fridays for Future movement in 2019, as indications that it is possible to mobilize citizens politically without appealing to their particular personal interests. However, the base of both movements was limited (the new middle class!), and in general there is the question of how such political mobilization could be sustained.

Bibliography

Adloff, Frank, et al. *Convivialist Manifesto: A Declaration of Interdependence.* Trans. Margaret Clarke. Duisburg: Käte Hamburger Kolleg / Centre for Global Cooperation Research, 2014.

Altmeyer, Martin. *Auf der Suche nach Resonanz: Wie sich das Seelenleben in der digitalen Moderne verändert.* Göttingen: Vandenhoeck & Ruprecht, 2016.

Amable, Bruno, and Stefano Palombarini. *L'Illusion du bloc bourgeois: Alliances sociales et avenir du modèle français.* Paris: Raisons d'agir éditions, 2018.

Anderson, Benedict. *Imagined Communities: Reflections on the Origin and Spread of Nationalism.* 2nd edn. London: Verso, 1991.

Antweiler, Christoph. *Inclusive Humanism: Anthropological Basics for a Realistic Cosmopolitanism.* Trans. Diane Kerns. Göttingen: Vandenhoeck & Ruprecht, 2012.

Arcidiacono, Davide et al. *Foundational Economy: The Infrastructure of Everyday Life.* Manchester University Press, 2018.

Ash, Amin, ed. *Post-Fordism: A Reader.* Oxford: Blackwell, 1994.

Bahl, Friederike. *Lebensmodelle in der Dienstleistungsgesellschaft.* Hamburger Edition, 2014.

Bauer, Thomas. *Die Vereindeutigung der Welt: Über den Verlust an Mehrdeutigkeit und Vielfalt.* Stuttgart: Reclam, 2018.

Beck, Ulrich. "Jenseits von Stand und Klasse? Soziale Ungleichheiten, gesellschaftliche Individualisierungsprozesse und die Entstehung neuer sozialer Formationen und Identitäten." In *Soziale Ungleichheiten.* Ed. Reinhard Kreckel. Göttingen: Schwartz, 1983. Pp. 35–74.

Beck, Ulrich. *Risk Society: Towards a New Modernity.* Trans. Mark Ritter. London: SAGE, 1992.

Beckert, Jens. *Imagined Futures: Fictional Expectations and Capitalist Dynamics.* Cambridge, MA: Harvard University Press, 2016.

Beckert, Jens, and Patrik Aspers, eds. *The Worth of Goods: Valuation and Pricing in the Economy.* Oxford University Press, 2011.

Bell, Daniel. *The Coming of Post-Industrial Society: A Venture in Social Forecasting.* New York: Basic Books, 1973.

Berlant, Lauren. *Cruel Optimism.* Durham, NC: Duke University Press, 2011.

Berlin, Isaiah. *The Roots of Romanticism.* Ed. Henry Hardy. Princeton University Press, 2014.

Biebricher, Thomas, ed. *Der Staat des Neoliberalismus.* Baden-Baden: Nomos, 2016.

Blade Runner 2049. Directed by Denis Villeneuve. Burbank, CA: Warner Bros. Pictures, 2017.

Boltanski, Luc, and Ève Chiapello. *The New Spirit of Capitalism.* Trans. Gregory Elliott. London: Verso, 2005.

Boltanski, Luc, and Arnaud Esquerre. *Enrichment: A Critique of Commodities.* Trans. Catherine Porter. Cambridge: Polity, 2020.

Bolte, Karl Martin et al., eds. *Deutsche Gesellschaft im Wandel*. Opladen: Leske, 1967.

Bomsel, Olivier. *L'Économie immatérielle: Industries et marches d'expériences* (Paris: Gallimard, 2010).

Bourdieu, Pierre. "The Forms of Capital." In *Handbook of Theory and Research for the Sociology of Education*. Ed. John G. Richardson. Westport, CT: Greenwood Press, 1986, pp. 241–58.

Brinkmann, Svend. *Stand Firm: Resisting the Self-Improvement Craze*. Trans. Tam McTurk. Cambridge: Polity, 2017.

Bröckling, Ulrich. *The Entrepreneurial Self: Fabricating a New Type of Subject*. Trans. Steven Black. London: SAGE, 2016.

Brooks, David. *Bobos in Paradise: The New Upper Class and How They Got There*. New York: Simon & Schuster, 2000.

Brooks, David. *The Road to Character*. New York: Random House, 2015.

Brown, Wendy. *Undoing the Demos: Neoliberalism's Stealth Revolution*. New York: Zone Books, 2015.

Bude, Heinz. *Die Ausgeslossenen: Das Ende vom Traum einer gerechten Gesellschaft*. Munich: Hanser, 2008.

Bude, Heinz. *Deutsche Karrieren: Lebenskonstruktionen sozialer Aufsteiger aus der Flakhelfer-Generation*. Frankfurt am Main: Suhrkamp, 1987.

Bude, Heinz, and Philipp Staab, eds. *Kapitalismus und Ungleichheit: Die neuen Verwerfungen*. Frankfurt am Main: Campus, 2016.

Butterwegge, Christoph et al. *Kritik des Neoliberalismus*. Wiesbaden: Verlag für Sozialwissenschaften, 2007.

Cassirer, Ernst. *The Philosophy of Symbolic Forms*. Trans. Ralph Manheim. 3 vols. New Haven, CT: Yale University Press, 1955–7.

Castells, Manuel. *The Power of Identity*. Cambridge, MA: Blackwell, 1997.

Charim, Isolde. *Ich und die Anderen: Wie Pluralismus uns alle verändert*. Vienna: Paul Zsolnay Verlag, 2018.

Christensen, Jens. *Global Experience Industries: The Business of the Experience Economy*. Aarhus University Press, 2009.

Cohen, Daniel. *Three Lectures on Post-Industrial Society*. Cambridge, MA: MIT Press, 2009.

Collier, Paul. *The Future of Capitalism: Facing the New Anxieties*. New York: HarperCollins, 2018.

Conrad, Sebastian. *What Is Global History?* Princeton University Press, 2016.

Crouch, Colin. *Can Neoliberalism Be Saved from Itself?* London: Social Europe, 2017.

Crouch, Colin. *Post-Democracy*. Cambridge: Polity, 2004.

Dahrendorf, Ralf. *Gesellschaft und Demokratie*. Munich: R. Piper & Co., 1965.

Dahrendorf, Ralf. "Die globale Klasse und die neue Ungleichheit." *Merkur* 11 (2000): 1057–68.

Davis, Gerald F. *Managed by the Markets: How Finance Re-Shaped America*. New York: Oxford University Press, 2009.

Despentes, Virginie. *Vernon Subutex*. Trans. Frank Wynne. 3 vols. London: MacLehose Press, 2017–20.

Dewey, John. *Democracy and Education: An Introduction to the Philosophy of Education*. New York: Macmillan, 1916.

Doering-Manteuffel, Anselm, and Lutz Raphael. *Nach dem Boom: Perspektiven auf die Zeitgeschichte seit 1970*. Göttingen: Vandenhoeck & Ruprecht, 2008.

Drucker, Peter. *Post-Capitalist Society*. New York: HarperCollins, 1993.

Durkheim, Émile. *The Elementary Forms of Religious Life*. Trans. Joseph Ward Swain. London: G. Allen & Unwin, 1915.

Eagleton, Terry. *The Idea of Culture*. Oxford: Blackwell, 2000.

Ehrenberg, Alain. *Le Culte de la performance*. Paris: Calmann-Lévy, 1991.

Ehrenberg, Alain. *The Weariness of the Self: Diagnosing the History of Depression in the Modern Age*. Trans. David Homel et al. Montreal: McGill-Queen's University Press, 2010.

Ennenbach, Matthias. *Buddhistische Psychotherapie: Ein Leitfaden für heilsame Veränderungen*. Oberstdorf: Windpferd, 2010.

Eribon, Didier. *Returning to Reims*. Trans. Michael Lucey. Cambridge, MA: MIT Press, 2013.

Esping-Andersen, Gøsta. *Changing Classes: Stratification and Mobility in Post-Industrial Societies*. London: SAGE, 1993.

Fawcett, Edmund. *Liberalism: The Life of an Idea*. Princeton University Press, 2014.

Featherstone, Mike. *Consumer Culture and Postmodernism*. London: SAGE, 1990.

Flaig, Berthold B. "Migrantische Lebenswelten in Deutschland." In *Praxis der SINUS-Milieus: Gegenwart und Zukunft eines modernen Gesellschafts- und Zielgruppenmodells*. Ed. Bertram Barth et al. Wiesbaden: Springer, 2018, pp. 113–24.

Flassbeck, Heiner, and Paul Steinhardt. *Gescheiterte Globalisierung: Ungleichheit, Geld und die Renaissance des Staates*. Berlin: Suhrkamp, 2018.

Florida, Richard. *Cities and the Creative Class*. New York: Routledge, 2005.

Florida, Richard. *Who's Your City? How the Creative Economy Is Making Where You Live the Most Important Decision of Your Life*. New York: Basic Books, 2008.

Foucault, Michel. *The Birth of Biopolitics: Lectures at the Collège de France, 1978–1979*. Trans. Graham Burchell. New York: Palgrave Macmillan, 2011.

Foucault, Michel. *Security, Territory, Population: Lectures at the Collège de France, 1977–1978*. Trans. Graham Burchell. New York: Palgrave Macmillan, 2007.

Fourastié, Jean. *Le Grand Espoir du XXe siècle: Progrès technique, progrès économique, progrès social*. Paris: Presses universitaires de France, 1949.

Fourastié, Jean. *Les Trente glorieuses, ou la revolution invisible de 1946 à 1975*. Paris: Fayard, 1979.

Franck, Georg. *Ökonomie der Aufmerksamkeit: Ein Entwurf*. Munich: Hanser, 1998.

Frank, Robert, and Philip Cook. *The Winner-Take-All Society: Why the Few on the Top Get so Much More Than the Rest of Us*. London: Virgin Books, 2010.

Frank, Thomas. *Listen, Liberal: Or, Whatever Happened to the Party of the People?* New York: Picador, 2016.

Fraser, Nancy. "From Progressive Neoliberalism to Trump – and Beyond." *American Affairs* (Winter 2017): https://americanaffairsjournal.org/2017/11/progressive-neoliberalism-trump-beyond.

Fuchs, Thomas, and Lukas Iwer, eds. *Das überforderte Subjekt: Zeitdiagnose einer beschleunigten Gesellschaft*. Berlin: Suhrkamp, 2018.

Fukuyama, Francis. *The End of History and the Last Man*. New York: The Free Press, 1992.

Fuller, Robert W. *All Rise: Somebodies, Nobodies, and the Politics of Dignity*. San Francisco: Berrett-Koehler, 2006.

Funk, Rainer. *Der entgrenzte Mensch: Warum ein Leben ohne Grenzen nicht frei, sondern abhängig macht*. Gütersloher Verlagshaus, 2011.

Gay, Peter. *Pleasure Wars: The Bourgeois Experience, Victoria to Freud*. New York: W. W. Norton, 1988.

Giesen, Bernhard. *Kollektive Identität: Die Intellektuellen und die Nation 2*. Frankfurt am Main: Suhrkamp, 1999.

Goodhart, David. *The Road to Somewhere: The Populist Revolt and the Future of Politics*. London: Penguin Books, 2017.

Goos, Maarten, and Alan Manning. "Lousy and Lovely Jobs: The Rising Polarization of Work in Britain." *Review of Economics and Statistics* 89 (2007): 118–33.

Greco, Monica, and Paul Stenner, eds. *Emotions: A Social Science Reader*. London: Routledge, 2008.

Groh-Samberg, Olaf. "Sorgenfreier Reichtum: Jenseits von Konjunktur und Krise." *Wochenbericht DIW Berlin* 35 (2009): 590–612.

Guilluy, Christoph. *La France périphérique: Comment on a sacrifié les classes populaires*. Paris: Flammarion, 2015.

Gundermann. Directed by Andreas Dresen. Cologne: Pandora Filmproduktion, 2018.

Han, Byung-Chul. *The Burnout Society*. Trans. Erik Butler. Stanford University Press, 2015.

Han, Byung-Chul. *Hyperkulturalität: Kultur und Globalisierung*. Berlin: Merve, 2005.

Haskel, Jonathan, and Stian Westlake. *Capitalism Without Capital: The Rise of the Intangible Economy*. Princeton University Press, 2018.

Häußermann, Hartmut. *Dienstleistungsgesellschaften*. Frankfurt am Main: Suhrkamp, 1995.

Heiss, Sonja. *Rimini*. Cologne: Kiepenheuer & Witsch, 2017.

Heitmeyer, Wilhelm. *Autoritäre Versuchungen*. Berlin: Suhrkamp, 2018.

Helbig, Marcel, and Stefanie Jähnen. "Wie brüchig ist die soziale Architektur unserer Städte? Trends und Analysen der Segregation in 74 deutschen Städten," WZB Discussion Paper (2018): http://dennymoeller.de/wp-content/uploads/2018/10/WZB-Segregation.pdf.

Herrendorf, Berthold et al. "Growth and Structural Transformation." In *Handbook of Economic Growth*. Vol. II. Ed. Philippe Aghion and Steven Durlauf. Amsterdam: Elsevier, 2014, pp. 855–941.

Herzog, Lisa. *Freiheit gehört nicht nur den Reichen: Plädoyer für einen zeitgemäßen Liberalismus*. Munich: C. H. Beck, 2013.

Hillenkamp, Sven. *Negative Moderne: Strukturen der Freiheit und der Sturz ins Nichts*. Stuttgart: Klett-Cotta, 2016.

Hochschild, Arlie Russell. *Strangers in Their Own Land: Anger and Mourning on the American Right*. New York: The New Press, 2016.

Honneth, Axel, ed. *Kommunitarismus: Eine Debatte über die moralischen Grundlagen moderner Gesellschaften*. Frankfurt am Main: Campus, 1995.

Howkins, John. *The Creative Economy: How People Make Money from Ideas*. London: Penguin, 2001.

Huntington, Samuel. P. *The Clash of Civilizations and the Remaking of World Order*. New York: Simon & Schuster, 1996.

Hüther, Otto, and Georg Krücken. *Hochschulen: Fragestellungen, Ergebnisse und Perspektiven der sozialwissenschaftlichen Hochschulforschung*. Wiesbaden: Springer, 2016.

Illouz, Eva. *The End of Love: A Sociology of Negative Emotions*. Oxford University Press, 2019.

Illouz, Eva. *Saving the Modern Soul: Therapy, Emotions, and the Culture of Self-Help*. Los Angeles: University of California Press, 2017.

Illouz, Eva. *Why Love Hurts: A Sociological Explanation*. Cambridge: Polity, 2013.

Inglehart, Ronald. *Modernization and Postmodernization: Cultural, Economic, and Political Change in 43 Societies*. Princeton University Press, 1997.

Inglehart, Ronald. *The Silent Revolution: Changing Values and Political Styles Among Western Publics*. Princeton University Press, 1977.

Inglehart, Ronald F., and Pippa Norris. "Trump, Brexit, and the Rise of Populism: Economic Have-Nots and Cultural Backlash." Harvard Kennedy School Working Paper, no. RWP16-026 (2016).

James, Paul, ed. *Globalization and Economy*. London: SAGE, 2007.

Jameson, Fredric. *Postmodernism, or, the Cultural Logic of Late Capitalism*. London: Verso, 1991.

Jensen, Uffa. *Zornpolitik*. Berlin: Suhrkamp, 2017.

Jessop, Bob. *The Future of the Capitalist State*. Cambridge: Polity, 2002.

Jullien, François. *There Is No Such Thing as Cultural Identity*. Trans. Pedro Rodriguez. Cambridge: Polity, 2021.

Karpik, Lucien. *Valuing the Unique: The Economics of Singularities*. Trans. Nora Scott. Princeton University Press, 2010.

Kondratieff, Nikolai. *The Long Wave Cycle*. Trans. Guy Daniels. New York: Richardson & Snyder, 1984.

Koppetsch, Cornelia, and Günter Burkart. *Die Illusion der Emanzipation: Zur Wirksamkeit latenter Geschlechtsnormen im Milieuvergleich*. Konstanz: UVK, 1999.

Kopytoff, Igor. "The Cultural Biography of Things." In *The Social Life of Things: Commodities in Cultural Perspective*. Ed. Arjun Appadurai. Cambridge University Press, 1986, pp. 64–91.

Koselleck, Reinhart. *Futures Past: On the Semantics of Historical Time*. Trans. Keith Tribe. New York: Columbia University Press, 2004.

Kuhn, Thomas S. *The Structure of Scientific Revolution*. 4th edn. University of Chicago Press, 2015.

Kymlicka, Will. *Multicultural Odysseys: Navigating the New International Politics of Diversity*. Oxford University Press, 2007.

Lareau, Annette. *Unequal Childhoods: Class, Race, and Family Life*. Berkeley: University of California Press, 2011.

Largo, Remo H. *The Right Life: Human Individuality and Its Role in Our Development, Health, and Happiness*. Trans. Ruth Martin. London: Allen Lane, 2019.

Lash, Scott. *Sociology of Postmodernism*. London: Routledge, 1990.

Lash, Scott, and Celia Lury. *Global Culture Industry: The Mediation of Things*. Cambridge: Polity, 2007.

Lash, Scott, and John Urry. *Economies of Signs and Space*. London: SAGE, 1994.

Lash, Scott, and John Urry. *The End of Organized Capitalism*. Cambridge: Polity, 1987.

Lazzarato, Maurizio. "Immaterial Labor." In *Radical Thought in Italy: A Potential Politics*. Ed. Paolo Virno and Michael Hardt. Minneapolis: University of Minnesota Press, 1996, pp. 133–48.

Leinberger, Paul, and Bruce Tucker. *The New Individualists: The Generation after the Organization Man*. New York: Harper Collins, 1991.

Levitsky, Steven, and Daniel Ziblatt. *How Democracies Die*. London: Penguin, 2019.

Lorey, Isabell, and Klaus Neundlinger, eds. *Kognitiver Kapitalismus*. Vienna: Turia + Kant, 2012.

Luhmann, Niklas. *Observations on Modernity*. Trans. William Whobrey. Stanford University Press, 1998.

Lupton, Deborah. *The Emotional Self: A Sociocultural Exploration*. London: SAGE, 1998.

Malik, Kenan. *Multiculturalism and Its Discontents: Rethinking Diversity After 9/11*. University of Chicago Press, 2013.

Manow, Philip. *Die politische Ökonomie des Populismus*. Berlin: Suhrkamp, 2018.

Marazzi, Christian. *Capital and Affects: The Politics of the Language Economy*. Trans. Giuseppina Mecchia. Cambridge, MA: MIT Press, 2011.

Marx, Karl. *Capital: Volume One*. Trans. Ben Fowkes. New York: Vintage Books, 1977.

Maslow, Abraham H. *Motivation and Personality*. New York: Harper & Row, 1954.

Mason, Paul. *Postcapitalism: A Guide to Our Future*. New York: Farrar, Straus & Giroux, 2015.

Mau, Steffen. *The Metric Society: On the Quantification of the Social*. Trans. Sharon Howe. Cambridge: Polity, 2019.

Mazzucato, Mariana. *The Value of Everything: Making and Taking in the Global Economy*. London: Allen Lane, 2018.

Menger, Pierre-Michel. *The Economics of Creativity: Art and Achievement under Uncertainty*. Cambridge, MA: Harvard University Press, 2014.

Menke, Christoph. *Critique of Rights*. Trans. Christopher Turner. Cambridge: Polity, 2020.

Merkel, Wolfgang. "Kosmopolitismus versus Kommunitarismus: Ein neuer Konflikt in der Demokratie." In *Parties, Governments, and Elites: The Comparative Study of Democracy*. Ed. Philipp Harfst et al. Wiesbaden: Springer, 2017, pp. 9–23.

Merkel, Wolfgang. *The Struggle over Borders: Cosmopolitanism and Communitarianism*. Cambridge University Press, 2019.

Milanović, Branko. *Global Inequality: A New Approach for the Age of Globalization*. Cambridge, MA: Harvard University Press, 2016.

Mishra, Pankaj. *Age of Anger: A History of the Present*. New York: Farrar, Straus & Giroux, 2017.

Moldaschl, Manfred, and Günter G. Voß, eds. *Subjektivierung von Arbeit*. Munich: Hampp, 2003.

Moulier-Boutang, Yann. *Cognitive Capitalism*. Cambridge: Polity, 2011.

Mounk, Yascha. *The People vs. Democracy: Why Our Freedom Is in Danger and How to Save It*. Cambridge, MA: Harvard University Press, 2018.

Müller, Jan-Werner. *Contesting Democracies: Political Ideas in Twentieth-Century Europe*. New Haven, CT: Yale University Press, 2011.

Müller, Jan-Werner. *What Is Populism?* Philadelphia: University of Pennsylvania Press, 2016.

Nachtwey, Oliver. *Germany's Hidden Crisis: Social Decline in the Heart of Europe*. Trans. David Fernbach and Loren Balhorn. London: Verso, 2018.

Ngai, Sianne. *Ugly Feelings*. Cambridge, MA: Harvard University Press, 2007.

Niemann, Hans-Werner. *Europäische Wirtschaftsgeschichte: Vom Mittelalter bis heute*. Darmstadt: Wissenschaftliche Buchgesellschaft, 2009.

Nieswand, Boris. *Theorizing Transnational Migration: The Status Paradox of Migration*. London: Routledge, 2011.

Norris, Pippa, and Ronald Inglehart. *Cultural Backlash: Trump, Brexit and Authoritarian Populism*. Cambridge University Press, 2019.

Ortega y Gasset, José. *The Revolt of the Masses*. Trans. Anthony Kerrigan. Notre Dame University Press, 1985.

Paoli, Guillaume. *Die lange Nacht der Metamorphose: Über die Gentrifizierung der Kultur*. Berlin: Matthes & Seitz, 2017.

Perez, Carlota. "Technological Revolutions, Paradigm Shifts and Socio-Institutional Change." In *Globalization, Economic Development and Inequality*. Ed. Erik Reinert. Cheltenham: Edwin Elgar, 2004, pp. 217–42.

Perez, Carlota. *Technological Revolutions and Financial Capital: The Dynamics of Bubbles and Golden Ages*. Cheltenham: Edward Elgar, 2002.

Phillips, Adam. *Missing Out: In Praise of the Unlived Life*. London: Hamish Hamilton, 2012.

Pieterse, Jan Nederveen. "Globalization as Hybridization." In *Global Modernities*. Ed. Mike Featherstone et al. London: SAGE, 2002, pp. 45–68.

Piketty, Thomas. *Capital in the Twenty-First Century*. Trans. Arthur Goldhammer. Cambridge, MA: Harvard University Press, 2014.

Pine, Joseph B., and James Gilmore. *The Experience Economy: Work Is Theatre & Every Business a Stage*. Boston: Harvard Business Review Press, 1999.

Piore, Michael J., and Charles F. Sabel. *The Second Industrial Divide: Possibilities for Prosperity*. New York: Basic Books, 1984.

Plamper, Jan. *The History of Emotions: An Introduction*. Trans. Keith Tribe. Oxford University Press, 2012.

Plessner, Helmuth. *The Limits of Community: A Critique of Social Radicalism*. Trans. Andrew Wallace. New York: Humanity Books, 1999.

Polanyi, Karl. *The Great Transformation: The Political and Economic Origins of Our Time*. New York: Farrar & Rinehart, 1944.

Popper, Karl. *The Open Society and Its Enemies: New One-Volume Edition*. Princeton University Press, 2013.

Prebish, Charles S., and Martin Baumann, eds. *Westward Dharma: Buddhism Beyond Asia*. Berkeley: University of California Press, 2002.

Prisching, Manfred. *Die zweidimensionale Gesellschaft: Ein Essay zur neokonsumistischen Geisteshaltung*. Wiesbaden: Verlag für Sozialwissenschaften, 2006.

Putnam, Robert D. *Our Kids: The American Dream in Crisis*. New York: Simon & Schuster, 2015.

Raphael, Lutz. *Jenseits von Kohle und Stahl: Eine Gesellschaftsgeschichte Europas nach dem Boom*. Berlin: Suhrkamp, 2019.

Reckwitz, Andreas. *Das hybride Subjekt: Eine Theorie der Subjektkulturen von der bürgerlichen Moderne zur Postmoderne*. New edn. Berlin: Suhrkamp, 2020.

Reckwitz, Andreas. *The Invention of Creativity: Modern Society and the Culture of the New*. Trans. Steven Black. Cambridge: Polity, 2017.

Reckwitz, Andreas. *The Society of Singularities*. Trans. Valentine A. Pakis. Cambridge: Polity, 2020.

Reckwitz, Andreas. *Die Transformation der Kulturtheorien: Zur Entwicklung eines Theorieprogramms*. Weilerwist: Velbrück Wissenschaft, 2000.

Reckwitz. Andreas. "Zwischen Hyperkultur und Kulturessenzialismus." *Soziopolis* (October 24, 2016): https://soziopolis.de/beobachten/kultur/artikel/zwischen-hyperkultur-und-kulturessenzialismus.

Riesebrodt, Martin. *Rückkehr der Religionen? Zwischen Fundamentalismus und der "Kampf der Kulturen."* Munich: Beck, 2000.

Riesman, David. *The Lonely Crowd: A Study of the Changing American Character*. New Haven, CT: Yale University Press, 1950.

Rödder, Andreas. *21.0: Eine kurze Geschichte der Gegenwart*. Munich: C. H. Beck, 2015.

Rosa, Hartmut. *Resonance: A Sociology of Our Relationship to the World*. Trans. James Wagner. Cambridge: Polity, 2019.

Rosa, Hartmut. *The Uncontrollability of the World*. Trans. James Wagner. Cambridge: Polity, 2020.

Rosanvallon, Pierre. *The Society of Equals*. Trans. Arthur Goldhammer. Cambridge, MA: Harvard University Press, 2013.

Rose, Stephen J. "Manufacturing Employment: Fact and Fiction," Urban Institute (April 2018): www.urban.org/sites/default/files/publication/97776/manufacturing_employment_fact_and_fiction_2.pdf.

Rousseau, Jean-Jacques. *Discourse on the Origin of Inequality*. Trans. Donald A. Cress. Indianapolis: Hackett, 1992.

Runciman, Walter G. *Relative Deprivation and Social Justice: A Study of Attitudes to Social Inequality in Twentieth-Century Britain*. London: Routledge & Kegan Paul, 1966.

Sassen, Saskia. "Vive l'economie réelle!" *Le Monde* (February 21, 2009): www.lemonde.fr/idees/article/2009/02/21/vive-l-economie-reelle-par-saskia-sassen_1158611_3232.html.

Schelsky, Helmut. "Die Bedeutung des Schichtungsbegriff für die Analyse der gegenwärtigen deutschen Gesellschaft." In *Auf der Suche nach Wirklichkeit: Gesammelte Aufsätze*. Düsseldorf: E. Diederichs, 1965, pp. 331–6.

Schiller, Friedrich. *On the Aesthetic Education of Man in a Series of Letters*. Trans. Elizabeth M. Wilkinson and L. A. Willoughby. Oxford: Clarendon Press, 1983.

Schimank, Uwe, and Ute Volkmann. *Das Regime der Konkurrenz: Gesellschaftliche Ökonomisierungsdynamiken heute*. Weinheim: Juventa, 2017.

Schimank, Uwe et al. *Statusarbeit unter Druck? Zur Lebensführung der Mittelschichten*. Weinheim: Beltz Verlagsgruppe, 2014.

Schultz, Duane. *Growth Psychology: Models of the Healthy Personality*. New York: Van Nostrand Reinhold, 1977.

Schultz, Patricia. *1000 Places to See Before You Die*. New York: Workman, 2003.

Schultz, Tanjev, and Klaus Hurrelmann, eds. *Die Akademiker-Gesellschaft: Müssen in Zukunft alle studieren?* Weinheim: Juventa, 2013.

Schulze, Gerhard. *Die beste aller Welten: Wohin bewegt sich die Gesellschaft im 21. Jahrhundert?* Munich: Hanser, 2001.

Schulze, Gerhard. *Die Erlebnisgesellschaft: Kultursoziologie der Gegenwart*. Frankfurt am Main: Suhrkamp, 1992.

Schumpeter, Joseph A. *The Theory of Economic Development: An Inquiry into Profits, Capital, Credit, Interest, and the Business Cycle*. Trans. Redvers Opie. Cambridge, MA: Harvard University Press, 1934.

Scott, Allen J. *A World in Emergence: Cities and Regions in the 21st Century*. London: Edward Elgar, 2012.

Serres, Michel. *C'était mieux avant!* Paris: Le Pommier, 2017.

Shklar, Judith N. *Der Liberalismus der Rechte*. Berlin: Matthes & Seitz, 2017.

Simmel, Georg. *Sociology: Inquiries into the Construction of Social Forms*. Trans. Anthony J. Blasi et al. Leiden: Brill, 2009.

Smith, Adam. *An Inquiry into the Nature and Causes of the Wealth of Nations*. Ed. W. B. Todd et al. Oxford University Press, 1976.

Spengler, Oswald. *The Decline of the West*. Trans. Charles F. Atkinson. New York: Oxford University Press, 1991.

Srnicek, Nick. *Platform Capitalism*. Cambridge: Polity, 2016.

Staroske, Uwe. *Die Drei-Sektoren-Hypothese: Darstellung und kritische Würdigung aus heutiger Sicht*. Regensburg: Roderer, 1995.

Stearns, Peter N. *American Cool: Constructing a Twentieth-Century Emotional Style*. New York University Press, 1994.

Stegemann, Bernd. *Das Gespenst des Populismus: Ein Essay zur politischen Dramaturgie*. Berlin: Theater der Zeit, 2017.

Stehr, Nico. *Wissen und Wirtschaften: Die gesellschaftlichen Grundlagen der modernen Ökonomie*. Frankfurt am Main: Suhrkamp, 2009.

Streeck, Wolfgang. *Buying Time: The Delayed Crisis of Economic Capitalism*. Trans. Patrick Camiller and David Fernbach. London: Verso, 2014.

Streeck, Wolfgang. *How Will Capitalism End? Essays on a Failing System*. London: Verso, 2016.

Taylor, Charles. *Sources of the Self: The Making of Modern Identity*. Cambridge, MA: Harvard University Press, 1989.

Thrift, Nigel. *Knowing Capitalism*. London: SAGE, 2005.

Trentmann, Frank. *Empire of Things: How We Became a World of Consumers, from the Fifteenth Century to the Twenty-First*. London: Allen Lane, 2016.

Vannini, Phillip, and Patrick J. Williams, eds. *Authenticity in Culture, Self, and Society*. London: Routledge, 2016.

Vertovec, Steven. "'Diversity' and the Social Imaginary." *European Journal of Sociology* 53:3 (2012): 287–312.

Voswinkel, Stephan. *Welche Kundenorientierung? Anerkennung in der Dienstleistungsarbeit*. Berlin: Edition Sigma, 2005.

Wagner, Peter. *A Sociology of Modernity: Liberty and Discipline*. London: Routledge, 1994.

War for the Planet of the Apes. Directed by Matt Reeves. Los Angeles: 20th Century Fox, 2017.

Weber, Max. *The Protestant Ethic and the Spirit of Capitalism*. Trans. Talcott Parsons. New York: Charles Scribner's Sons, 1930.

Wetzel, Dietmar J. *Soziologie des Wettbewerbs: Eine kultur- und wirtschaftssoziologische Analyse der Marktgesellschafte*. Wiesbaden: Springer, 2013.

Whyte, William H. *The Organization Man*. New York: Simon & Schuster, 1956.

Wilkinson, Richard, and Kate Pickett. *The Inner Level: How More Equal Societies Reduce Stress, Restore Sanity, and Improve Everyone's Well-Being*. New York: Penguin, 2018.

Williams, Joan C. *White Working Class: Overcoming Class Cluelessness in America*. Boston: Harvard Business Review Press, 2017.

Williams, Raymond. *Culture and Society, 1780–1950*. New York: Columbia University Press, 1958.

Windolf, Paul, ed. *Finanzmarkt-Kapitalismus: Analysen zum Wandel von Produktionsregimen*. Wiesbaden: Verlag für Sozialwissenschaften, 2005.

Wolitzer, Meg. *The Interestings*. New York: Riverhead Books, 2013.

Young, Michael. *The Rise of Meritocracy, 1870–2033: The New Elite of Our Social Revolution*. London: Random House, 1958.

Yúdice, George. *The Expediency of Culture: Uses of Culture in the Global Era*. Durham, NC: Duke University Press, 2003.

Index